The Cleveland Street Scandal

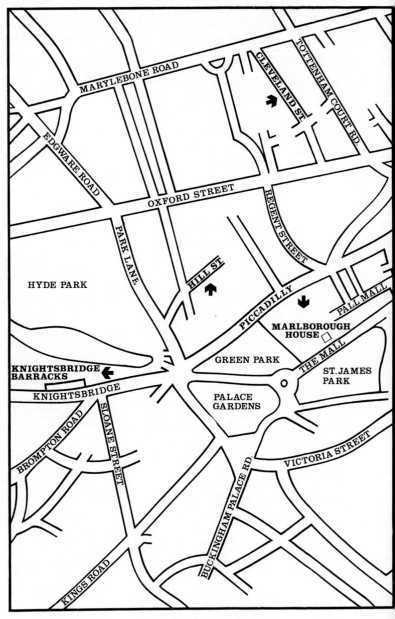

The West End of London at the time
of the Scandal

The
Cleveland Street
Scandal

by

H. Montgomery Hyde

W. H. ALLEN · LONDON
A division of Howard & Wyndham Ltd
1976

Printed and bound in Great Britain by
W & J Mackay Limited, Chatham
for the publishers W. H. Allen & Co. Ltd.,
44 Hill Street, London W1X 8LB

ISBN 0 491 01995 5

To Phyllis Grosskurth
friend and fellow worker
in admiration

'The Government did not wish for revelations; they wished to hush up the matter.
. . . What is this case but a criminal conspiracy by the very guardians of public
morality and law, with the Prime Minister at
their head, to defeat the ends of justice?'

Henry Labouchere in the House of
Commons, 28 February 1890.

Contents

Illustrations

Acknowledgements

I WISH TO THANK the Home Secretary, the Rt. Hon. Roy Jenkins, MP, and his official staff for enabling me to see the departmental files on the Cleveland Street case which are still closed to the general public. I am also grateful to the staff of the Public Record Office, and particularly Mr. E. K. Timings, Principal Assistant Keeper, for facilitating my researches among the papers on the case which were formerly in the custody of the Director of Public Prosecutions and are now available for study without restriction in the PRO. I am likewise indebted to Sir Robert Mark, Commissioner of Metropolitan Police, and his staff for their assistance, and similarly to the staffs of the British Library and the London Library.

My thanks are due to a number of private individuals for kindly allowing me access to papers and correspondence in their possession or which they control, namely Viscount Esher, Mr. Victor Montagu and the Marquess of Salisbury. In this connection I would like to thank the librarians and archivists of Churchill College, Cambridge, and Christ Church, Oxford, for their facilities. For information and other help I wish to thank the Duke of Beaufort, Mrs. Georgina Battiscombe, Viscount Chilston, the Duke of Grafton, Mr. Anatole James, Commander Harold Lewis, Mr. John Peskett, Mr. Cecil Roberts, and Mr. D. J. Swan.

ACKNOWLEDGEMENTS

The source of each illustration is indicated in the list of illustrations at the beginning of the book, and I am grateful to the owners of the pictures for permission to reproduce them here.

H. M. H.

Westwell House,
Tenterden,
Kent.

Introduction

ONE OF THE most remarkable and least attractive features of the Victorian social scene was the prevalence of prostitution, particularly in its juvenile form, and the so-called 'white slave' trade in young girls for work in foreign brothels, which flourished in the second half of the nineteenth century. A House of Lords Commission appointed on the initiative of the Home Office in 1881 to investigate the subject produced an alarming report which moved the philanthropist Lord Shaftesbury to conclude that 'nothing more cruel, alarming or detestable could be found in the history of crime all over the world.' From the day of her thirteenth birthday, it was a sufficient defence to any charge of carnal assault or procuring for the purposes of prostitution if the alleged seducer could show that the girl had consented to her seduction.

A bill to amend the criminal law by raising the age of consent was introduced by Mr. Gladstone's Liberal Government, but in spite of the Prime Minister's known interest in reclaiming 'fallen women', the measure failed to arouse much enthusiasm in Parliament and was dropped. Similar measures suffered the same fate in succeeding sessions, and this was the position when the Conservatives under the Marquess of Salisbury came into office in June 1885. Once again it looked as if the bill would be sacrificed. At this point its supporters enlisted the help of W. T. Stead, the editor of the *Pall Mall Gazette*, an influential Liberal daily, which furnished its readers with a carefully chosen political diet of Radicalism and sensationalism.

From his father, who was a Congregational Minister in Northumberland, William Thomas Stead, destined later to lose his life in the *Titanic* disaster, had inherited the strong Puritan emotions and beliefs of the manse. Consequently he advocated with a passion, which was to develop into a positive obsession with sex, the current and widely held view of 'fallen women' that these 'unhappy creatures' had descended from a state of maidenly innocence solely by reason of male depravity. Seeking enlightenment from the former head of the Criminal Investigation Department at Scotland Yard, Stead was horrified to learn how easy it was for a teen-age girl to be inveigled into a brothel where she could be violated without any possible hope of redress, because, if she had freely consented to enter the brothel, she was held to have consented to her own 'ruin', although she might at that time be, and probably was, absolutely ignorant of what 'vice' meant.

Stead asked whether the innocent victims did not cry out or scream. Was not their shouting enough to raise hell?

'It doesn't even raise the neighbours,' was the reply.

'Then *I* will raise hell!' declared Stead.

He was as good as his word. His plan was to institute an investigation into juvenile prostitution in London, and he hoped that the resultant disclosures, when published in the *Pall Mall Gazette*, would be such as to compel the Tory Government of the day, however reluctant it might be, to suspend all other business until the Criminal Law Amendment Bill had reached the statute book. In order to demonstrate how easily a man could have a girl over thirteen procured for him as a prostitute, he would himself personate the man, playing the part in every detail short of actually consummating the act which he was pretending to do. The evidence which Stead obtained in this way formed the subject of a series of astonishing articles entitled 'The Maiden Tribute of Modern Babylon', which appeared in his newspaper during the first fortnight of July 1885.

The articles created an immense sensation at home and abroad. An immediate result was that, while they were still running, the Government rushed through the second reading of the Criminal Law Amendment Bill, designed in the words of its title 'to make further provision for the protection of women and girls, the suppression of brothels and other purposes.' Unfortunately for himself, Stead allowed his zeal in the cause of purity to outrun his discretion. Apart from the fact that there was no hint in the articles that the procuring incident was a stage-managed operation, the editor failed to take the precaution of securing the consent of the girl's father, although her mother had given hers. In the result Stead found himself charged with criminal abduction at the Old Bailey, where he was duly convicted and sent to prison for two months. However, we are not concerned here with the unhappy sequel to 'The Maiden Tribute of Modern Babylon' which befell the author. What does concern us is the course of the Criminal Law Amendment Bill in the House of Commons after its second reading and before it became law, when it was popularly styled 'Stead's Act'.

At this stage another editor comes into the story. This was the Radical Member of Parliament, Henry Labouchere, whose upbringing and social background were very different from Stead's and who had none of Stead's religious Nonconformist conscience—in fact he was an agnostic—although the two men united in their respective journals, attacking successive Governments regardless of their political complexion, and exposing current abuses and injustices. Futhermore, while Stead was a serious 'do gooder', in some ways too serious, Labouchere was a brilliant wit and man of the world, whose weekly journal *Truth*, which he had founded a decade previously, was recognised as by far the most successful of personal organs in the press at this period.

A rich man, who had inherited a fortune through his family's connection with the Dutch banking firm of Hope, Henry du Pré Labouchere, nicknamed 'Labby', was now in his middle fifties. He had had an adventurous and varied career, which included working in a circus in Mexico, living in a camp of Chippewa Indians, and spending ten years in the British diplomatic service, before winning fame as a journalist by his spectacular coverage of the siege of Paris in 1870. Six years earlier, his diplomatic career had ended abruptly when he happened to be on leave at Baden-Baden and was informed by the Foreign Secretary that he had been appointed second secretary in the British legation in Buenos Aires; he replied that he would be delighted to accept the post if he could fulfil its duties in Baden-Baden.

Like today's *Private Eye*, with which it merits comparison, *Truth* and its fearless editor were frequently sued for libel, many of which actions he won, although he usually failed to recover his costs. Nevertheless, he regarded the actions as an excellent advertisement for his journal, which indeed they were. Since 1880 he had shared the parliamentary representation of Northampton with the professed atheist Charles Bradlaugh and would jokingly refer to himself as 'the Christian member for Northampton', although he preferred to keep quiet about the fact that he himself was a lifelong agnostic. Besides his interest in the Criminal Law Amendment Bill, Henry Labouchere made a substantial contribution to the cause of Home Rule for Ireland, and he assisted in exposing the forgeries of Richard Pigott which sought to implicate the Nationalist Charles Stewart Parnell in acts of terrorism, notably the Phoenix Park murders. While always treating his party leader Gladstone with respect, in private he ridiculed his political fervour and 'mystifications'. He did not object, he said, to Gladstone always having the ace of trumps up his sleeve, but only to his pretence that God put it there. Labouchere was a born rebel and eccentric.

After the Criminal Law Amendment Bill had been given an unopposed second reading in the Commons—it had already passed through all its stages in the Lords—Stead sent Labouchere a report of the prevalence of male homosexuality, which suggested to Labouchere that he might put down an amendment on the order paper designed to make homosexual acts between men not amounting to buggery or sodomy a criminal offence, whether in public or *private*. Buggery, or sodomy (as it was called in Scotland), had been a capital offence from the time of Henry VIII in 1533 until 1861, when life imprisonment was substituted as the maximum penalty. In respect of homosexual acts not amounting to buggery, the only possible proceeding was by indictment for conspiracy to commit the graver offence, and this could only be proved by the evidence of an accessory, which it was rarely possible to obtain. Accordingly Labouchere put down an amendment to insert a new clause in the Bill in the following terms:

> Any male person, who in public or private, commits, or is a party to the commission of, any act of gross indecency with another male person, shall be guilty of a misdemeanour, and being convicted thereof, shall be liable, at the discretion of the court, to be imprisoned for any term not exceeding one year with or without hard labour.

At the same time Labouchere drew the attention of the Home Secretary, Sir Richard Cross, and the Attorney General, Sir Henry James, to his proposed new clause which he hoped the Government would accept. He afterwards admitted that he had taken it from the French penal code, which appears to suggest that he had primarily in mind the corruption of youth (*détournement de mineurs*) since the French code did not penalise homosexual acts between consenting adults in private and in fact had not done so since the Revolution. But Labouchere's clause proposed no age limit. Also, if Labby had stuck to the term 'indecent assault' as expressed in the French code in regard to minors rather than the vague and undefined 'act of gross indecency', a vast amount of unnecessary trouble and suffering might have been avoided. In the event, the Government intimated that it would accept the so-called 'Labouchere amendment' in principle. 'In doing so,' said Labouchere afterwards, 'they recognised that the offence was on the increase, and they expressed their desire that it should be stamped out; and, presumably, it was intended that the law should be used equally against high and low.'

After its second reading, the draft Bill was considered sufficiently important to be referred to a committee of the whole House, instead of being sent 'upstairs' to a standing committee for detailed consideration. The committee stage was thus taken late at night on 6 August 1885, and this was to prove a fateful date in the history of English criminal jurisprudence.

When Labouchere rose to move his amendment, another back-bench member intervened on a point of order to ask the Deputy Speaker, who was chairman of the committee, whether 'the clause about to be moved by the Hon. Member for Northampton, and which dealt with a totally different class of offence to that against which the Bill was directed, was within the scope of the Bill.' The Deputy Speaker replied that, at this stage of the bill, anything could be introduced into it by leave of the House.

Labouchere, in moving the amendment, explained briefly that at present, in order to involve punishment, any person on whom 'an assault of the kind here dealt with' was committed must be under the age of thirteen, and the object with which he had brought forward the new clause was 'to make the law applicable to any person, whether under the age of thirteen, or over that age'. He went on to say that he did not think it necessary to discuss it at any length, as he understood the government was willing to accept it. He therefore left it for the House and the government 'to deal with as might be thought best'. The Attorney General did accept it on behalf of the government, subject to an amendment which he moved increasing the maximum penalty from one year to two years imprisonment with or without hard labour. Labouchere had no objection to this minor change, and the clause, which was somewhat illogically entitled 'Outrages on public decency', was agreed to without any further discussion and incorporated in the bill as section 11. The measure became law on 1 January 1886.

Looking back in old age, Sir Travers Humphreys, the well-known English criminal judge, had some pertinent remarks to make about the 1885 Act and in particular section 11.

> It is doubtful whether the House fully appreciated that the words 'in public or private' in the new clause had completely altered the law, but as soon as the Royal Assent had been given and the Act was published, there began a spate of correspondence in the newspapers,

both legal and lay, and references to the subject on various public platforms, which were duly reported. A learned Recorder dubbed it 'The Blackmailer's Charter', and an eminent Q.C. prophesied that juries would refuse to convict where the alleged acts were in private and not visible to any member of the public. On the other hand, those interested in the welfare of girls welcomed the Act as a whole so warmly (and indeed it was an excellent Act apart from section 11), and it was so clearly impossible to do anything except to let the law take its course, that after a few weeks the clamour died down and the public interest became centred upon some more savoury topic. The criticisms proved to be not without foundation. The reluctance of juries to convict in such cases is notorious, while no one having experience in such matters would deny that the words 'in private' have materially assisted the blackmailer in his loathsome trade.

One of the first prosecutions to be brought under section 11 of the new Act, certainly the first to receive wide notoriety, was in respect of acts which took place in a male brothel in Cleveland Street, a thoroughfare in the West End of London situated between the Middlesex Hospital and Tottenham Court Road. By a curious piece of irony, the street got its name from Barbara Villiers, Countess of Castlemaine and Duchess of Cleveland, one of King Charles II's most rapacious mistresses. When Barbara's influence at court began to wane, she concentrated on obtaining titles and arranging profitable marriages for her numerous royal bastards. Her second son, Henry Fitzroy, Earl of Euston and Duke of Grafton, married the heiress to Tottenham Court Manor, and the old lane which separated this estate from the neighbouring manor of Marylebone thus came to be called Cleveland Street.

CHAPTER I

The House in Cleveland Street

I

THE CLEVELAND STREET scandal, as it was generally known, first came to light as the result of the theft of a sum of money from a room in the Receiver-General's Department in the Central Telegraph Office, which was then situated in the building known as the General Post Office West in St. Martin's-Le-Grand in the City of London. Suspicion fell upon a fifteen-year-old telegraph messenger-boy named Charles Thomas Swinscow, who had been seen leaving the room and to have more money in his possession than might be expected of a boy whose weekly earnings amounted to a few shillings.

On 4 July 1886, Police Constable Luke Hanks, who was attached to the Post Office, sent for young Swinscow and in the presence of Mr. Phillips, a senior Post Office official, told him of the theft and asked him to explain how he had as much as eighteen shillings in his possession.

'I did not have so much as that,' said the boy, 'but I had fourteen shillings.'

'Where did you get it?' asked Hanks.

'I got it for doing some private work away from the office.'

'For whom?'

'For a gentleman named Hammond.'

'Where does he live?'

'19 Cleveland Street.'

'What did you do for him?' the policeman persisted.

The boy hesitated and at first refused to answer. Eventually, on being pressed by Hanks, he admitted: 'I will tell you the truth. I got the money for going to bed with gentlemen at his house.'

Swinscow went on to give some details which were taken down in the form of a statement which the boy subsequently signed. A fellow employee named Henry Newlove, who worked as a clerk in the GPO Secretary's office, had persuaded him to go with him to the lavatory in the basement, he said, after which he shut the door and 'behaved indecently'. Newlove later induced him to visit the house in Cleveland Street, where he got into bed quite naked with a gentleman in the back parlour. What happened then seems to have been more or less paraphrased in police language. 'He put his person between my legs and an emission took place.' They were together for about half an hour, Swinscow went on, after which he got up and the gentleman gave him a half-sovereign. This the boy handed over to Hammond, who gave him four shillings for himself. He never saw the gentleman again, he said. However, about a month ago, he went again to the house, where the same performance took place as before but with another gentleman. 'This gentleman after we had got out of bed told me I ought not to come to the house again,' he added. According to him, he never did go there again. He was not in uniform on either occasion. Nor did he give Newlove any share of the money he had received.

Swinscow also volunteered the information that two other telegraph boys named Wright and Thickbroom had gone to Cleveland Street at the instance of Newlove. The constable then sent for these boys and took statements from each of them.

The first was George Alma Wright, aged 17, who said he lived with his parents in the East End of London. 'There was a boy messenger in the Secretary's office who used to speak to me in the lobbies,' he continued. On Newlove being sent for, Wright identified him as the youth whose acquaintance he had made about four months previously and who persuaded him to go with him several times to the basement lavatory. 'On one or two occasions, certainly more than once,' he stated, 'Newlove put his person into me, that is to say behind only a little way and something came from him. I never did this to him. He never gave me any money.'

Wright went on to say that one afternoon when they met in the corridor of the Post Office during the dinner hour, Newlove said to him: 'I know a gentleman I go with sometimes and if you like to come I will show him to you. He wants to have a game of spooning with you.'

Wright's statement continued:

> We went up to Cleveland Street. I don't know the number. We went into the house after ringing the bell and Newlove introduced me to a man whose name I don't know who said he was the landlord. The man was of middling size, rather black hair, bald on the top of his head, black eyebrows and a full moustache. I think I should know him again.
>
> Another gentleman came in whom I should know again, I think a rather foreign looking chap. I went with the latter into a bedroom on the same floor and we both undressed and we got into the bed quite naked. He told me to suck him. I did so. He then had a go between my legs and that was all. He gave me half a sovereign which I gave to the landlord who gave me four shillings. This was the first and only time I have ever been to the house.

Wright also stated that Newlove once asked him if he knew of 'another nice little boy', younger and shorter than himself, whom he could get to visit the house. 'I introduced him to Thickbroom. I don't know what passed between them.' Wright added, what apparently Newlove had admitted in his presence, that 'on one occasion at least I put my person into his hinderparts. I could not get it in, though I tried and emitted. I was not in uniform except for the trousers.'

The third boy to make a statement was Charles Ernest Thickbroom, aged 17. He said that Wright introduced him to Newlove, whose name he did not know at the time. Newlove persuaded him to go to bed with a man, although at first he refused, but agreed when he was told that he would get four shillings for it. He then went to

Cleveland Street where he met Hammond, and another gentleman, with whom he went to bed, quite naked. 'We got into bed and played with each other. He did not put his person into me.' After he had got up, the gentleman gave him half a sovereign, which he gave Hammond who let him have four shillings, as he had done with the other two boys. According to Thickbroom's statement, Hammond said he hoped he would visit the house again and that he should send a message by Newlove to announce his arrival. He went on another occasion, when the same performance took place as before. He was in uniform both times.

Newlove admitted the truth of the three statements when they were shown and read over to him. He and the three boys were immediately suspended from duty and told to go home. Newlove who lived with his mother, lost no time in seeking out a youth named Hewitt, who had introduced him to Hammond more than two years previously, and telling him what had happened. Together they went to Cleveland Street early next morning and warned Hammond, who told them that he would go away and urged Newlove 'to stoutly deny everything'. Later that morning Hammond was seen leaving the house with a black portmanteau and accompanied by another man who from his dress appeared to be a clergyman. The latter turned out to be an individual named George Veck who had been living with Hammond under the name of the Rev. G. D. Veck, although in fact he had never been in holy orders. Hammond then went off to Gravesend where he had a brother living, while Veck took lodgings in Howland Street, near Cleveland Street, under the name of the Rev. George Barber.

Meanwhile the Postmaster General, Mr. C. H. Raikes, MP, was informed of what had happened in the office, and he immediately reported the facts to the Metropolitan Police Commissioner, to whom the statements taken by P.C. Hanks from the three telegraph boys were also sent. In those days, and indeed for many years afterwards, the office of Chief of the Metropolitan Police was never occupied by a career police officer but invariably filled by someone outside the police ranks, usually a senior army officer but sometimes a high-ranking member of the Indian civil service. The present Commissioner was Mr. James Monro, who had only held the office for a few months. He was an energetic and conscientious Scot who had served as a judge and police commissioner in Bengal before returning to Britain in 1884 to become head of the CID at Scotland Yard. Although he then held the rank of Assistant Commissioner, Monro claimed that his department was independent and directly responsible to the Home Office. This brought him into conflict with the then Commissioner, General Sir Charles Warren, who forced him to resign in the summer of 1888 when the notorious Jack the Ripper murders of prostitutes were at their height. However, two months later, Warren wrote an article for a magazine, stressing that the head of the CID should be subordinate to the Commissioner. Since this was in flagrant violation of a Home Office directive forbidding police to discuss internal matters in the press, Warren was in turn obliged to send in his resignation. This enabled the Home Secretary, Mr. Henry Matthews, to recall Monro to Scotland Yard and install him as Warren's successor.

On 5 July 1889, Monro instructed Chief Inspector Frederick Abberline of the CID to apply to the magistrate at Great Marlborough Street Police Court for warrants for the arrest of Hammond and Newlove on charges of criminal conspiracy. Abberline, already well known for his investigations in the Jack the Ripper case, was a soft-spoken portly man rising fifty, who looked more like a bank manager than the formidable detective he was. He duly laid the facts before the magistrate on the following day and was granted the warrants for 'that they did unlawfully, wickedly and corruptly conspire, combine, confederate and agree to incite and procure George Alma Wright and divers other persons to commit the abominable crime of buggery against the peace of Her Majesty the Queen.'

When the detective went to Cleveland Street next morning to arrest Hammond, he found the house shut up and no trace of the proprietor. Abberline then went on to Camden Town where he arrested Newlove about 1.30 p.m. in his mother's house.

On his way to the police station, Newlove remarked to Abberline:

'I think it is hard that I should get into trouble while men in high positions are allowed to walk about free.'

'What do you mean?' asked the detective.

'Why,' Newlove replied, 'Lord Arthur Somerset goes regularly to the house in Cleveland Street, so does the Earl of Euston and Colonel Jervois.'

Asked who Colonel Jervois was, Newlove answered that he lived at Winchester in the army barracks there.

After spending the night in the cells, Newlove was brought before the magistrate in Marlborough Street and remanded in custody for a week so that further inquiries could be made by the police.

Next day, 9 July, P.C. Hanks called to see Newlove's mother in Camden Town, apparently at the request of another son who also worked in the Post Office. As he was speaking to Mrs. Newlove, there was a knock at the front door, and Mrs. Newlove said: 'That's Mr. Veck, I know his knock.' Hanks at once left the room and went into the passage, where he could stand out of sight. He saw Veck enter and overheard him say to Mrs. Newlove: 'Have you heard anything further?'

On Mrs. Newlove saying she had not, her visitor remarked: 'Dear me, how strange! I saw Hammond at Gravesend yesterday and I have been down there today but he had flown. I cannot say where he is. I will see Henry is right and I will see you all right as well. Do you want any money? If so, let me know . . . I will instruct a solicitor to defend Henry in the morning.'

Meanwhile Inspector Abberline had been finding out something about Mr. Veck. 'He dresses as a clergyman but I know that he is not a clergyman of any sort,' the detective reported to the Commissioner. 'He was formerly a telegraphist in the Eastern District Post Office and I have been informed that he was dismissed from the service for improper conduct with telegraph messengers . . . He has a lad about eighteen years old living with him whom he passes off as his son, and who is occupying the same apartments. Since he left the Post Office service he has kept a coffee house at Gravesend where he is now wanted on a warrant for non-payment of rates.'

2

Observation was ordered by Scotland Yard to be kept on the house at 19 Cleveland Street, and a police constable named Sladden was detailed for the job. He began his duties on 9 July. At 4.50 p.m. on that day he saw a gentleman arrive and knock at the door. He was answered from the door but apparently did not go in. Shortly afterwards a corporal of the 2nd Life Guards arrived at the house. The gentleman and the corporal shook hands, talked for about five minutes and walked away without entering the house. Three days later a horse van arrived and all the furniture was removed from the house, being taken to Gravesend and stored by Hammond's brother Ted who lived there. Thereafter the house was unoccupied. On 13 July the gentleman and the corporal again appeared, and when they found the house empty they went away. P.C. Sladden later deposed that on the same day a great many other gentlemen called at the house with the same result.

In his report to the Commissioner, Inspector Abberline stated that he had lost no time in endeavouring to arrest Hammond but found he had absconded. His report, which was dated 18 July, continued:

> Observation has been kept on the house—19 Cleveland Street—and a number of men of superior bearing and apparently of good position have been seen to call there accompanied by boys in some instances, and on two occasions by a soldier, but after waiting about in a suspicious manner left without gaining admission. Some of them arrived in separate cabs, and evidently met by appointment at the house for unnatural purposes.
>
> From inquiries I am satisfied that Hammond for a considerable time past has obtained his livelihood by procuring boys and allowing persons to visit his house for unnatural purposes. Although at the present stage of the case (until Hammond is arrested) I have not deemed it prudent to interrogate other boys at the Post Office, I have every reason to believe that a large number have been defiled at this house. . . .

I have received information—confidentially—that Hammond is now in Paris. His postal address in Mme de Foissard, 8 Passages des Abbesses, Paris. I beg to ask that the French authorities be communicated with to ensure if possible his arrest.

An attempt was accordingly made through the Foreign Office to obtain Hammond's extradition on a charge of 'conspiracy to incite persons to commit unnatural offences.' But it appeared that this was not an offence which was covered by the current Anglo-French extradition treaty, and Scotland Yard was informed that 'the Foreign Secretary does not consider this to be a case in which any official application could justifiably be made to the French Government for assistance in surrendering the fugitive to this country.' The Foreign Secretary at this time was the fifty-nine-year-old patrician Marquess of Salisbury, who was also Prime Minister.

On 25 July, two of the telegraph boys who had been suspended, Swinscow and Thickbroom, met P.C. Sladden by prior arrangement in Piccadilly. Swinscow identified the gentleman whom he had seen calling twice at Cleveland Street at the same time as the Guards corporal, as Lord Arthur Somerset and as a person who had been with him (Swinscow) in the house. This was done when Lord Arthur came out of a club in Piccadilly. He was thereupon followed by Sladden with the boys to the Hyde Park Barracks in Knightsbridge where he was quartered with his regiment, his rank being that of major in the Royal Horse Guards (The Blues). He was again identified there by a sergeant. Thickbroom also identified Lord Arthur 'as the person who had acted indecently with him at 19 Cleveland Street.' Another of the boys, William Perkins, later described a tall man, answering to Lord Arthur's description, as having acted with him in a similar manner.

Constable Sladden subsequently had this to say about the boys:

I was with them many weeks keeping observation on different club houses. I had a bitter feeling towards them at first, but in time my feelings altered towards them through being in continuous conversation with them.

[27]

I found them very deficient in knowledge of simple things that surprised me [with the result] that I came to the conclusion that they were ignorant of the crimes they committed with other persons.

'I know that evidence of informers is generally tainted, but the evidence of the boys is not nearly so tainted as would have been the evidence of one of these professional wretches,' Labouchere afterwards remarked in the House of Commons when the case was under discussion. 'These boys were employed at the Post Office. They have been more sinned against than sinning, and it is not likely that they would have identified Lord Arthur Somerset unless they honestly believed that he was the man who tempted them.'

Henry Arthur George Somerset, known as Lord Arthur Somerset to distinguish him from his elder brother whose first name was also Henry, was the third son of the eighth Duke of Beaufort, who lived at Badminton in Gloucestershire, where he was a considerable landowner. The Duke was well known as a sportsman, a former Master of the Horse at the court of Queen Victoria, and besides devising the game resembling tennis played with shuttlecocks, he also gave the name of his country estate to the well-known series of works on sport of which he was co-editor and without which no country gentleman's library was complete in those days. At the time Arthur Somerset first came to the notice of the authorities in connection with the house in Cleveland Street, he was thirty-seven, and his career had hitherto followed the conventional lines of a peer's younger son. At Eton, where he spent two years at school, he formed a close friendship with Reginald Brett, whose father, the first Lord Esher, was an eminent lawyer who sat on the judicial bench for thirty years. After leaving Eton, Arthur Somerset was gazetted a cornet in the Blues at the age of eighteen, and during the next fourteen years rose to the rank of major, at the same time serving with his regiment in Egypt and the Sudan. When in London he stayed either in barracks or with his grandmother, the Dowager Duchess of Beaufort, who had a house in Hill Street, Mayfair. As a subaltern he was admitted into the intimate circle of the Prince of Wales and became a member of the Marlborough Club, which the

Prince had founded opposite his house in Pall Mall and which no one could join without the Prince's personal approval.

When trouble broke out in Egypt following the breakdown of the Turkish and native government in 1882, Somerset embarked for Alexandria with his regiment as part of the expeditionary force 25,000 strong which was despatched under the command of General Sir Garnet Wolseley. On the eve of their jubilant departure, the Prince of Wales gave a dinner for twenty-three officers of the Blues at the Marlborough Club, including the commanding officer, Colonel the Hon. Oliver Montagu, and Captain Lord Arthur Somerset. The decisive defeat of the Egyptian army by the expeditionary force a few weeks later at Tel-el-Kebir led to the British occupation of the country. Two years afterwards, Somerset, who had in the meantime been promoted to field rank, again saw active service with the relief expedition which went up the Nile with the object of rescuing General Gordon who was besieged by the Sudanese tribal forces in Khartoum. In January 1885, he took part in the engagement at Abu Klea with the Mahdi's troops who greatly outnumbered the British contingent and were successfully repulsed. On this occasion Somerset was wounded, but the British commander, Sir Herbert Stewart, and the war correspondent, Colonel Fred Burnaby, famous for his ride to Khiva, were both killed. For his services Somerset was awarded the campaign medal with two clasps and a bronze star.

Shortly after returning to England, Lord Arthur stood as a Conservative candidate at the General Election of 1885 for the Chippenham Division of Wiltshire. Although the Liberals suffered many losses at this election, among those defeated being Somerset's friend Reginald Brett, who had sat as a Liberal in the previous Parliament, Lord Arthur was not elected. He therefore went back to regimental soldiering. At the same time he was appointed an equerry to the Prince of Wales and superintendent of his stables, for which purpose he had an office in Marlborough House. He seems to have been generally popular in the regiment as well as being liked by the Prince who relied greatly on his judgment in buying horses for racing and breeding. In the words of the profile which accompanied his cartoon by 'Spy' (Leslie Ward) and which appeared in *Vanity Fair* on 19 November 1887, 'he is now Extra Equerry to the Prince of Wales and as such has the control of the Marlborough House stables, for which his knowledge of and affection for horses well fits him. He hunts much with his father's hounds, he is the best of sons, a true Somerset, a gentleman, a good sportsman, good natured, and of much solid sense. He is favourably regarded by the fair sex, and his irreverent brother officers long ago nicknamed him Podge.'

After the two telegraph boys had identified 'Podge' and had made additional statements to the police, thus confirming Newlove's admission to the police at the time he was first brought up before the magistrate in Great Marlborough Street, the authorities had to consider what further steps if any against Lord Arthur Somerset should be taken on the strength of this evidence. The initial opinion in the office of the Director of Public Prosecutions was that any prosecution 'in cases of this character' should be undertaken by the police. However, Commissioner Monro did not agree, now that the name of such a distinguished person as Lord Arthur had been introduced, and he appealed to the Home Secretary, Henry Matthews. 'I do not consider that his prosecution is in any sense a Police Prosecution,' he wrote on 22 July, 'and there are no funds at the disposal of the Metropolitan Police to meet the legal expense which must necessarily be incurred.' In the event Matthews ruled that the case should be undertaken by the Director of Public Prosecutions.

Before joining the Salisbury Government as the first Catholic to sit in the Cabinet since the passing of the Emancipation Act, Matthews, a man of substantial private means, had had a successful career at the Bar, his last case before becoming a minister being the sensational Crawford divorce in which he cross-examined the co-respondent and Liberal M.P., Sir Charles Dilke, with considerable skill and effect. On account of his education at the University of Paris, since his religion at that time debarred him from Oxford and Cambridge, he was somewhat unkindly known as 'the French dancing master'. In the House of Commons he was a failure; nor did he shine as a departmental minister. On the other hand, he was a man of wit and charm and he moved in fashionable social circles which his ample private means enabled him to do with ease. Lord Salisbury liked him and regarded him highly on account of his influence in Irish Catholic circles, and when he threatened to resign early in 1889 on account of what he thought was the Government's failure to honour its election pledges over Ireland, the Prime Minister was genuinely alarmed and he begged the Lord Chancellor, Lord Halsbury, to try to persuade Matthews to change his mind. 'The loss of him at this time would very seriously imperil the Government,' wrote Salisbury, 'and I think I am not putting our value too high when I say that the fall of the Government at this time would probably be fatal to the Union . . . Pray do what you can. The resignation of Matthews at this time involves something more than the defeat of the [Conservative] Party.' The upshot was that Matthews stayed and in the result was incidentally to play a part in the Cleveland Street affair.

The Home Secretary's decision meant that the matter strictly speaking came under the Treasury, since the Director of Public Prosecutions was Solicitor to the Treasury and had his office in the Treasury building in Whitehall. The then Director was Sir Augustus Stephenson, an elderly barrister near retiring age. The Assistant Director was the Hon. Hamilton Cuffe, later fifth and last Earl of Desart, an able and energetic lawyer of thirty-two, who was to be mainly responsible for the handling of the case since Stephenson was absent on leave for much of the time. A few years later Cuffe was to succeed his chief as Director, and shortly afterwards to initiate the proceedings against Oscar Wilde on homosexual charges under the Criminal Law Amendment Act.

Stephenson's first action was to send the papers down to the chambers of Horace Avory in the Temple with a request for an opinion. Avory, later a well-known judge, was at this time one of the Junior Treasury counsel responsible for the conduct of prosecutions at the Old Bailey. He gave his opinion on 3 August to the effect that it was 'not expedient to proceed against Newlove until all means have been exhausted to compel the attendance of Hammond to answer the charge,' and he advised that 'further application be made to the Foreign Office for assistance.' As a result Newlove, who had already been remanded three times, was again remanded for another week, and the procedure was repeated at regular weekly intervals until Newlove was eventually committed for trial five weeks later. As for the question of Hammond, pending any further move by the Foreign Office, Inspector Abberline was despatched to Paris to ascertain whether the French police would do anything to help. But the detective had little success and duly reported to the Commissioner that in his view, 'unless great weight is brought to bear upon the French Police, they are not likely to put themselves to much trouble in the matter.'

As from this date the police kept a watch on Lord Arthur Somerset's movements. On 7 August two constables interviewed him at Hyde Park barracks on the occasion of the German Kaiser's state visit to this country. No record of this meeting has survived, but presumably he was asked if he had ever been to Cleveland Street and whether he knew Swinscow and Thickbroom who had identified him as having been there with them, which in any case he later denied.

Stephenson's next move was to consult the two government law officers, Sir Richard Webster, the Attorney General, and Sir Edward Clarke, the Solicitor General. Accordingly a consultation took place in Webster's chambers in Pump Court on Saturday 10 August, the resulting opinion being written by the Attorney General and signed by all three.

> We are of opinion that proceedings should be taken against the man Veck alias Barber and also against Lord Arthur Somerset. There is not at present any sufficient evidence against the other parties except Hammond to justify proceedings. As regards Veck he should in our judgment be arrested on warrant founded on sworn information on the charge on which Newlove is now remanded.
>
> As regards Lord Arthur Somerset a Summons should in the first case be issued against him to appear to answer a charge under section 11 of the Criminal Law Amendment Act. The question whether any

further charge should be presented against Veck or Lord Arthur Somerset must depend upon the course of proceedings.

It is noteworthy that, so sensitive was the feeling in the Treasury Solicitor's office when this opinion was delivered, that pieces of paper were pasted over the name of Lord Arthur Somerset. At the same time, Godfrey Lushington, the Permanent Under-Secretary at the Home Office, wrote a brief note to Stephenson informing him that 'Mr. Matthews wishes you to stay your hand until he has seen Lord Salisbury on Monday.' Naturally Stephenson was none too pleased by this request which smacked of political interference with the course of law, and he only complied with considerable reluctance.

During the next week further papers were sent to the Attorney General, and in the result Webster wrote to Stephenson on 17 August as follows:

> I have read the further statements of Thickbroom, Swinscow and P.C. Sladden which have been taken since the Solicitor General, Avory and self advised on this case on the 10th inst. These statements differ on important points from those previously before us and I am not satisfied with the evidence of identification of Lord Arthur Somerset. I therefore give you directions that no proceedings be taken against him till further directions given. Directions against Veck in accordance with opinion of 10th.

Richard Everard Webster, later Viscount Alverstone and Lord Chief Justice of England, who figures prominently in this narrative as the senior government law officer, was not a very clever man, nor a learned lawyer, nor a good speaker, either in the courts or in parliament. But these defects were made up for by an imposing presence, a powerful personality and immense industry. He is said to have delighted in playing billiards and singing drawing-room songs, and was an assiduous churchgoer. At the same time he indulged in a somewhat boisterous geniality which gave his detractors the impression of a *faux bon homme*.

In accordance with the Attorney General's directive to Stephenson, in which the name of Lord Arthur Somerset was again pasted over, an information was sworn by the police against Veck on 19 August and a warrant granted by the Great Marlborough Street magistrate for his arrest. However, when the police went to his lodgings in Howland Street at seven o'clock the following morning, they found that Veck was away. But there was a boy there aged seventeen who gave his name as George Barber and described himself as Veck's 'Private Secretary'. He was sleeping in Veck's bed and in reply to police questioning he stated that Veck had gone to Portsmouth and was coming back the same day. Inspector Abberline and another police officer then went to Waterloo railway station where they arrested him as soon as his train arrived.

On the same day Lushington wrote from the Foreign Office to Stephenson that Lord Salisbury, 'having decided that it was impossible to move the French Government in the matter of the suggested surrender or expulsion of Hammond from France', was now of the opinion that 'the case against the other prisoners should be proceeded with in the usual way under the instructions of the Attorney General.'

3

When the police searched Veck on his arrest, some letters were found on him from a teen-age youth named Algernon Allies asking for money and mentioning a certain 'Mr. Brown' who had been helping him financially. Also in his pocket was a piece of paper with Newlove's address in Camden Town and above the address the following words: 'Let me urge upon you the extreme necessity of utmost secrecy'. In addition Veck was carrying a letter from Hammond in which the latter wrote to him: 'Let me know when it is safe to come back.'

It appeared that Algernon Allies had once lived with Hammond in Cleveland Street but was now living with his parents at their home in Sudbury, Suffolk, where his father was a coachman in service. Inspector Abberline thereupon sent P.C. Hanks down to Sudbury in plain clothes to take a statement from young Allies. The youth stated that he had received a number of letters from

Mr. Brown. He also admitted that as the result of an anonymous letter he had had the previous day, he had destroyed all Mr. Brown's letters that were in his possession. On being pressed, Allies confessed that Mr. Brown was really Lord Arthur Somerset, who had been supplying him with money for services rendered. This was confirmed when Hanks visited the local post office and found three postal orders for £1 each which had been despatched from the Knightsbridge district office and cashed by Allies.

On 22 August a police officer again saw Lord Arthur at Hyde Park barracks. After the first interview a fortnight previously, Lord Arthur had consulted his solicitor, Arthur Newton, whom he asked to undertake Newlove's defence and at his expense. Somerset was alarmed by the news of Veck's arrest and agreed to arrange for his defence as well. Then, after the police saw him for the second time, on 22 August, Lord Arthur obtained permission to go abroad on leave immediately. Before leaving, he wrote to his friend 'Redge' Brett, telling him he expected the defence would cost another £1,000 in addition to what he had already put up. 'Of course I would not drag any one into it for the world,' he assured Brett. He also thanked his friend for seeing 'that fellow yesterday', presumably Veck just before his arrest. 'How bored I shall be at Homburg!' he added. When he reached Dover, bad weather ('1,000 gales') prevented the packet-boat from sailing, so that he was able to write a few more lines from the Lord Warden Hotel. 'I expect others, very likely many others, will appear on the scene as this man (Veck) did the correspondence and knows everything.'

On 23 August Allies was brought up to London by P.C. Hanks and after making a statement, he was taken to the Treasury where he was seen by Sir Augustus Stephenson. There is no record of his statement or of his interview with the Public Prosecutor, but it is possible to piece his story together from other sources. He was a good-looking curly-haired youth of twenty who had been out of a job for the past six months or so and during that time had been living at home with his parents. Before that he had been employed as a house boy in the Marlborough Club, where he had attracted the attention of Lord Arthur Somerset. He had also stolen some money from the club premises as a result of which he was arrested and charged with theft. He appealed to Lord Arthur for help, and instead of being sent to prison, he was bound over, Lord Arthur going surety for his good behaviour. In the circumstances he was not given his job back in the club, where he had been provided with living quarters. Afraid to go home on account of the disgrace of his conviction, he againt went to Somerset for help. Lord Arthur said he would try to get him a job in a London tobacconist's shop which the lad had heard of. In the meantime he had to have somewhere to live. Accordingly Somerset wrote a letter from his grandmother's house in Hill Street to Hammond in Cleveland Street asking him to accommodate young Allies, and in the result Allies was put up there 'as a friend of Mr. Brown's.' He remained in Cleveland Street for three months, but left to go home before Hammond and Veck fled the house in July. Meanwhile he continued to pester Somerset for money, since he was still without work and nothing had come of the job with the tobacconist.

Allies's statement incriminating Lord Arthur was sent with other papers by Stephenson to the Home Secretary. At the same time, the Public Prosecutor asked the Attorney General for further directions in the case of Newlove and Veck. 'The prosecution wishes to avoid putting any witness into the box who refers to "Mr. Brown",' wrote Stephenson; at the same time he pointed out that 'it is of course impossible to say what course will be taken by the prisoner Veck', since the police were already in possession of letters from Veck to Newlove referring to 'Mr Brown'. Meanwhile a difference of opinion as to the wisdom of initiating criminal proceedings against Somerset developed between the Home Secretary and the Director of Public Prosecutions.

On 26 August, Matthews wrote to Stephenson after reading the additional papers:

> The principle accepted by the Attorney General was that a charge of this sort ought not to be preferred unless the evidence was complete and gave a moral certainty of a conviction. These additional

papers contain only the evidence of a participator (Allies) in the offence which would not be sufficient in law to warrant a conviction unless it was corroborated by untainted evidence. The evidence in question stands peculiarly in need of corroboration: the story of numerous letters, all destroyed, seems very suspicious.

So far as I am able to form a judgment, it appears to me that there is not sufficient evidence to justify proceedings against Lord Arthur Somerset.

P.S. This is a case in which I think any 'directions' should be given by the Attorney General himself.

Next day Stephenson wrote from the Treasury to Webster enclosing the additional papers:

In the Director's judgment it is the duty of the prosecution to submit to the magistrate in the prosecution of Newlove, Veck and Hammond without regard to what the consequences may be to this individual, be he 'Mr. Brown', Lord Arthur Somerset or any other man.

He therefore proposed to go ahead with the case but not to prefer a charge against anyone else without the Attorney General's express direction.

'I think the course you propose is quite right,' Webster replied. 'If Brown's name comes out at the Police Court it will be at once "name disclosed".' In this event he (the Attorney General) would consider whether or not to take proceedings against Somerset when he had seen the depositions sworn by the witnesses. On the other hand, if Brown's identity was not disclosed, he thought that all the documents affecting him ought to be communicated in confidence to the Secretary of State for War. In the event of proceedings, young Barber, who had been living with Veck at the time of his arrest and had previously been with him in Cleveland Street, should be able to identify the persons who frequented the house, since he was an 'untainted' witness. 'In my opinion,' Webster added, 'Brown's conduct must and ought to be brought home to him.'

From this view the Home Secretary emphatically dissented. There was still no case against Lord Arthur Somerset, he told

Stephenson. 'The duty of the prosecution,' he added, 'is to give evidence of the charge which has been made before the magistrate and to confine themselves to that: not to make fishing inquiries about other charges and other persons. In the "evidence" I have seen today, among a vast amount of irrelevant matter, I found nothing to suggest any fresh charge.'

By this time the subject of this correspondence had arrived in Homburg, the picturesque watering-place near Frankfurt which had become popular with English visitors through the patronage of the Prince of Wales. Besides its casino and gaming-rooms, which antedated their more famous counterpart at Monte Carlo, Homburg possessed sparkling chalybeate and saline springs, which were supposed to be particularly good for the stomach trouble regularly suffered by the Prince of Wales and his entourage through overeating. 'A lovely place full of English people who were much surprised to see me,' Somerset wrote to his friend Brett from the Villa Imperiale. 'I am living here over HRH with whom I lunched yesterday . . . I never tasted anything so nasty as the waters but I hope they will do me good . . . This is a highly moral place and all the ladies of pleasure are turned out!!' In the same letter he adjured his friend 'for Heaven's sake to make Newton keep the expenses down as much as possible.'

Arthur Newton, Somerset's solicitor, who had been instructed to undertake the defence of Newlove and Veck and of Somerset himself if it came to it, was a remarkable young attorney aged twenty-nine who claimed descent from the scientist Sir Isaac Newton and who had only been practising for five years. But during that period he had built up an extensive practice, particularly in the police courts, his office being conveniently situated opposite the Great Marlborough Street court. He was a persuasive advocate and had a charm and sense of humour which gained him many friends and clients. He had the advantage of a good appearance and a courteous manner, which contrasted favourably with the more common type of police-court advocate of the period. He also had the advantage of a good education, since his father, who was the manager of the Legal and General Assurance Society, had been able to send him first to a fashionable preparatory school and then to Cheltenham College, after which he was despatched on a voyage to New Zealand and back so that he could see something of the world before settling down to the law. Although his course seemed firmly set on the road to the peak of success in his profession—with the exception of George Lewis, and perhaps one other solicitor, he probably had the largest criminal practice in London at this time—unfortunately Arthur Newton was inclined to sail rather too near the wind on occasion, and this was to prove his undoing when he was eventually convicted of a serious charge of fraud and sent to penal servitude for three years. But this fate lay nearly a quarter of a century ahead, and until he began to act for Somerset his career was unclouded by any professional misfortune or setback.

Besides the fact that Allies had been picked up by the police, which he learned from Brett, Somerset was worried by the prolongation of the current dock strike in London. 'I hope this strike will soon cease or I may be recalled to join the regiment,' he wrote to Brett from Homburg on 1 September. 'It would be most inconvenient at the moment.' He went on:

> When you said that A[llies] had been carried off, you did not mean that he had been arrested, did you? Because I cannot see upon what charge that could be done. In case anything should be done about myself, I hope N[ewton] will prevent their going all over the place to search for me by saying that I am abroad. . . .
> I trust Webster gave good advice on the subject.

On the same day as Somerset wrote this letter, a police constable called at Hyde Park Barracks and learned for the first time that Lord Arthur had obtained four months' leave of absence and had gone abroad, taking no servant with him and leaving no address. This information was immediately reported to the Treasury Solicitor. 'It is quite possible (in my judgment it is probable) that he will not return,' Stephenson told Webster in passing on the news to him. 'It may be the best thing that could happen.' A week later Stephenson again wrote to Webster that other soldiers and an officer

Captain Montagu Barber, also a man named Ripley, might also have to be charged along with Somerset.[1] At the same time he pointed out that a summons could not be served upon the latter until he returned to England.

On 10 September, the Attorney General gave his opinion on the case to date as follows:

> In my opinion some action must now be taken respecting Lord Arthur Somerset. Upon the depositions already taken (particularly that of Allies) it is quite clear that Brown can be identified. . . .
>
> The person who sent Allies several times to Cleveland Street, whom Allies saw in Hill Street, and from whom Allies received postal orders, was undoubtedly Lord Arthur Somerset.
>
> The evidence is independent altogether of the identification in Piccadilly, and of the admission made by Newlove, and I note further that a description corresponding as I understand with that of Lord Arthur Somerset has been given by the witnesses Barber and Swinscow and Thickbroom and Perkins.[2]
>
> If it be the fact that Allies has for some time past been receiving money from Lord Arthur Somerset and that his mother knew the money came from that person (although her knowledge is not evidence), the truth of Allies's story is in my opinion strongly confirmed.
>
> I do not at present know what means exist of identifying [Captain] Barber or the Colonel from Winchester or any other person or whether there is sufficient evidence of any offence by Ripley, but in my opinion the proper course is to issue a summons or sworn information against such persons as can be identified including Lord Arthur Somerset for an offence under section 11 of the Criminal Law Amendment Act. There is not in my opinion any sufficient evidence of conspiracy to justify proceedings [on that count]. In my judgment some communication must be made to the military authorities.

[1] Although I have been unable positively to identify Ripley, it is possible that he was George Ripley (1845–95), a younger son of the Yorkshire baronet, Sir Henry Ripley.
[2] Barber was the boy who lived with Veck and is not to be confused with Captain Montagu Barber. William Perkins was one of the telegraph boys who was suspended from duty and eventually dismissed.

Evidence was given by the telegraph boys against Newlove and Veck at the preliminary proceedings before the magistrate in Marlborough Street on 27 August and 3 and 4 September, mention being made of Hammond and various persons who were alleged to have visited Cleveland Street, in particular Lord Arthur Somerset and the Earl of Euston. But this evidence passed unnoticed in the press apart from a vague reference which appeared in one London evening paper *The Star*.

Meanwhile a mutual friend of Somerset and Brett in the City, a stockbroker named Hugh Weguelin, had been trying to raise more money for the defence. He wrote to Brett on 9 September after he had seen Newton:

> Frankly, Reggie, the only person seriously implicated is A[rthur] S[omerset]. That is perfectly evident and I am afraid you will have to warn him that he must produce the sum required by hook or by crook. I certainly think that for him it is of importance that the affair should go through as quietly as possible. You may have seen *The Star* on Friday night; it mentioned a 'sporting nobleman'. I should strongly advise him to come home, and see Leo Rothschild or someone like that and borrow if he can. I think it very unfair that other people whose names are mentioned in this business should not bear some of the heat of the day. I think Eric Barrington, Howard Sturgis and one or two others should be called upon to assist and that money whatever it amounted to should be given him to repay the loan.[1]
>
> The constant description of him in the court is the one thing, as far as I can make out from Newton, that he has to fear and that has come about entirely because he did not have confidence at first and has allowed the second brat to be *pincé*. According to Newton the money should be forthcoming the end of this week, so the important thing is to get it somehow at once. I suggest a line from Leo to AS

---

[1] Eric Barrington was Lord Salisbury's Private Secretary at the Foreign Office. Howard Sturgis (1865–1919) was a well-off American homosexual, whose father was a partner in Baring's Bank. He wrote one outstanding novel called *Belchamber*, did embroidery and entertained his friends in his luxurious house near Windsor Great Park, where he was a neighbour of Brett's. A. C. Benson has written an account of him in *Memories and Friends* (1924).

and subscriptions after to repay as much of it as possible. Can you get him to do this? I shall be very glad with you or anyone else to 'back his bill', but I am not inclined to trust myself any further in Mr. Newton's hands. I am writing to N today to say that I cannot personally go in deeper but that I will use every endeavour to assist in getting the sum needed or as much as possible.

There is no doubt we can get a lot of money together from personal friends later on, but as the need for AS is pressing I think he should really come back at once and see to it. You see, Reggie, we cannot blind ourselves to the fact that *he* is primarily in this mess and that principally through his own act. We are only hangers-on and there is only a distant probability involving an immense stirring up of mud of our being injured. Therefore he must come back and do all he can to fight the battle. Telegraph him today and impress your strong opinion that this is his best method.

In fact Brett had already written to his friend in this sense. Somerset immediately replied from Homburg on 10 September: 'Your letter is very serious. Try if possible to enable me to return by Thursday week (the 19th) as my mother wishes me to go there (Badminton) before I go to Newmarket. As she has been very ill I should like to do so.' He added that the Prince of Wales wished him to go to Hanover and Berlin to see some horses on his way home and that he had to meet the Prince on the latter's way through London to Denmark with the Princess of Wales by the 21st, 'so please mind that all is clear by that time if possible.'

On the same day Brett wrote to the solicitor Newton with a clear hint that it would be best for all concerned if Veck and Newlove were to plead guilty:

At present my strong suspicion is that efforts should be concentrated upon the two men in custody, i.e. to simplify and shorten the inquiry and arrange for their fate on the lines of least hardship.

With regard to the other person not in custody [Hammond], I confess that it goes against the grain to see him profit by his villainies, and if he could be 'procrastinated' with and then cavalierly dealt with it would be no more than he deserves. I am not at all sure that

in the long run it would not have been better had he been in a similar
position to the other two. . . .

I confess I shall be glad when this odious affair is disposed of and
I have no doubt that you share the sentiment.

Were you acquainted with the mother of our friend and were you
to know all she has suffered in life, you would feel that no stone ought
to be left unturned to spare her any blow.

It is true that the Duchess of Beaufort's life had never been
particularly happy from the day when as Lady Georgiana Curzon,
'The Old Blue 'Un', as her husband was popularly known, had proposed to her at Badminton in the middle of a thunder storm from
which she was hiding between two big double doors. The Duke was
notoriously fond of other women and he retained his bachelor rooms
in London to facilitate his love affairs. On one occasion, when he
was away, there was a party at Badminton and just as the guests
were going into lunch the butler told the Duchess that a large case
had arrived which he had unpacked; it contained a picture, and the
butler wished to know where to hang it. So the whole party went into
the corridor after lunch to inspect the portrait which was that of a
pretty young woman whom everyone knew to be the Duke's mistress.
With complete self-possession the Duchess looked at it admiringly
and said: 'Is it not charming? A fancy portrait, I suppose.' At first
she thought it might do very well on the corridor wall. Then, chang-
ing her mind, she said to the butler: 'His Grace might like it in his
own room perhaps. You had better hang it there.' And there it was
hung as a pleasant surprise for the Duke when he returned.

The next cross which the Duchess had to bear was the trouble
which occurred between her second son, Lord Henry Somerset,
known in the family as 'Penna', and his wife Isabella, who was the
heiress daughter of the last Earl Somers. After five years of marriage
Isabella, who was very straitlaced, left her husband, allegedly on
account of his homosexual inclinations, taking their only child with
her. 'We have nothing whatever to say in defence of Penna and unless he is mad cannot understand his behaviour', the Duchess wrote
to her daughter-in-law at the time, while the Duke told his son that

'a man may get tired of his wife but your conduct and language is not that of a gentleman.' He added that in his view Lord Henry would 'never get the child in any Court of Law.' However, Lord Henry was determined to try. The result was a long drawn out legal battle for the custody of their infant son which began in 1877 and terminated a year later in Isabella being awarded the infant's custody subject to the father having reasonable access. Isabella made no attempt to get a divorce, which was contrary to her religious beliefs, and she devoted the remainder of her life to the cause of temperance and other good works, after she had been ostracised by society for violating the code of womanly reticence in marital relationships. At the same time her husband retired first to Monaco and later to Florence, then a fashionable resort for expatriate homosexuals, where he made a name for himself as a sentimental songwriter, his compositions (which his behaviour did not prevent being frequently sung in Victorian drawing-rooms) including 'Hush me, O Sorrow', 'All through the Night' and 'Dawn'.

Finally, the Beauforts' youngest child and only daughter Blanche, an unusually beautiful and gifted woman, who married the widower Marquess of Waterford in 1874, developed cancer from which she eventually died, while her husband became a cripple as the result of a hunting accident and ultimately committed suicide by shooting himself.

4

On 11 September, Veck and Newlove were again brought up before the magistrate, Mr. James Hannay, at Marlborough Street for a final hearing. They were formally committed for trial at the next Old Bailey sessions which were due to start immediately. Bail was refused. The facts were briefly reported in *The Times*, the only morning newspaper to do so, Veck being described as a well-dressed man of middle age and Newlove as a youth, both charged on remand with 'conspiring to induce boys to go into a house in Cleveland Street'. *The Times* noted that 'it was mentioned in evidence that Veck occasionally assumed the garb of a clergyman and was addressed as such.' It was also noted that during the proceedings the Public Prosecutor sat beside the magistrate on the bench. During the various police-court hearings, Horace Avory, the Junior Treasury counsel, led for the prosecution, while Newton appeared for Newlove and Charles Gill for Veck.

Charlie Gill, a hard-headed and hard-hitting Irishman, who was shortly to join the team of Junior Treasury counsel at the Old Bailey and was later to prosecute Oscar Wilde, had been frequently briefed by Newton in police-court cases. He had acquired a considerable reputation for securing acquittals, particularly for sexual offences in the London parks. When the lighting in Hyde Park was considerably improved, which it was at this period, he complained that he had lost £2,000 a year in fees as a consequence.

'I must say I despair of a secret known to many being kept especially in these days,' Somerset wrote to Brett next day before he had seen *The Times*. 'Hang *The Star*! What a curse the press is!' On 14 September, he wrote again to his friend, saying that no words could describe his horror on seeing a paragraph in the *Pall Mall Gazette* which appeared later on the same day as *The Times* notice and which he had read in the train on his way from Homburg to Hanover. 'I see the *Pall Mall* has got hold of it,' Eric Barrington wrote from the Foreign Office to Brett, who was staying at Studley Royal, the country house in Yorkshire of the liberal leader, Lord Ripon. Barrington was keeping Brett posted with the latest developments in the case. 'A nasty paragraph this evening. I don't like the looks of things,' he added.

The paragraph in question, undoubtedly written by the editor, read as follows:

> We are glad to see that Sir Augustus Stephenson, Solicitor to the Treasury, was present at the Marlborough-street police-court yesterday, when two prisoners were committed for trial in connection with a criminal charge of a very disgraceful nature. Mr. Hannay refused bail for both the accused, and no doubt if found guilty by a jury they will receive exemplary punishment. But the question which Sir Augustus Stephenson will have to answer is whether the

two noble lords and other notable persons in society who were accused by the witnesses of having been the principals in the crime for which the man Veck was committed for trial are to be allowed to escape scot free. There has been much too much of that kind of thing in the past. The wretched agents are run in and sent to penal servitude; the lords and gentlemen who employ them swagger at large and are even welcomed as valuable allies of the Administration of the day.

'I fear from that all is lost,' Somerset wrote to his friend from the Hotel Continental in Hanover, 'because our names must have been mentioned in court and therefore are common property. It makes my position awfully difficult having letters of introduction to everyone here. I really dread presenting them and yet I can hardly do my business without doing so.'

He went on to tell Brett that he had called at the Post Office in Hanover for his mail but 'found nothing', which 'rather relieved' him, as he was expecting 'every moment to hear from HRH or [his Comptroller Sir Dighton] Probyn or the Regiment on the subject.'

> I have even got so far as to wonder what I am to do with myself in case of the worst. Stead and *The Star* will never leave us now they have got our names, even if matters can be stopped where they are, which I take it seems very doubtful as I see by the *Pall Mall* that the Treasury Solicitor prosecuted.
>
> The Kaiser is here and the whole place full and illuminated with arches etc. Very pretty, but I can think of only one thing.

On the same day, Brett wrote from Studley Royal to Newton, telling him that he thought he had succeeded in stopping any further reference to the case in the *Pall Mall Gazette*, no doubt owing to his influence with the proprietor and the Liberal party leaders. But he regretted that he had no influence with *The Star* and its editor T. P. O'Connor, the Irish Nationalist MP, who had left the *Pall Mall Gazette* to start an evening paper with a new look. 'As to funds which are essential and urgent,' Brett went on, 'I have written to Mr. W[eguelin] expressing a hope he will make a temporary sacrifice to enable you to meet the immediate demand.' Weguelin immediately responded with a cheque for £1,200 but stipulated that it was to 'cover everything'.

'I am sure that a speedy settlement of the case is essential,' Brett now assured the solicitor, 'and that your success in carrying it through will be warmly recognised by all concerned.'

5

In those days indictments were lengthy and complicated documents which had to be engrossed on parchment before they were presented to the Grand Jury. The indictment in the case of Newlove and Veck had already been drawn by Avory, but in the light of the news received by the Treasury Solicitor that the French intended to expel Hammond, the Crown counsel applied to the Recorder of London, Sir Thomas Chambers, who was the judge appointed to try the case at the Old Bailey, to have Hammond's name added. The Recorder agreed on being told that his name appeared throughout the depositions 'so that having absconded he could be arrested if he came over.'

Hammond was thus indicted along with Newlove and Veck on thirteen counts of procuring six boys—Wright, Swinscow, Thickbroom, Perkins, Barber and Allies—'to commit divers acts of gross indecency with another person' between 20 December 1888 and 25 March 1889. There were also counts charging conspiracy to commit the same offence. In addition Veck was specifically charged with committing acts of gross indecency with Allies and Barber, contrary to section 11 of the Criminal Law Amendment Act, and Newlove with similar acts with Swinscow as well as the attempted buggery of Wright.

In the light of the indictment and the evidence given at the police court, Newton and the counsel he had briefed, Gill for Veck and Willie Mathews for Newlove, advised the two prisoners as to the best course they should adopt when the trial came on. As a result Veck decided to plead guilty to the charges relating to Allies and Barber but not guilty to those of conspiracy and procuring. 'Avory thinks we ought to accept this plea,' Cuffe informed Stephenson on 17 September. As for Newlove, he decided to plead guilty to everything except the attempted buggery.

Next morning, before the prisoners were brought to court, Cuffe received the following telegram from the Attorney General:

> If both prisoners plead guilty do not proceed with charges of conspiracy unless counsel strongly advises.

Consequently Cuffe agreed with Harry Poland, QC, the Senior Treasury Counsel who was to lead Avory for the Crown, that it would be best to accept the pleas of both prisoners in regard to the indecency charges under the Act and not to press the charges of conspiracy and procuring, and in Newlove's case, that of attempted buggery. The latter charge, as Cuffe afterwards told Stephenson, was 'in the process of "messing about" and added little if anything morally to his offence and would not, as we all thought, affect the sentence.'

In view of the accusation subsequently made by Labouchere and others that the prosecution had made a bargain with the prisoners' counsel that if the prisoners pleaded guilty to certain counts in the indictment, which would mean that they would not give evidence and mention names, the other charges would be dropped and they would receive light sentences, it is perhaps as well to quote from the written statement which Poland wrote and signed at the Attorney General's request and which Webster later read out in the House of Commons when Labouchere raised the matter.

> Mr. Avory, my junior, was informed by Mr. Gill, who defended Newlove, or by Mr. Mathews, who defended Veck, that the prisoners intended to plead guilty, and that the case would be disposed of in the course of the day. I went to the Old Bailey between 3 and 4 o'clock, that being the time when pleas of guilty are taken, when convenient. I addressed the Recorder, and Mr. Gill and Mr. Mathews addressed him also.
>
> I wish to say that I neither directly nor indirectly made any arrangement with the prisoners' counsel as to what counts the pri-

soners should plead guilty to, and that there was no undertaking of any kind, either express or implied, as to what should be done by me or by the prisoners' counsel.

Also, Poland was of the opinion—'an opinion which I entirely share', said the Attorney General afterwards—that no good was done by reporting cases of this description, 'and it is greatly to the credit of the reporters of the Press', Webster added, 'that they almost invariably refrain from reporting them.' Futhermore, Webster had Poland's assurance in writing that he took no steps to get the Court cleared or to prevent the proceedings from being reported in the newspapers. 'I was specially careful', Poland emphasised, 'to do nothing in this case out of the usual and ordinary course.' The only noteworthy incident occurred just after Poland had begun to address the Court. The Recorder noticed that there was a woman in court, and the judge of his own accord ordered her to leave.

Sir Thomas Chambers, who was nearly seventy-five, had sat on the Bench at the Old Bailey for the past thirty-two years. In those days the Recorder could also sit in Parliament, and Chambers had also been a Liberal MP for over a quarter of a century before 1885, but he did not stand again at the General Election. In the House of Commons he had made a name for himself as a law reformer, persistently advocating legislation to provide for the inspection of convents and to permit marriage with a deceased wife's sister. His ideas on penal matters and the rehabilitation of convicted prisoners were in advance of his time, and he was noted for the lenience of his sentences. Indeed it may have been for this reason that an attempt was made to have the case heard by one of the High Court judges who habitually sat at the Old Bailey sessions, but these judges primarily dealt with felonies, leaving the Recorder and Common Serjeant to deal with cases of misdemeanour such as the offence of 'gross indecency', which came within the latter category under the 1885 Act. 'I may say we tried to get the case into the Judge's list originally,' Cuffe afterwards reported to Stephenson, 'but the Recorder said there were twenty-two cases in the Judge's list and he could not depart from the rule about misdemeanours.' In the event, when Poland got on his feet in court, 'he stated the facts clearly and temperately (perhaps *too* temperately having regard to the temperament of the judge),' according to Cuffe, 'telling the story so that the Recorder should know Veck's connection with the house and all he did.'

The Crown counsel set the scene in his opening words:

> 19 Cleveland Street, which is a house close to the Middlesex Hospital, has for some time been in the occupation of a man named Charles Hammond who is not now in custody. The evidence shows that for a considerable time that house has been used as a brothel, except that women do not go there but boys, and the house is used for immoral purposes.

Poland then went on to describe the events from the police first being called in, following the theft of money in the General Post Office, to the arrest of Newlove and Veck. He emphasised that Newlove induced the telegraph boys in the Post Office to go to Cleveland Street, in addition to himself committing acts of gross indecency with two of the boys there.

> Dealing with his case first, I desire to point out that, having procured these boys to go to this place, the boys did go there. They were paid sometimes a sovereign, sometimes half a sovereign; four shillings was kept by themselves and the rest given to Hammond or kept by Newlove. After this [the police being called in] he communicated this information to Hammond which induced him to move the furniture and go abroad to evade justice.

'Where did the money come from?' the Recorder asked at this point.

'From the persons who are described as gentlemen who went to the bedroom with the boys,' replied Poland. 'They were asked what they had received. He has admitted that he induced them to go there, and no doubt the policy was to let the boys know that they would receive money for the acts of indecency.'

Coming to the case of Veck, counsel pointed out that, although Hammond was the landlord, there was no question but that Veck had lived in the house and assumed the garb of a clergyman, having cards printed indicating his religious status. Then, when he was taken into custody, a piece of paper with Newlove's address, a warning about the necessity for secrecy, as well as letters from Allies who had admitted to committing acts of indecency with him, were found in his possession.

Although two witnesses named Joseph Taylor and William Lovelock, who lived near by, had stated that they had seen Veck take boys and soldiers into the house, their recollection was vague and Poland was inclined to disregard it. But he stressed that Veck was in the house when Newlove caused the lads to go there. 'He has pleaded guilty to the most serious charge of committing acts of indecency with these two persons (Barber and Allies),' Poland concluded, 'and section 11 gives your Lordship very full powers. He is no clergyman at all. He was in the service of the Post Office and left in 1880, and although he pretended to be a clergyman it appears to be a sham for purposes best known to himself.'

Charles Gill then rose to explain why he had advised Veck, on whose behalf he appeared, to plead guilty to the statutory offence. 'He never asked the boys to go to the house, there is not a particle of evidence of procuring the boys or of conspiring on his part,' he said, 'but there is evidence of his committing the offence created by section 11 of the Criminal Law Amendment Act with regard to Barber and Allies. I therefore came to the conclusion that after a long inquiry and great public scandal, the jury would come to the conclusion that there was some evidence on these two counts and he would be convicted. As regards these acts of indecency, they were acts of indecency only and that was long after they (Barber and Allies) had, according to their own account, been doing this kind of thing, and they were only isolated instances.'

His client had known Hammond 'in respectable circumstances', Gill went on, and at one time had been employed by him. In July, when he was supposed to have taken boys and soldiers into the house, according to Taylor and Lovelock, he was actually out of London.

The only boy whom he had accompanied to and from the house,

was Hammond's son and that was when he was going to school. 'There was not a single boy who said he had gone into the house in Veck's company.'

'I submit to your Lordship that this man has never had a charge brought against him before,' Gill concluded his short speech in mitigation. 'He simply pleads to the offence under the new statute. He is in no way connected with bringing boys to the house. He has adopted the course of pleading guilty and so saved a long and most unpleasant inquiry . . . He is not in a position to call witnesses as to character under the lamentable circumstances in which he finds himself. He has been some time in custody—six weeks—and is in a bad state of health.'

Willie Mathews was equally brief on behalf of Newlove. 'I must ask your Lordship to exercise as much clemency as you can,' he pleaded with the Recorder. 'He is not yet nineteen—not till next month; he has been four years in the employ of the Post Office and he is a boy of excellent character. What may be his failings I am not in a position to give you evidence of, but he has been more or less under the control of persons older than he is. Mr. Hammond is a man of mature age and your Lordship may think he has had some effect on him. As to the charge to which he has pleaded guilty as to the boys Wright, Thickbroom and Swinscow, he does admit that he did take them to this house, knowing what might happen to them.' On the other hand, the three boys had admitted that they had all indulged in indecent practices before Newlove approached them, and Mathews went on to read from the statements to this effect that they had made to the police. He also asked the Recorder to take into account the fact that Newlove had already been in prison for nearly three months. 'I sincerely hope that the fact that he did not corrupt boys who had been blameless but rather made suggestions to boys who had not been blameless, that he has pleaded guilty to the charge under section 11 of the Criminal Law Amendment Act, which has avoided a public investigation, will all weigh with your lordship,' defence counsel concluded, 'and that looking at his age you will give him some chance of redeeming his character.'

[52]

'In justice to the boys,' Poland broke in here, 'I wish to say that they had played with other boys but had not committed these acts.'

'They said that they had done such acts with boys before but not with men,' Mathews retorted. 'That goes to the degree.'

This difference of opinion was not pursued, and the Recorder immediately proceeded to pass sentence. He did this in characteristically few words:

> Prisoners at the bar, you have pleaded guilty to these offences, all of them offences created by a recent Statute making such acts as these misdemeanours. The learned counsel very properly stated all that is necessary on both sides of the question. The sentence of the Court upon you Veck is that you be kept at hard labour for nine calendar months and upon you Newlove that you be kept at hard labour in the House of Correction for four calendar months.

What Cuffe called 'the travesty of justice at which I assisted at the Central Criminal Court' finished at ten minutes to six, so that he only just had time to catch the 6.15 train from Waterloo so as to be able to dine with Webster at the latter's house in Cranleigh and give him an account of the proceedings. 'The Recorder said hardly anything,' he also reported to Stephenson next morning, 'and the only reason for the ridiculous sentences that could be drawn was that by pleading guilty they had saved him the trouble of reading the depositions. Well! we can't help the sentences and as regards the other matters the case has neither advanced nor prejudiced the situation.' In his letter to Stephenson, who was on leave, Cuffe added that the Attorney General took the view that the case against Lord Arthur Somerset should go on, 'sharing our opinion that whatever happens the man cannot be allowed to walk about as a respectable member of society.'

On the same day, Hugh Weguelin, who had also been in court, wrote to Brett: 'The whole thing was hustled through in half an hour. The younger got only four months and the elder nine. Newton considers this very light. He wishes to get one or two people out of the country but this he will see to. It is *most* important that your friend should tell the truth and say whether he has written any letters, as now the enemy is defeated is the time to get him. I do not think he will have any more trouble.'

Brett's informant was mistaken. Somerset's troubles were really just beginning. At the same time, the name of a much more illustrious personage than his own was introduced into the case—in fact that of a prominent member of the Royal Family.

CHAPTER II

Prince Albert Victor
and Lord Arthur Somerset

I

'I AM TOLD that Newton has boasted that if we go on a very distinguished person will be involved (PAV). I don't mean to say that I for one instant credit it—but in such circumstances as this one never knows what may be said, be concocted or be true.' Thus Hamilton Cuffe, the Assistant Public Prosecutor, wrote to his chief, Sir Augustus Stephenson, on 16 September 1889. What Cuffe had heard and what was being talked about in the London clubs gave a new and disturbing twist to the Cleveland Street case.

The initials 'PAV' in Cuffe's letter stood for Prince Albert Victor, generally known at this time as Prince Eddy or Eddie, more familiarly as 'Collars-and-Cuffs', and later as the Duke of Clarence and Avondale, which he was created on his return from a tour of India in the following year. He was the elder son of the Prince and Princess of Wales and as such stood next to his father in the direct line of succession to the English throne. The story was now spreading that the twenty-four-year-old Prince used to visit the house in Cleveland Street and that his name appeared in the book of aristocratic and noble customers which the establishment's proprietor kept there.

Albert Victor Christian Edward, to give Prince Eddy his full names, had been a seven months' baby and he had suffered from feeble health ever since his premature birth. After a trip round the world with his younger brother George, followed by a spell at Cambridge under a private tutor, he went into the 10th Hussars. Although he seems to have got on well enough with his fellow officers, Prince Eddy disliked army life, particularly the routine of a cavalry regiment. His health was not improved by a pronounced love of pleasure of various kinds. On the other hand, he had considerable charm, his manners were polished if languid, and he was attractive to women. There is no evidence that he was homosexual, or even bisexual. On the contrary, he formed several romantic attachments to women, of which the first was to Princess Alix of Hesse who turned him down for the future Tsar Nicholas II of Russia. 'Dear nice boy,' Somerset's sister, Lady Waterford, called Prince Eddy. He had brown, wavy hair, an oval face, aquiline nose, large, gentle, doe-like eyes, and a little cavalry moustache which was waxed and turned up at the ends. He also had an unusually long neck, 'like a swan', as one of his family called it, and as a result, when not in uniform he was obliged to wear a very high, starched collar, which led to his being nicknamed 'Collars-and-Cuffs' by Labouchere. The name stuck and was even teasingly applied to him by his father.

'I think HRH [Prince Eddy] has far more in him than he is generally given credit for,' wrote Sir Garnet Wolseley, then Adjutant-General of the army, to the Commander-in-Chief, the Duke of Cambridge, 'but I should describe his brain and thinking powers as maturing slowly . . . Personally I think he is *very much* to be liked, has most excellent manners, thoughtful for others and always anxious to do the right thing. He is, however, young for his age and requires to be brought out. I studied him closely when staying in a country house with him, and this is the result of my study.' Much has been made of his alleged dissipation and emotional instability by various royal biographers, notably those of his mother and of the future Queen Mary, to whom he was to be briefly engaged. He was an enthusiast for shooting and fishing and other field sports, particularly big game, and if his health was progressively undermined, it was as much the result of the pleasures of the gun and rod and hunting field as those of the boudoir, although his indulgence in the latter was known to have resulted in at least one attack of venereal disease. He was also an incessant cigarette smoker—Turkish were the rule in those days—and he was warned by his doctor of the risks he was running. He also suffered from gout, which made his younger brother George remark that 'it sounds as if one was talking of an old man.'

The regimental depot was in York, where Prince Eddy had a regular doctor. On one occasion, when the doctor was away and had left his practice in the charge of a young *locum* of the Prince's age, named Alfred Fripp, the latter was sent for to Scarborough where Prince Eddy was running a high temperature and was ordered to bed. Young Fripp, who later became a famous surgeon, impressed his patient so much that he was regularly called in and later presented to his father and to Queen Victoria, who both thanked him. Fripp wrote to his parents at this time:

> HRH seems to take kindly to me. We get on very well together, but my ingenuity is sorely taxed to exhibit the right mixture of firmness and politeness. You would be amused to see Colonel This and the Hon. That dancing around and asking me the most minute directions—what time he is to take his meals; then the menu for each meal is submitted for me. I have to have long talks with each, and then again with HRH who pours out all his little woes and always makes me smoke in his room. He smokes himself until he is stupid. I have knocked him down to three cigarettes and one cigar a day . . .
>
> Don't mention HRH's illness outside our house as the Prince of Wales particularly wants it not to get into the papers. He is afraid the public will get the impression that his son is a chronic invalid.

Fripp did not specify the nature of his patient's malady, apart from describing it as 'a sharpish attack of fever', but a prescription found among Fripp's papers by his biographer after his death indicated that the Prince suffered from a gonorrhoeal infection. Another surgeon named Thomas Stowell, who died in 1970, claimed that Prince Eddy had contracted syphilis in the West Indies during his world tour some years previously and that this had caused paresis or softening of the brain which led Prince Eddy to be confined for a time in a private mental home near Sandringham. This information Stowell claimed to have got from the papers of Queen Victoria's personal physician, Sir William Gull. In an article published in *The Criminologist* in November 1970, and also in a subsequent television interview, Stowell hinted that in a fit of insanity brought on by his alleged syphilis, Prince Eddy had committed the terrible murders of prostitutes in Whitechapel in the autumn of 1888 and could thus be identified with Jack the Ripper. Stowell declined to be more specific, apparently on the grounds of not wishing to embarrass the present Royal Family. And as he died shortly afterwards, having burned all his notes on which the article was based, posterity is none the wiser.

If Stowell really had Prince Eddy in mind as Jack the Ripper—he refers throughout the article to the Whitechapel killer as 'S'—the absurdity of his theory can easily be demonstrated by indisputable circumstantial evidence as to Prince Eddy's movements when the murders were being committed. For instance, in the case of two of the unfortunate victims, Prince Eddy was shooting with Prince Henry of Battenberg in Scotland, and on the occasion of the last murder, that of Mrs. Kelly, he was celebrating his father's birthday at Sandringham. On the other hand, there are some grounds for believing that 'S' may have been Prince Eddy's Cambridge tutor, James Kenneth Stephen, who subsequently went mad and died in an asylum. Prince Eddy's biographer, Michael Harrison, suggests that Stephen, a son of the judge Sir James FitzJames Stephen and cousin of Vanessa Bell and Virginia Woolf, had had a homosexual relationship, though not necessarily a physical one, with the Prince at Cambridge, and that the murders were committed by Stephen out of a perverted desire for revenge because of a gradual cessation of this relationship. This theory may be regarded by some as far-fetched, but not nearly so far as Mr. Stowell's identification of Jack the Ripper with Prince Eddy.

Although it can easily be shown that Prince Eddy was never in the East End of London at the time of the Whitechapel murders, there

[58]

are grounds for believing that he did visit the house in Cleveland
Street on at least one occasion, but not in the company of Lord
Arthur Somerset, as was alleged at the time. 'Please correct any impression that Arthur and *the boy* ever went out together,' Somerset's
sister, Lady Waterford, was to write to Reginald Brett. 'Arthur
knows nothing of his movements and was horrified to think he might
be supposed to take the Father's money and lead the son into mischief of *any* kind. I am sure the boy is as straight as a line, and as to
George Holford [Prince Eddy's equerry who was thought to have
accompanied him to Cleveland Street], even the blackguard
[Hammond] who "chantaged" A[rthur] never mentioned him or
thought of him. I am so glad—dear nice boy.'

Somerset was also to write from abroad to Brett on the subject in
similar terms:

> I can quite understand the Prince of Wales being much annoyed
> at his son's name being coupled with this thing, but that was the
> case before I left and nothing to do with me than the fact that we
> (that is Prince Eddy and I) must both perform bodily functions
> which we cannot do for each other. In the same way we were both
> accused of going to this place but not together, and different people
> were supposed to have gone there to meet us.

It is possible that Prince Eddy went to Cleveland Street under a
similar misapprehension to that which Lord Euston later claimed to
have done. When he was running the establishment, Hammond had
had cards printed, which he gave his touts to distribute, with his
name and the address in Cleveland Street and also the words '*Poses
plastiques*' at the top. *Poses plastiques* were the Victorian equivalent
of striptease, and they were what Prince Eddy may have thought he
was going to see and indeed may have seen, since it seems unlikely
that Hammond would have advertised his house thus if he did not
occasionally provide female entertainment as well as boys for his
customers. For many years Hammond had been associated with
women prostitutes, particularly those who used to come over from
Paris. His wife, known as Madame Caroline, was a French prostitute.

Another prostitute named Emily Baker is said to have lived with Hammond for several years. According to one witness, 'she used to write all his correspondence as he was a very bad scholar', and she was consequently in a position to 'give the names of all the gents who used the house, as she used to write them and make appointments for their visits.' On the other hand, Lord Euston, who said he had received one of Hammond's cards, was later to swear that when he arrived at the house Hammond told him that there were no '*poses plastiques*' and offered him boys instead. Also, there is a reference in the letter to Brett quoted above which suggests that it was Lord Euston who accompanied Prince Eddy to the house. 'I have never even mentioned Euston's name,' wrote Somerset, 'nor have I ever told *any one* with whom Prince Eddy was supposed to have gone there. I did not think it fair as I could not prove it, and it must have been his ruin.'

Exactly when the stories of Prince Eddy's alleged visits to Cleveland Street reached his father's ears is unclear. But there is no doubt that his general behaviour had been causing his parents worry for some time. Indeed the Prince of Wales had already decided that his elder son's remaining in the army was 'simply a waste of time— and he has not that knowledge even of Military subjects which he ought to possess. His education and future has been a matter of some considerable anxiety for us and the difficulty in rousing him is very great.' Hence the decision to despatch him on a tour of India for several months. His parents arranged to travel part of the way with him, their pretext being the wedding in Athens in October of the heir to the Greek throne, the Prince of Wales's nephew, Constantine Duke of Sparta, to the German Kaiser's sister, Princess Sophie—an occasion which attracted what Queen Victoria used to describe as 'the royal mob'. Then, while the Princess of Wales returned to Copenhagen with her parents, her husband arranged to go on with Eddy in the royal yacht *Osborne* to Port Said to see how Egypt was settling down under the new British dispensation.

When Lord Arthur Somerset met the Prince of Wales at Marlborough House on his way through London, as he had arranged to do, the Prince knew nothing of the whispered scandal involving his son and the superintendent of his stables. He merely told the latter to see that Prince Eddy was properly fitted out with saddlery and similar equipment for the forthcoming tour. He also asked Somerset to meet him again in a week's time and see him off to Denmark where he was taking his wife on a visit to her parents before the royal wedding in Athens which they all planned to attend.

After this meeting at Marlborough House, Somerset went on to Newmarket for the autumn sales. But he only spent two or three days there instead of the week or more he had expected to do. What caused his hurried change of plan appears from a letter his solicitor wrote to Brett on 26 September:

> I do not think it advisable in writing to go into details but when I was at home in the country last night at 11 o'clock I received information of the most reliable nature that on Friday (tomorrow) a warrant will be applied for against your friend. I immediately came up to town and was up till 3 this morning trying to find his whereabouts and sent down at 6 o'clock this morning to Windsor to find you. Kindly let me know where I can see you tomorrow.

Presumably Newton saw Brett in the latter's London house and between them they were able to let Somerset know in Newmarket that he should lose no time in getting out of the country. Somerset immediately acted on this unpleasant news, which in the event turned out to be a false alarm. He made for Dieppe, which he reached after a somewhat hectic journey, which he described in a letter to Brett on his arrival at the Hotel Royal:

> I had an awful drive to Cambridge, the axle heated and I had to take off the wheel. Of course it ran very heavy in consequence and the horse stopped a mile out of Cambridge and I had to run with two bags and a rug in a very thick coat a mile at least. However, I just caught the Kings Cross train, took a ticket to Hitchin but travelled on to Finsbury Park and paid excess there and thence to Brondesbury by road and thence by train to Willesden and thence to Addison Road, thence to Clapham Junction and so to Newhaven and

Dieppe and was not sick once—too much worried. I had a fright at Clapham, a man with black whiskers in a grey coat and white hat walked up to a policeman near me and said, 'I am not sure whether I shall want you or not'—but nothing happened.

It was suggested by either Brett or Newton that Somerset should change his name to Mr. Winter. 'I thought over the name,' Somerset wrote in the same letter, 'and it struck me that it might lead to awkward complications, as all my linen is marked AS and they might think Winter was a thief. Also my umbrella has A. Somerset on it, so I suppose I must stick to my name as Lytton and several people are here I see by the hotel book.' (Lord Lytton was British ambassador in Paris at this time.) 'I know you and Newton will do your best for me,' Somerset added. 'Let me know if anyone else is mixed up in this new phase and what the new phase is.'

2

Ever since the Home Secretary had expressed the view, which he did after he had read the statement taken from young Allies, that there was not sufficient evidence to prosecute Somerset, the question had continued to exercise the mind of the Public Prosecutor. On 15 September, while on leave at his home in Wiltshire, Stephenson wrote in the strongest terms to Webster:

> I have no apprehension that either the Secretary of State or that you as Attorney General will allow the responsibility of not proceeding against Lord Arthur Somerset, Ripley or Captain Barber to rest upon myself whether with the public or in Parliament; but there is one responsibility of which you cannot relieve me nor can I relieve myself except by distinctly disclaiming, as I now do most respectfully and most decidedly, any agreement with *the opinion* that the evidence in our possession does not justify nor call for the prosecution of Lord Arthur Somerset.
>
> My opinion is that Lord Arthur Somerset ought to be charged and proceeded against by warrant for conspiring with Hammond with respect to the boy Allies, as Newlove, Veck and Hammond have been charged with respect to the boy Wright.

I think in the interest of public justice this charge ought to be preferred, for if it is not, the evidence of Allies as to the statement made by Hammond to him, when he took the letter written by Lord Arthur Somerset at 19 Hill Street to 19 Cleveland Street and Hammond admitted him 'as a friend of Mr. Brown's', would be excluded.

In my opinion there is at present direct and overwhelming moral evidence against Lord Arthur Somerset for conspiring to procure and incite young Allies to commit the felony in addition to the offences under the Criminal Law Amendment Act. There is at present some evidence of the same description against Ripley and Captain M. Barber, and it is my duty as Director of Public Prosecutions (unless otherwise directed by the Attorney General) having undertaken at the direction of the Secretary of State the prosecution of Newlove and Hammond on the charge of conspiracy, to include in that prosecution any other person or persons to whom the evidence already obtained points, as it clearly does to Ripley and Captain M. Barber as co-conspirators with Newlove and Hammond.

I am also of the opinion that excepting as to the 6 persons above mentioned there is no evidence—nothing beyond the uncorroborated statements of accomplices—which would justify criminal proceedings against any others who have been referred to either by name or description as frequenting No. 19 Cleveland Street, but I think it extremely probable that further inquiries would furnish corroboration of those statements with respect of some of such persons.

Whether or not such inquiries should be made depends upon considerations of public policy or expediency. In my judgment much can be said both for and against prosecuting such inquiries—but unless and until further evidence should come to light in the prosecution of such inquiries re the 6 persons above mentioned I do not consider it my duty to prosecute such inquiries.

But I do consider it my duty either as Director of Public Prosecutions or as Solicitor to the War Office, unless I am expressly prohibited from doing so by the Home Secretary or the Attorney General, to furnish the War Department with all the information which has come to my knowledge affecting persons under War Office control.

Although no criminal charge could be preferred or conviction obtained in a criminal court against a commissioned officer for shaking hands with a private soldier at the door of a house known to be frequented by sodomites, or against private soldiers for entering such a house, I cannot think that a public official can be justified in witholding information which he believes to be worthy of credit of such occurrences from another public Department responsible for the observance of the Articles of War.

The question of public policy is not for me, assuming as I do that the entire responsibility for *not* preferring a charge—if no charge is to be preferred—or of not communicating with the War Office is taken from me by the Home Secretary or by yourself. Nor do I discuss again the sufficiency or otherwise of the evidence. The Secretary of State and you know all that I know and, although some of it may be technically inadmissible on the particular charge, in my opinion the moral effect of it leaves no reasonable doubt that Lord Arthur Somerset was a frequent visitor at 19 Cleveland Street *for immoral purposes*.

The public scandal involved in a criminal charge against a man in his position in Society is undoubted. But in my opinion the public scandal in declining to prefer such a charge and in permitting such a man to hold Her Majesty's Commission and remain in English society is much greater.

In my opinion the attempt to avoid such publicity—even if such attempt were justifiable which in my judgment it is not—must absolutely fail and the public scandal will then be infinitely aggravated.

Whatever may be said—and much may be said—as to the public policy of allowing *private* persons being full grown men to indulge their unnatural taste in private or in such a way as not necessarily to come to public knowledge, in my judgment the circumstances of this case demand the intervention of those whose *duty* it is to enforce the law and to protect the children of respectable parents taken in the service of the public, as these unfortunate boys have been, from being made the victims of the unnatural lust of full grown men —and no consideration of public scandal owing to the position in society or sympathy with the family of the offender should in my judgment militate against *this paramount duty*. (Stephenson's italics.)

[64]

This must be one of the strongest letters ever addressed by a Director of Public Prosecutions to a Government Law Officer on the subject of a case involving unusual political and social features.

Cuffe warmly sympathised with his chief, although he also appreciated the delicate position of the Home Secretary. 'My principal reason for hesitating to again force on the Secretary of State the weakness, not to use stronger language (as we think), of his position is we may hardly know *what* his position is. I should agree that, if you had not done it, it must have been done. But need it be repeated?' There was another view, Cuffe pointed out. 'If Lord Arthur Somerset is to be tried by court martial, he may get an exemplary sentence as in any other way, and the Attorney General thinks it seems rather to point to that. It *cannot* be left to slide whatever the case may be.'

Poland was also consulted, and Cuffe told Stephenson: 'He agrees with us, although with his usual caution he does not confidently say that the witnesses will be believed, that Lord Arthur Somerset's case ought to go to a jury and he ought to be taken by warrant . . . I certainly concur. A summons is like giving him notice to get away if in England and is futile if he is not.'

Meanwhile the Attorney General endorsed Stephenson's views, which he passed on to the Home Secretary. The minister thereupon shifted his ground and wrote back to Webster that he 'on consideration was not prepared to differ from and accepted the Attorney General's opinion as to the institution of proceedings [against Somerset] but before he could assent he must communicate with Lord Salisbury.' He did so by letter from the Home Office on 17 September as follows:

> Fresh evidence has come to the hands of the Director of Public Prosecutions against Lord Arthur Somerset, and the Attorney General writes to me now that in his opinion 'the case against Lord Arthur Somerset is complete;' that there is 'no doubt whatever as to his identity,' and that he 'cannot, on the information before him, take the responsibility of saying that proceedings shall not be taken against Lord Arthur Somerset.'
> Although I do not take quite so strong a view of the new evidence,

I think it is sufficiently cogent to make it impossible to interfere with the ordinary course of the law.

The magistrate (Hannay) informed the Attorney General that, if the case had not been under the Attorney General's control, he should have directed the persons implicated and identified to be brought before him.

As you have taken an interest in this case, I am anxious that no decisive step should be taken without your having the opportunity of expressing your opinion. I have requested the Attorney General to delay if possible until I or he receive a reply from you . . .

The first step would be to give notice of the charge to the military authorities. The next to apply for a summons or warrant.

I am informed that Lord Arthur Somerset has gone abroad; and, if so, proceedings will be suspended until his return.

It is a hateful business; but upon the whole the risk of interference with this charge is greater than the mischief it will do.

Salisbury replied that he thought the case should be referred to Lord Halsbury, the Lord Chancellor, for his opinion. On 21 September Matthews replied that he had asked Webster to communicate directly with Halsbury, who was in Scotland, in order to save time, and send him all the papers. The Home Secretary added for the Prime Minister's information: 'The new evidence was principally that of a youth who could not possibly be mistaken as to identity as he had known Lord Arthur Somerset at a Club where he had been a waiter; and whose narrative was corroborated by postal orders etc received from Lord Arthur Somerset.'

As Cuffe told his chief at the time, 'the position therefore has so far advanced that Matthews now accepts the Attorney General's opinion as to the correct view of the case and has presumably told this to Lord Salisbury.' Cuffe went on to reassure Stephenson as to the correctness of the line he had taken:

> Whether the Attorney General is personally responsible or whether the Home Secretary or Lord Salisbury or the Cabinet are responsible, all responsibility is taken off your shoulders. You have done your best that we think right should be done, and there it must rest for the moment.

[66]

My impression is that, while it is by no means certain we shall be authorised to prosecute Lord Arthur Somerset, steps will certainly be taken to remove him from the army and consequently 'society'.

There were no fresh developments for several days. Then, late in the afternoon of 25 September, Inspector Abberline called at the Treasury, as Cuffe put it, 'to say that a man (probably from Newton the solicitor) offered Allies today passage to America, £15 on landing, and £1 a week till he got work.' The Attorney General was immediately informed.

Meanwhile Somerset, who was chafing from inactivity in Dieppe, had been pressing for action over Allies. 'Make N[ewton] look sharp and get A[lgernon] A[llies] away, as if I could return in time before going to Newmarket it would certainly be all the better,' he wrote to Brett. 'In fact I cannot stay away without exciting curiosity. For the first time in the memory of man the stables don't know where the Master of the Horse is and they can't get a brush or an oat without my initials.' Unfortunately Newton's plan to get Allies away misfired and rebounded on the solicitor with most embarrassing consequences for himself.

Since the date he had been brought up to London from Sudbury a month previously, young Allies had been provided by the police with board and lodging at a coffee-house in Houndsditch called the Rose and Crown in case he should be needed to give evidence in court against Hammond and Somerset. According to Abberline, Allies came to his office about 4.30 in the afternoon of 25 September and told him that he had just received a call from a man sent by Newton who said he had been down to Sudbury the day before and obtained his address from his parents. 'You see they haven't paid your mother's expenses yet,' the man was alleged to have told the youth. 'They will tell you that you ought to be glad that you were not locked up and then you can go to the devil.' According to Allies when examined later in court, he said the man, who was in fact Newton's managing clerk, Frederick Taylorson, told him: 'The reason we want you to go abroad is because we don't want you to appear against you know who.' Allies also admitted that at first he thought he would like to go, but directly Taylorson had gone, 'I changed my mind because I did not think the agreement was quite substantial and I went and told Inspector Abberline.'

Abberline immediately brought Allies to the Treasury, where Cuffe saw them and directed a member of his staff to take a statement from Allies. This was done and read as follows:

Treasury 4.45 p.m. 25 September 1889

I am now staying at 38 Houndsditch, E.C. About a quarter past two this afternoon a man came to me at my lodgings. He was tall and fair and about 25, dressed like a gentleman with a thin light moustache and light trousers, light spats and a black jacket and waistcoat and high hat. He came upstairs by himself to the Dining Room where I was. There was another gentleman whom I don't know at dinner at the time. The person said to me, 'Mr. Allies?' I said, 'Yes.' He then said he would like to speak to me for a minute.

I took him into the Sitting Room where no one else was. He then said, 'I've come to persuade you to go away.' I said, 'Well, I must refer you to Mr. Abberline.' He said, 'If you go away to America, you will be found everything, clothing and everything you want, and I will give the Captain about £15 to give you when you get there to go on with.'

I said I would go and told him I should want underlinen, two suits, a pair of boots and a hat. He said, 'All right,' and took a piece of paper out of his pocket and wrote down the articles I wanted. He said it would be all right. I asked him how I should get on when I got there. He said, 'Oh, unless you can get work you will be allowed about £1 a week.'

I asked him where he came from and at first he would not tell me. Afterwards I remarked that Mr. Newton seemed to be very much against the witnesses and then he said, 'You must not take any notice of that—that is where I come from.' He then asked me to meet him this evening at 9 o'clock outside the A1 Public House in Tottenham Court Road to go to Liverpool tonight and he would get my clothing here and see me off tomorrow for America.

I agreed to meet him and I asked him to let me have the money to get a shirt, collar and tie and he gave me six shillings and then left. I then went at once to Inspector Abberline and told him and he brought me here. The man told me he had been down to my home in the country the day before.

A. E. ALLIES

After Allies had signed this statement, Cuffe asked Abberline to arrange to see who met him at nine o'clock that night and 'if possible to provide him with lodgings where he would not be interfered with.' P.C. Hanks then undertook to lodge him in his own house pending further arrangements being made for his safekeeping. Allies was also instructed to keep the appointment and he duly did so, while the police kept watch.

Allies arrived first and was standing in the passage outside the door of the private bar, when Taylorson came up and said, 'Oh, you have come then?' He went on to say that he had left his bag at another pub, the Marlborough Head in Great Marlborough Street and that they must go there for it. 'We'll jump into a cab.'

They then went out, crossed Oxford Street and hailed a passing cab. On the way to the other pub, Taylorson asked, thinking they might be followed by the police, 'Did you see any of them hanging about?' Allies said, 'No, have you?' Taylorson replied, 'No, it's all clear.' On entering the private bar of the Marlborough Head, he asked Allies if he had bought the shirt, collar and tie, and Allies told him that he had thought it best not to as it might arouse his landlady's suspicions. Taylorson then remarked that it was very cold and that he would buy him an overcoat on the way to the station.

At this moment Abberline and Hanks appeared. They had recognised a man named De Gallo, whom Newton employed as an enquiry agent, standing in the outside doorway of the private bar, and they both went inside. After telling Hanks to take charge of Allies, the detective turned to the other man and asked him, 'What is your name?'

At first he refused to give it but eventually admitted, 'My name is Frederick Taylorson. I am over the way at No. 24.'

'Are you not Mr. Newton's clerk?'

'Yes,' replied Taylorson.

'What are you doing with this lad?'

'I will answer no questions,' said Taylorson, who thereupon left the pub.

Hanks also claimed to have recognised Newton standing a few yards outside the pub with a tall fair man, after which they both walked away together in the direction of Regent Street. But in this the policeman was mistaken, since Newton at this very moment was entertaining some friends to dinner at his home in New Malden, some forty miles from London. In fact, Taylorson went straight off there, arriving at eleven o'clock the same night, thus being the source of the information about Somerset's possible arrest which caused Newton to return to London in the circumstances described in his letter to Brett already quoted, since Allies had told him what he had presumably gathered from Abberline that 'process was going to be taken.'

On 27 September, Newton wrote from his office at 24 Great Marlborough Street to the Treasury Solicitor about Allies, referring to the fact that 'he had given evidence in a case that had finally been disposed of' and complaining that the police were holding him in a small coffee house in Houndsditch in a state of duress. The police, Newton alleged, had even threatened him and had told him what to write in letters to his father.

> Acting on instructions from the boy's father our managing clerk called on him and told him it was his father's wish to remove him from the surroundings into which he had unfortunately fallen. The boy said he was in a state of terror and fright owing to the threats of the police.

Newton went on to state that young Allies had met his managing clerk and that they were followed by Inspector Abberline, 'who had the audacity' to take the boy away. Counsel's opinion had been taken, the solicitor added, and it was to the effect that the action of the police was entirely illegal. Consequently Newton asked for an appointment when the father could see and obtain possession of his

[70]

son, and as Mr. Allies was coming to Newton's office next morning, he suggested that young Allies should be produced there then.

To this letter Hamilton Cuffe replied that the case was not 'finally disposed of', since Hammond's name was still on the indictment; that it might be necessary at any moment for young Allies to give evidence against Hammond; that he was nineteen years of age and, so far from being in 'duress', he had expressed his willingness to remain in Detective Inspector Abberline's charge, and that the necessary arrangements had been made with his consent. 'I am sure,' Cuffe added, 'that you will feel as an officer of the Court that everything should be done to keep the boy in this country as long as there is a prospect that his evidence may be wanted in furtherance of public justice.' Newton was further reminded that 'any persons who were parties to sending the lad out of the country with the view of preventing him from giving evidence would render themselves liable to criminal proceedings.'

At the same time Allies made a further statement in Cuffe's office, denying that he was 'in a state of terror and fright owing to the threats made by the police and was most anxious to get away.' Nor had he told his father he was held under duress. 'I have no complaint about the way I have been treated by the police,' he added. 'I do not consider that I am detained forcibly and prevented from going away.' The statement continued:

> I consider it my duty to stay as long as I am wanted for this case. I should like to see the case out.
>
> If Mr. Newton or anyone else asks me to go away I shall refuse.
>
> I say that from a sense of duty and not because I believe I am under any compulsion . . .
>
> I have no wish to go to America.

Allies also stated that he had 'no special wish to see his parents', but if they pressed it he would be satisfied with any arrangements the Treasury Solicitor might make.

Next day, 1 October, the statement was read over to him in Cuffe's office and Allies was asked again whether he wished to see his father. 'I have nothing particular to see my father about,' he told

Cuffe, 'but I am willing to see him. I think I had better see him here or somewhere hereabouts so that Mr. Newton doesn't know anything about it.' Then, after a few moments' pause, he said: 'Do you think I'd better see my father?'

'I don't wish to express any opinion,' answered Cuffe. 'It is for you to say if you wish to see him. I don't want to exercise any influence or to do anything to prevent your seeing your father.'

Allies hesitated and said nothing for a minute or two. Then, having made up his mind, he declared: 'No, I don't wish to see him.'

Cuffe was then called out of the room. When he returned about five minutes later, he asked Allies whether he was quite sure about not wishing to see his father. 'That is my final conclusion,' said Allies. He then confirmed that his statement, which had been read over to him, was 'correct' and he added his signature to it.

The same day Somerset returned from Dieppe to England, none too pleased to have learned from Newton that Allies was the source of the story that a warrant had been about to be issued for his arrest. He warned Newton that Allies was 'the greatest liar in Europe and always knows everybody's business. Had I known it was only A[lgernon] A[llies] I should have stayed where I was and it would have been worth anything to have seen HRH off without exciting any comment.'

3

By this time Hammond was in Belgium preparing to sail from Antwerp to New York. On 4 October, Newton, who had just returned from a brief visit to Brussels where he had seen Hammond, told Hugh Weguelin that he could not settle 'the man in Paris', as he called Hammond, for less than £2,000. The same day Weguelin wrote to Brett with this unpalatable news, which in effect amounted to blackmail on Hammond's part:

> The 'man' aforesaid has an excellent position in that by remaining away himself but sending over a person who is with him he can strengthen the enemy's hands. Your friend will know to whom I refer. Ask him.

Practically N[ewton] has drawn the money as the boat starts
tomorrow morning in which the 'man' is to sail. He (Newton] had
an interview with your friend and is acting (as I understand) practically on the faith of what passed at that interview backed by a
verbal arrangement from me to see that he was not done out of his
money, i.e. that if it could not be promptly paid I would advance it
to him (N). For reasons explained to you I don't want to do this.
Capital is everything to me but I know you will use me gently. The
facts, however, which you must bear in mind whatever you do are
these:

1. It is not necessary for the 'man' to appear to upset plans. He
   has a deputy who could make a great fuss and suffer little if at
   all himself.
2. N[ewton] is acting on the faith of what he agreed with your
   friend.

The person or deputy in question appears to have been Newton's
clerk Taylorson, who had bought the steamship tickets for Hammond
and the boy travelling with him, and who in the event was to accompany them on their voyage as far as New York. To understand how
these events came about it is necessary to notice Hammond's
activities and movements from the time of his abrupt departure for
France immediately after Newlove's arrest in July.

Evidently unaware that an attempt was being made through the
Foreign Office to extradite him from France to stand trial on conspiracy charges, he wrote to his wife after he had been in Paris
for about a fortnight, under the impression that the trouble over his
house in Cleveland Street would blow over and he might eventually
be able to return to England.

Paris,
17 July 1889

My dear Caroline,
    A few lines to tell you that I have written to Bob and to Mr. Rip-
ley to ask them to find everything out for me, as I do not think things
are so bad as what people tell you. For if they wanted to find your

mother or Florence [Mrs. Hammond's sister] they could have followed
the furniture and they would soon have found you. You must remember that whatever was done was not done in our house; it was
done in the Post Office.

I think you have been very silly to let Florence or yourself fall
out with Mr. Veck. You ought to have been friends with him till all
the trouble had blown over. I had a letter from him this morning.
He tells me that Florence insulted him and has not told him anything, so he has not known what to do about money for me. You
remember I told you to take him to Gravesend with you, for you
know he has got all the addresses of my friends. I have written to
him to ask him to come over to France to see me. He wants me to
come to London, but that I shall not do until I can see that everything is all right . . .

Yr ever loving husband,
CHARLIE

Caroline Hammond's response to this letter was to visit Paris
herself. After she had arrived there, her husband wrote on 23 July
to their son, who was staying with Hammond's brother Ted in
Gravesend, and asked for news of 'how things are going on.'

Tell your uncle not to tell Mr. Veck that your mama is over here
with me. Tell him to write to him, and ask him why he does not
come over to see me or send me any money. I think there must be
something wrong as he has changed his name and [is] living under
the name of George Barber at 2 Howland Street, Tottenham Court
Road, London. If we do not get any news me and mama think of
coming back. Ask your uncle to send me a newspaper if there is anything in it about Henry [Newlove] . . .

Hammond stayed on in France, warned no doubt by their friends
at home that it would be dangerous for him to come back. Although
pressed by Commissioner Monro, who sent over Abberline and
another detective, the French police did not seem particularly keen
to help their opposite numbers in Scotland Yard. Eventually as the
result of a good deal of prodding, they agreed to expel Hammond
from France, but they declined to return him to England or to put
him on board a British vessel at any of the Channel ports. The most

they would do was to inform Hammond that he must leave French
territory. As a result he crossed the north-eastern frontier with
Belgium and Luxembourg on 12 September and left the train at the
first habitable place he reached a few miles inside Belgian territory.
This was Halanzy, where he took a room in the local hotel. A few
days later Caroline Hammond returned to England, leaving her
husband and the boy Ames at Halanzy.

Hammond was aware that he was being watched by the Belgian
police, as well as by an official from the GPO in London who was
trying to persuade the Belgian police to arrest him. But they intimated that they could only do so as the result of an extradition order,
and this was not forthcoming.

On 22 September, Hammond wrote to his sister-in-law from
Halanzy:

> A line to let you know we are still at the same place. One of the 2
> men that followed us from France has gone away and a Belgium
> [*sic*] man has come in his place. If we only go across the road from the
> Hotel they follow us. If I ask any questions they go and ask the
> people what I said to them. It makes me feel so ill I can scarcely eat
> my meals. I wish to god I knew what they are going to do. But I
> expect they will hunt us about from place to place.
>
> I hope poor Caroline is home. . . . Dear Florence, try and do all
> you can to make Caroline as happy as she can be. You must all stick
> to one another and do all you can for each other. For things may
> soon come to the worst and I may be turned away at a minute's
> notice and I have but very little money left and travelling is so ex-
> pensive. I wish Mr. Newton would send some one over with money
> at once . . . I hope you went to Mr. Newton and showed him my
> letter I sent you the other day.

This appeal had some effect, as Hammond showed signs of relief
in his next letter which was to his wife. 'Try and take courage for
they cannot touch me where I am,' he wrote to her on 30 September.
'I am waiting to see what they are going to give me. They sent me
over £30 for my present expenses. I have just received a telegram
from them asking me to go on nearer to Brussels so as he [Newton]

can come over to see me. I suppose it means to arrange with me what money I am to have.'

Thereafter events moved swiftly for Hammond, whose next letter to his wife was written three days later when he was preparing to embark for the United States:

> Just a line to let you know that we have arrived in Antwerp. And being happy to tell you that we have escaped without being followed after twelve hours hard journey.
>
> I must tell you my Solicitor met me at Brussels this morning. And then we went to his hotel and had a long talk about everything. He wants me to start for *America* on Saturday by the American Steamer that sails under the American Flag for *New York*. He said he wd pay all expenses for first Class Passage. And give me *Three Hundred Pounds*. But I refused to take such a little money. I told him he must pay all my Family's Expenses First Class Passage And give me *Eight Hundred Pounds* to start business with. He asked me how many there was to pay for. I told him there was three of you . . . He will come down and see you.

If Hammond was not actually followed, his movements were certainly observed by police agents and reported to Scotland Yard. In the event Newton and his clerk met Hammond and the boy Ames when they arrived at the Northern Railway Station from Halanzy and were observed going to the Hotel Bordeaux where the solicitor was staying. Evidently it was thought that Hammond and the boy might be stopped if they took the Antwerp train from the Brussels terminus, so Newton had them driven to Vilvorde, a small station about five miles from Brussels on the Antwerp line. Here they boarded the train, while Newton and his clerk followed on from Brussels.

In the same letter which Hammond wrote to his wife on reaching Antwerp, he gave her directions as to how to dispose of their household effects:

> You must sell all the things off by Auction. Ted will tell you how to do it. Sell all the Birds . . . You must buy another large basket

like the one you have got to pack the Bed Linnen [*sic*] and Velvet Curtains in And the two yellow silk Pillows. You can pack the best Dresden Vases that are on my Mantle Glass And the few best plates —there are the 2 large round ones and the Blue Dresden Dish that hangs on the wall. If Ted can get our Oil Paintings packed nicely I should like him to send them to me later on when I send my address or any thing you would like him to keep to send out to us.

As an afterthought he asked his wife to get Ted to find out how much it would cost to ship his piano to America 'properly packed'. The piano apparently was for his son's use, as in another letter Hammond told his son: 'Stick to your music for that will be useful by and by.'

Next morning he wrote again to his wife that he was expecting Newton any minute to tell him whether he could have the £800 for which he had asked. 'Of course I shall want my money before I sail.' Evidently the money was forthcoming as well as first-class tickets on board the SS *Pennland* of the Red Star Line, the tickets being bought at the local branch of Thos. Cook & Son by Newton's clerk Taylorson who was to accompany Hammond and the boy Ames as far as New York. 'A few lines to let you know that we have started for America,' Hammond wrote to Caroline as they were sailing down the Scheldt to the Hook of Holland. 'Mr. Newton wants you to come over in a week's time but of course if you have not sold your things you must say you cannot come over for a fortnight.'

According to Labouchere, Commissioner Monro wrote a strong letter from Scotland Yard to the Treasury Solicitor on 6 October, 'drawing attention to the stigma which would rest on the English police if Hammond were allowed to escape.' But it was too late. 'On that day he did escape.'

A week or so later the fugitive brothel-keeper wrote to Madam Caroline that 'we arrived quite safe in New York after a very nice voyage.' He was leaving for the west coast next day, he added, and would be staying with a mutual friend in Seattle called Adele Gayet, whose vocation it is not difficult to guess.

In the columns of *Truth* and later on the floor of the House of

Commons, Labouchere bitterly attacked Lord Salisbury's Government for their alleged laxity in allowing Hammond to get away. This
is what he had to say on the subject in the House:

> During the time Hammond had been in Belgium, the Belgian
> police reported that he was accompanied by an English boy. This
> boy had been abstracted from his parents presumably for vile
> purposes. Now, whilst Hammond was in Belgium, whilst the
> English and Belgian police were surrounding him, Mr. Newton, the
> solicitor to Lord Arthur Somerset and also to Veck and Newlove,
> either went to Belgium or sent someone there. This Mr. Newton,
> or the other person, gave Hammond a large sum of money, and
> also paid for the ticket not only of Hammond, but also of the boy
> who had fallen into such a terrible position. Any one can find that
> out by going to Cook's office . . .
>
> I cannot help thinking that if the Government had been in
> earnest, they might have obtained the extradition of Hammond,
> because our Extradition Treaties, both with France and Belgium,
> cover such charges as those of indecent assault, either by the princi-
> pal or by accessories. It was put in evidence before the magistrate,
> and I do not think it was questioned, that Hammond induced boys
> to come into a room and handed them over to the creature who was
> going to assault them. I should say that was being an accessory to
> an indecent assault . . .

Labouchere had spent ten years in the diplomatic service and he
knew what he was talking about. He had no doubt in his mind that
the French or Belgian Governments could have been induced to
expel Hammond by putting him on board a British ship which
would have brought him to England. 'If it had not been intended to
extradite Hammond, if the Government had no plan by which they
intended to get rid of him,' he asked, 'what was their object in
hunting this man from France to Belgium and from Belgium to
America, and then leaving him alone?'

Labby easily supplied the answer to his rhetorical question. 'I
think the object is pretty obvious,' he said. 'They wanted to send
him as far as possible from this country. Their object, in fact, was

much the same as that of Mr. Newton, who gave him money and paid his passage, and also that of the boy with him, to America. Both of them, each for different reasons, wanted him not to turn up in England. The Government did not wish for revelations; they wished to hush up the matter.'

It was a formidable challenge that the Government would have to meet if Lord Salisbury and its members were to retain any credibility with the public.

4

We must now return to Lord Arthur Somerset. Before leaving Dieppe for England, which he did on 30 September by the night boat to Newhaven, he had sent a telegram to the Prince of Wales, excusing himself for being unable to see the Prince off to Denmark as arranged, since (so he informed his royal master) he had been obliged to go 'on urgent private affairs' to Dieppe, where he had been detained. To this telegram he received a reply from HRH in person to the effect that the Prince regretted his absence but understood the reason. 'Of course that may mean that Matthews has told him all, or it may mean that my reason was sufficient,' Somerset wrote to Brett the day before he left France. 'Anyhow HRH or rather all T[heir] R[oyal] H[ighnesses] are abroad now until the second week in November, so that disposes of them for the present . . . My great hope is that if HRH had known all he would not have wired himself but I should have received a wire from Probyn or an equerry.'

Somerset travelled from Newhaven to Badminton by a route which avoided London. His solicitor, who met him somewhere along the route, had been against his returning to England at all, but now he had done so, Newton advised him to keep away from London, at any rate for a while, and in this he was supported by Brett. Hugh Weguelin, on the other hand, was more optimistic. 'There is a great deal of gossip,' he told Brett, 'but if the next week or two can be got over, all that will die out, mainly on account of his presence in England. We shall win but more money must be found . . . The ship mustn't be spoiled for a ha'porth of tar. We can easily raise the money for A[rthur] and he can repay either out of his own resources or by applying eventually to Papa by easy instalments . . . N[ewton] has seen him and now only waits for a telegram telling him of the whereabouts of the man in Paris and I have finally closed the matter. A[rthur] must be ready to repay N[ewton] and that is where our assistance will be wanted.' Weguelin was confident that he could get the money on loan at five per cent.

'Everything most successful here,' Somerset wrote to Brett on his arrival at Badminton. Apparently when tackled by his father about his leaving Newmarket without telling him, he had 'passed the thing off' to everyone's satisfaction. He now considered going racing with Brett at Kempton Park and was only prevented by a sudden death in the family. 'How gladly would I avail myself of your advice and go to Kempton,' he wrote to Brett on 3 October, 'but unfortunately my father's old mother aged 89 died in the night, so here of course I must stay—very tiresome!'

'One is almost glad that the old Duchess of Beaufort should have died before all this comes to light,' Cuffe wrote next day to Stephenson who was still on leave. 'She was I believe devoted to L[ord] A[rthur] S[omerset] who lived in her house in London when not in barracks.'[1] Cuffe added that apparently nothing had come from the Lord Chancellor. 'There can be no doubt lots of people know the

---

[1] She was a rich heiress, named Emily Frances, daughter of Charles Culling Smith and his wife born Lady Anne Wellesley, sister of the 1st Duke of Wellington. The Marquess of Worcester, as the 7th Duke of Beaufort (1792–1853) then was, had previously been married to her half-sister Georgiana Fitzroy, so that his second marriage came within the 'prohibited degrees of affinity', and as such was voidable by the Ecclesiastical Court. As it was, the wedding took place very quietly in St. George's, Hanover Square, in 1822, the bridegroom signing the register as 'Henry Somerset, widower'. Had the Ecclesiastical Court declared the marriage void—and anyone, whether interested or not, could set the ecclesiastical law in motion—the future 8th Duke of Beaufort would have been illegitimate, and it was to prevent this possibility that Lord Worcester persuaded his friend, the ex-Lord Chancellor Lord Lyndhurst, to bring in a remedial measure in 1835 designed, in the words of its title, 'to render certain marriages valid'. As originally drafted, Lyndhurst's Bill would have made all such marriages legal, future as well as past, but owing to strong opposition by the bishops and some of the lay peers, only those marriages solemnized before 31 August 1835 were declared

names and there are some MPs who would delight in the case.'

Somerset now decided to pay a hurried visit to London before his grandmother's funeral on the 8th so as to put matters right with his commanding officer, whom he guessed might have heard the rumours about him which were now beginning to circulate in the clubs. On 5 October, he wrote to Brett from Hyde Park Barracks:

All went well today and Oliver Montagu and Algie Lennox have promised to help all they can in refuting the scandal. Oliver has kindly promised to go to Fredensborg and see the Prince so as he may hear the right story first, and Algie says he will delay everything at Newmarket.

Algie went to see Monro and he said he did not feel justified in saying anything one way or the other. He said these things are secrets of the office and cannot be divulged . . .

My grandmother is to be buried on Tuesday at Badminton. I shall come up Wednesday and go to Sandringham on Thursday, stay there till about Saturday night and then come here and stay in barracks . . .

I have asked Newton to draft me a careful letter to write to him [the Prince of Wales] and Probyn. He must be told by me and not by any one else.

---

valid; any subsequent marriages were absolutely null and void. It was not until the law was again changed, in 1907, that a widower was legally able to marry his deceased wife's sister.

As a young man Lord Worcester, who succeeded his father as 7th Duke of Beaufort a few months after the passing of Lord Lyndhurst's Act, had been in love with and (according to her) wished to marry the famous Regency courtesan, Harriet Wilson, in whose frank memoirs he figures prominently. After he came into his inheritance in 1835, he made the Badminton Hunt famous, as Nimrod's *Sporting Reminiscences* testify. His second wife Emily, according to her great-granddaughter, Lady Clodagh Anson, 'had a vile temper, and was not a very pleasant woman'. For example, when she was out driving in her victoria and the coachman went in any direction she did not approve of, she would suddenly spring up and belabour him on the back with her umbrella. According to the same source, 'she had an enormous Wellington nose, which descended more or less to all her children', to whom she was 'very cruel', particularly her only son, the 8th Duke. 'When they sent him to school it was such an awful place and he was so miserable that he ran away home, but she had him well beaten and then sent straight back with a letter, asking the schoolmaster to thrash him, which he did with great gusto.' Lady Clodagh Anson. *In Victorian Days* (1957), pp. 78–79. However, she seems to have been very fond of her grandson Arthur.

Oliver Montagu, younger son of the Earl of Sandwich, was the Colonel of the Blues. He was also on terms of considerable intimacy with the Princess of Wales, although he was not her lover. But he was her ardent admirer, so that it was no hardship for him to make the journey on Somerset's behalf to the Danish royal castle where she and her husband were staying.

Somerset also gave his version of what had happened to Lord Algernon Lennox, whose father was the Duke of Richmond; he was Colonel of the Grenadier Guards, and also ADC to the Duke of Cambridge, commander-in-chief of the army. Lennox and Montagu had been staying at Gordon Castle, the Duke of Richmond's Scottish seat, and the party included Lord Cranbrook, the Lord President of the Council in the Salisbury Government, and Colonel Richard Pearson, the Assistant Commissioner of Police, who was a former officer in the Grenadier Guards. 'I suppose he let it out,' Somerset told Brett. 'If so he ought to be trounced. I rather hope that Algie Lennox, having gone to Monro about it, will put two and two together and tell Pearson what he thinks of him. What I should like to do would be to write and tell him I could prosecute him for slander, but I will write to no one except through Newton.'

Immediately after Lennox had seen Monro, the Commissioner wrote to Cuffe: 'I learn on the best authority that Lord Arthur Somerset is in town. I cannot take any steps to arrest without a warrant. I must leave it to you to say whether I am to have that warrant that it may be executed while the accused is within my jurisdiction.'

In view of this communication from Scotland Yard, Cuffe, who was determined (as he put it) that '*we* should not be responsible for delay in action', sent a special messenger with the substance of the Commissioner's letter to the Attorney General, who was at his home in Cranleigh. Webster immediately replied, directing Cuffe to telegraph the information to the Lord Chancellor in order to expedite his opinion which had been requested a fortnight before. He did so in these terms:

Brown is in England. Can you send opinion to Attorney General or to me? I write by tonight's post. Time may be of importance.

In his following letter to Halsbury, who was the minister in attendance upon the Queen at Balmoral, Cuffe wrote that Somerset was probably in the country for his grandmother's funeral. He went on:

> After the failure of the attempt to get the witness Allies out of the country I am surprised that LAS should have returned . . . I think it is known to many people in London that LAS's name has been mentioned in connection with the case.
>
> Newton, the solicitor for the defence, is a man who talks a great deal and no doubt the names of the frequenters of the house are known to people of whom we know nothing. I have strong reason to believe the rumour has reached the ears of his (LAS's) friends.

Harry Poland, the Senior Treasury counsel, also wrote to Halsbury, probably at the latter's request for his views. 'I don't know what Poland wrote to the Lord Chancellor,' Cuffe told Stephenson, 'but he feels the difficulty of not prosecuting as much as we do as well as the difficulties as to prosecuting.' So too did Halsbury himself, who telegraphed on 7 October in reply to Cuffe's telegram:

> Opinion goes tonight's post. Cannot recommend as to B[rown] unless corroboration of A[llies].

The Lord Chancellor's considered opinion, which Halsbury wrote in his own hand, was as follows:

> Balmoral Castle
> [7 October 1899]
> I have very carefully considered the matter and I am unable on the present materials to advise further proceedings.
>
> I entirely concur in the views so forcibly put forward in Mr. Poland's letter that an unsuccessful prosecution would be a most serious injury to the public morals without any compensating advantage.
>
> The offence alleged to have been committed is an offence created by a recent Statute and only a misdemeanour.

[83]

The punishments already inflicted seem to me very inadequate and more likely to do harm than good. If, as is alleged in these papers, the social position of some of the parties will make a great sensation this will give very wide publicity and consequently will spread very extensively matter of the most revolting and mischievous kind, the spread of which I am satisfied will produce enormous evil.

If a successful prosecution could be reasonably looked for, and if the sentence could be penal servitude for life, or something which by its terrible severity would strike terror into such wretches as the keeper of such a house or his adult customers, I should take a different view—but as I have pointed out, the only offence alleged is the new misdemeanour and at present I doubt very much the success of a prosecution.

If material corroboration of Allies can be obtained, proof that the PO orders were actually sent would be some corroboration if the sending could be traced to the person accused (though I agree with Mr. Poland that it might be susceptible of explanation) then the question will remain purely one of policy in the public interest, but at present I see no corroboration whatever and though in strictness of law this is a question for the jury and not one of law yet I do not think there is a judge upon the Bench who would allow a jury to convict upon such a charge without some real corroboration of the accomplices in the alleged offence.

If untainted witnesses can be obtained that any of the parties were seen going into or coming out of the house, this I think would be a real corroboration, but as it is the sole evidence offered 'has to be tainted' with the very guilt which is in question here and not to be relied on alone for an accusation made on the responsibility of the Public Prosecutor.

With respect to a prosecution of those attempting to get rid of Allies, I am certainly under the belief that someone other than his father is endeavouring to make him leave the country but it will be extremely difficult to prove this. It cannot be truly said that the keeper of the house is expected to return and the father might very well try to get his son to leave the country and endeavour to commence a new career and he could not be supposed to know the possibility of a prosecution upon which the Public Prosecutor has not yet entered, and to make the proposal to Allies an offence it must have been made with the intention of defeating Public Justice.

If the father himself disowns the act and denies that it is done with his authority then I think a prosecution might be proper—otherwise not.

This opinion was regarded as something of a bombshell when it was delivered at the Treasury Solicitor's office. Cuffe greatly deplored it. 'If identification by respectable witnesses is a condition precedent,' he protested to Stephenson, 'it comes to saying there shall be no prosecution.' He also wrote in like strain to the Attorney General on 10 October:

> The Lord Chancellor's opinion rather affects my position as regards the witness Allies. My reason for providing for him and keeping him as far as possible free from solicitations to leave the country, and his reason for declining to see his father at present is that he may be required to give evidence. On this ground he refused the offer made to him by Newton's clerk and in writing to Newton I have dwelt on this as the reason for my action and that of the Police in the matter.
>
> Substantially the Lord Chancellor's advice is that there shall be no prosecution. I have little hope that any corroboration can be obtained at present beyond what appears in the papers sent to the Lord Chancellor. Hammond has gone to America, so there is little chance of his being tried.
>
> The Lord Chancellor's opinion is silent as to whether the papers should be sent to the War Office or whether nothing should be done. If the papers are to go to the War Office, the authorities may wish to see the witnesses, and Allies and the other boys ought not to be sent out of the way . . .
>
> I think I ought to tell you that the fact that L[ord] A[rthur] S[omerset] is suspected is known to the Colonel of the Blues and I believe LAS knows this.

Cuffe continued to complain to Stephenson that 'none of the bigwigs who are conducting this case are in town or accessible to one another which does not expedite matters.' In another letter (11 October) he wrote to the Public Prosecutor:

The Attorney General feels *very strongly* I know as to the result of doing nothing and that LAS cannot be left where he is—but I think the march of events will prevent this.

Of course our inaction has led to all sorts of rumours about persons whose names have never even been suggested, and I pointed out to the Attorney General when I saw him that this must be the case. But he agrees with me so entirely that it is almost unnecessary to press him as I have done.

If they had boldly said at first they would not prosecute on grounds of Policy and sent the papers to the War Office—whether it was the best course or not—it would have been intelligible. But to go on punching holes in the evidence and suggesting nothing else on such a case as there is on the whole seems incapable to me of justification.

Cuffe's sense of grievance was shared by Monro of Scotland Yard. 'I can only deplore the delay which is being made in high quarters about this horrible case,' the Commissioner wrote to Cuffe. He had sent P.C. Hanks down to Badminton but the policeman was powerless to act. The policeman could only report that in accordance with his instructions he had 'attended the funeral of the late Dowager Duchess of Beaufort, and saw Lord Arthur Somerset was present at the obsequies.' A few days later Cuffe told Stephenson that the Home Office had sent the Attorney General without comment a violent protest from Monro. 'I must say the Attorney General is in a terribly difficult position,' Cuffe added, 'and I can see he is terribly worried at the course events have taken.'

Cuffe had seen Webster, who said he was not in a position to give any instructions. Finally, on being pressed by Cuffe, he sent the Lord Chancellor a telegram asking him for a plain yes or no as to whether the papers should be sent to the War Office. On 16 October Halsbury telegraphed his reply: 'Certainly not.'

'I confess I am aghast at the Lord Chancellor's decision,' was Cuffe's reaction to this news. However, although he did not know it, what he had called the march of events was to result in the most drastic and far-reaching change in Lord Arthur Somerset's position during the next forty-eight hours.

5

Somerset returned to London from Badminton on 9 October after his grandmother's funeral. The same evening he met Newton and counsel whom the solicitor had retained in the event of his client being prosecuted, and the conference went on until two o'clock in the morning. The advice given to him was that he should leave the country. But Somerset was inclined to stay and fight it out.

Later in the day Newton gave Brett an account of what had passed between them:

> I saw him last night and explained the exact position to him which is this. I am informed on what I believe to be the most reliable authority that it is the intention of the police to apply for a warrant for his arrest unless he resigns his appointments and goes away—this information is corroborated by the fact that the persons who recently gave evidence are still in the hands of the police and also A[llies] who cannot be required only on the chance of Hammond being arrested. Moreover my office has been watched for two days I am told to see if he comes here . . .
>
> This being the position of affairs he stated most emphatically that if he were to take leave now without any strong reason that of a certainty he would lose both his appointments and that under these circumstances he has definitely decided to trust that the authorities will not injure him by applying for process against him on the uncorroborated evidence of ruffians, one of whom admitted to blackmailing him but if the worst comes to fight it out. He would be certain to be allowed bail.

'I am afraid things look as black as it is possible for them to do,' Somerset wrote to Brett the same day from Hyde Park Barracks. 'So much so that Newton is very anxious that I should go abroad again for a good long while. But of course I might as well cut my throat at once. The only question is whether everything is not really over and that therefore I should just as well make up my mind to it and be off. A very kind letter from HRH but of course he says he must know why I left Newmarket without letting my father know and why I went to Dieppe just when he particularly wanted to see me. I saw Probyn today. He evidently knows nothing and asked me to go to Sandringham tomorrow which I shall do. Anything to get away from here.'

On his way to Sandringham, Somerset continued to worry about 'this awful Dieppe incident' which made things 'very difficult'. Evidently he had seen Newton again before leaving London, since he noted that the solicitor was 'very uneasy and thinks they are opening letters that are passing between us, consequently of course one can write nothing.' While he was at Sandringham, Somerset received a telegram from his commanding officer, Oliver Montagu, who had been to Fredensborg, saying he wished to see him as soon as he got back to London. Somerset himself wanted to see the Prime Minister, who was in Paris, and also Arthur Balfour, regarded as the strong man in the Cabinet. 'I should like to see Lord Salisbury as soon as he returns,' Somerset wrote to Brett from Sandringham on 13 October, 'and if possible Mr. Balfour if you thought well and have the thing thoroughly thrashed out, as it is worse than death and makes life impossible.' He also wished to meet Newton and Brett at the latter's London house next day after he had been to his office in Marlborough House.

Among others whom he met on his return to London was John Oswald, a friend of Brett's who worked in the Foreign Office. 'Have seen LAS who is in good spirits,' Oswald reported to Brett on 15 October. 'He had quite a demonstration at the Turf and Marlborough Clubs last night. Everybody got up and shook hands and all his friends have expressed their feelings.' On the same day Somerset told his friends that Sir Dighton Probyn, the Prince of Wales's Comptroller, was going to see Monro at Scotland Yard and that Montagu would see Pearson, the Assistant Commissioner, who was expected back from Scotland within the next day or two. Montagu also undertook to tackle Lord Cranbrook, who had likewise 'blabbed'. At the same time Somerset wrote to Cranbrook and Pearson, threatening legal action against them for 'spreading disgusting rumours' about him at Gordon Castle.

Somerset met the Prince's Comptroller and Private Secretary by appointment the following morning. Later that day he reported progress to Brett:

Marlborough Club
16 October [1889]

Sir Dighton [Probyn] and Francis Knollys met me at 9.15 this morning and I suggested they should see Newton. They agreed and I sent for him. He told all just as he had told Colonel Montagu and they went off to Monro. He told them nothing but they hunted him a bit and told him it was a scandal that these rumours were entirely circulated by the police. He denied it, whereupon Sir Dighton said they were and as evidence he knew that Abberline had been to the *Pall Mall Gazette* and tried to make them write up the case and that two inspectors had told two gentlemen in society in the street all about the case.

Monro pretended to be furious with Abberline, but then said the matter was in the hands of the Public Prosecutor, so off they went. Stephenson was out but they saw Cuffe who said, 'Of course I ought to tell you that I know nothing, but I know all about it but am telling you nothing. However now you have come to ask I think we shall manage to let you know all about it.'

'I have had no unpleasantness of any sort at present,' Somerset added in this letter. However, there was one result of his meeting with Probyn and Knollys which caused him some concern. Both these courtiers were not at all favourably impressed by Newton, and they advised Somerset to go to George Lewis, the well-known solicitor of the firm of Lewis & Lewis, which had a reputation for being able to settle awkward society cases out of court. Somerset said he would think it over but he did not want to hurt Newton's feelings.

In a memorandum of his interview with Probyn and Knollys, Cuffe noted that they said that the Prince of Wales was 'in a great state', that he 'did not believe a word of it and wished he could come himself to clear LAS', and that he 'must have something settled'. On being strongly pressed that 'an answer and some decision should be come to', Cuffe told his callers that he understood their feelings, that he could tell them nothing without instructions and 'that as we were all public servants . . . and that as they were already informed, it was useless to deny all knowledge of the case.'

After they had gone, Cuffe wrote to the Lord Chancellor:

> This afternoon Sir Dighton Probyn and Sir Francis Knollys called here and stated that they were directed by HRH the Prince of Wales to make inquiry as to the rumours about Lord Arthur Somerset, that the matter ought to be cleared up and that the present state of the case was unjust and cruel to Lord Arthur Somerset. They informed me that they had been to the Commissioner of Police who informed them that the case was in our hands and also that Lord Arthur Somerset's legal advisers had so stated.
>
> They pressed me strongly as they said the Prince firmly believed in Lord Arthur Somerset's innocence and that his character ought to be cleared. They had seen Lord Arthur Somerset himself who urged them to go to the Police and the Treasury.
>
> I said that in my position I was unable to give them any information, but the fact of their inquiry should be known to my superiors and that it was impossible for me to say more than this.
>
> They then left urging me to send some answer as HRH was very anxious about it.

The Prince of Wales was as incredulous as he was anxious. 'I don't believe it,' he wrote to Probyn when the rumours first reached his ears, presumably from Montagu. 'I won't believe it any more than I would if they had accused the Archbishop of Canterbury. Go and see Monro, go to the Treasury, see Lord Salisbury if necessary.'

As soon as he had despatched his letter to Halsbury, Cuffe went off to the Temple, where fortunately he found the Attorney General in his chambers. Webster approved of the line he had taken with Probyn and Knollys and instructed him to make a further communication to them, if possible verbally in preference to a letter, in the following terms as from Cuffe:

> That all papers in Veck and Newlove's case have been before the Attorney General under whose directions I am acting in that

case, that I have seen him since you called and that he is unable to authorise me to make any communication to you respecting the contents of those papers. No inference to be drawn from this refusal.

If he was pressed, Cuffe was told he might point out that the Director of Public Prosecutions and his staff were not responsible for paragraphs appearing in the newspapers and they had no duty cast upon them in connection with such paragraphs.

Cuffe immediately went off to Marlborough House where he found Sir Francis Knollys and 'read to him the purport of the Attorney General's message of which he took note.'

Next morning, 17 October, Somerset went as usual to his office in Marlborough House where he wrote to Brett that he supposed that Cuffe would 'submit a statement of the evidence before the police and I shall have to answer it.' He went on:

> Meanwhile I am on hooks of expectation. I had half a mind to go and see Lewis but Newton spontaneously entreated me not to. I have a very strong conviction that Newton is very nervous about any trial on his own account but of course I know nothing. He is certainly not the man he was. He is and looks worried and repeats himself.
>
> My friends here are bent on my prosecuting someone, but whom? The only person who has thought fit to cut me is Lord Dudley from which I shall recover. All the Regiment and the household are charming about it. If it does not end soon, I shall go mad.

He wrote again to Brett after he had met Knollys at the Turf Club in the afternoon:

> Just seen Francies K[nollys]. The Treasury refuses all information at present and so it is likely they will be some time before they can say anything. So K has wired to Lord Salisbury making an appointment for Probyn tomorrow. What will he do? Sir Dighton Probyn arrives at Marlborough House at 11.40 tomorrow morning. Can anything be done? What on earth are they waiting

for? To try and catch someone else or what? I have a very shrewd idea that our legal friend [Newton] must have overstepped the ordinary etiquettes or something of that kind. Meanwhile I suppose we can do nothing . . .

I must say I wish they would look sharp and do something as these long constant interviews are very trying. By the time anything comes on, if it ever does, my nerves will be in such a state that I shall be unable to do myself and my case justice.

Sir Dighton Probyn and Knollys were very strongly impressed against my legal adviser yesterday and if Lord Salisbury refuses information want to take me to see Russell tomorrow and get him to squeeze the Government. All this is very difficult and unpleasant.

Before they parted, Knollys arranged to meet Somerset at the Marlborough Club the following afternoon with Probyn so that they could go together to the Temple to see Sir Charles Russell, the Liberal lawyer, later Lord Russell of Killowen and Lord Chief Justice of England. After that Probyn intended to go on to King's Cross station, where he was to have a brief meeting with the Prime Minister on his way home from Paris.

Meanwhile Stephenson had returned from leave to the Treasury and had resumed charge of the Somerset case. In telling Webster, as he did on 18 October, that he agreed with Cuffe's actions 'on every point', he remarked that a new incident had occurred which might affect him (Stephenson) personally in the event of further inquiries being made on behalf of the Prince of Wales.

I have the honour to be known personally to HRH. My brother is one of his equerries and in my judgement it is most probable that if HRH were in England some inquiries would be made of me either directly or indirectly through my brother confidentially which would put me in a position of difficulty.

This is not a case in which I could treat any communication as confidential in the sense of withholding it from you or make any communication to anybody without your knowledge or sanction.

Of one thing I feel certain—that is that HRH will not allow the matter to rest as it is.

As will be seen, the conscientious Public Prosecutor was worrying unnecessarily. Such inquiries as the Prince did make were to be directed elsewhere, notably towards the Prime Minister.

When Knollys and Probyn arrived at the Marlborough Club during the afternoon of 18 October, there was no sign of Somerset. But they noticed that there was a cab piled high with luggage waiting outside the club in Pall Mall. After waiting for some time, Probyn went off to King's Cross to keep his appointment with the Prime Minister.

Salisbury had no idea of the real reason why Probyn wished to see him. He imagined it had something to do with Foreign Office business connected with the journeys of the Prince of Wales. In the short talk they had at the station, before the Prime Minister caught the 7.30 p.m. train to Hatfield, Probyn told him that he wished to know, as Salisbury afterwards put it, 'whether there was any ground for certain charges which had been made in the newspapers against sundry persons whom he named', including apparently Prince Albert Victor and the Earl of Euston as well as Lord Arthur Somerset. The Prime Minister replied that, so far as he knew, 'there was no ground whatever for them, no vestige of evidence against anyone except one person', namely Somerset, and that, as against that person, he understood that 'the evidence was not thought to be sufficient in the judgment of those whose business it was to decide.'

The Prime Minister was subsequently accused by Labouchere on the floor of the House of Commons of having told Probyn that a warrant for Somerset's arrest was about to be issued and that Probyn immediately passed on this news to Somerset with the result that Somerset fled to France the same night. This was wholly untrue and explicitly denied by Salisbury in a statement he later made in the House of Lords.

> The interview was brief and hurried; and, as far as I know, the rest of the conversation principally consisted of expressions on the part of Sir Dighton Probyn of absolute disbelief in the charges which were levelled against the person whom I have indicated, and of answers of a more reserved character on my part.

I cannot give your Lordships any positive information as to the precise language that was used at that interview; but I can give you negative information. I am quite certain that I never said, as has been imputed to me, that a warrant was about to be issued the next day, because such a statement would have been absolutely inconsistent with what I am certain I did say, that, in the judgment of the legal authorities, the evidence was insufficient. You cannot issue a warrant against a person if the evidence is insufficient.

I certainly conveyed no secrets to Sir Dighton Probyn, for the best of all possible reasons, that I had no secrets to convey. I had been abroad, and I had no further information except mere rumour of the precise condition in which the affair stood; and I may add that I can aver in the most confident manner that the suggestion which has been made that a man of Sir Dighton Probyn's character and career could have appointed an interview with me for the purpose of worming out matter which he might use for the purpose of defeating the ends of justice is the wildest and most malignant imagination that has ever been conceived.

Probyn, whose many military decorations included the Victoria Cross, had had a most distinguished service career before joining the Prince of Wales's household, and it is highly unlikely that he would have 'tipped off' Somerset even if he had been in a position to do so. But in fact he was not. In the Attorney General's words when rebutting Labouchere's allegations in the House of Commons, 'Sir Dighton Probyn came back from the interview with Lord Salisbury; he never saw Lord Arthur Somerset again, and he never, directly or indirectly, communicated with him through any person. Nobody was more surprised than Sir Dighton Probyn that Lord Arthur Somerset had gone, for up to that moment he believed emphatically in the innocence of Lord Arthur Somerset.'

So far as Somerset was concerned, the 'answers of a more reserved character' which Salisbury gave Probyn seem to have been a euphemism for what the Prime Minister had learned from Matthews about Allies and the postal orders. At all events Probyn was stunned by what he heard. 'I fear what you told me last night was all too true,' he wrote to Salisbury next morning. 'Until I saw you last night, I always thought it was a case of *mistaken identity*. I would not let myself believe (and tried to check myself from thinking) that it was anything else. But after my conversation with you, I drove home a miserable man. I knew the story must be true.'

Meanwhile tongues were busy wagging in the officer's mess at Hyde Park Barracks, where Somerset was expected for dinner. He did not appear, and some of his fellow officers, thinking that in the circumstances he might have taken the honourable way out by killing himself, went to his quarters. They found the room empty both of its occupant and of his belongings. 'He had bolted,' was how Labouchere put it to Brett when he heard the news.

Four days later, Brett received a letter from his friend who was now lying low in Rouen, saying he was very sorry not to have seen him before he 'came away', if only to thank him for all the trouble he had taken on his behalf. 'O[liver Montagu] was very kind the day I left and helped me to get away quietly,' he told Brett, and added: 'Please let me know what is being done. I hope I shall not be cashiered but I am very much afraid of it. I suppose my coming away has alienated most of my friends but they were certainly very good and stuck to me well through evil report.'

As usual the letter was signed 'Podge'. But on second thoughts the writer scratched out 'Podge' and substituted 'Arthur Short'.

6

As late as the afternoon of 17 October Lord Arthur Somerset appeared to be prepared to face any legal proceedings that might be taken against him and fight the case to the end. What, therefore, happened to cause him to change his mind during the next twenty-four hours, throw up the sponge, and seek refuge in flight abroad?

According to Probyn, who learned the news from Newton next morning, Somerset wrote a letter to his father before leaving England, 'saying that his brain could not stand the anxiety of this awful scandal, that he feared he would be prosecuted and that even if he got off with flying colours he could never, having been accused of this awful crime, live in England again.' In this letter he is stated to have asked his father to tell Montagu and Probyn of his 'determination' and that 'he would write to us both resigning his appointments under us.' Probyn added that Newton had seen the Duke of Beaufort 'who is of course broken hearted.' However, it appears that after writing this letter, Somerset saw his commanding officer who helped him to get away quietly.

At the same time Probyn besought the Prime Minister to have the case against Somerset dropped:

> I write now to ask you, to implore of you if it can be managed to have the prosecution stopped. It can do no good to prosecute him. He has gone and will never show his face in England again. He *dare* never come back to this country.
>
> I think it is the most hateful, loathsome story I ever heard, and the most astounding. It is too fearful, but further publicity will only make matters worse. I have of course telegraphed to the Prince, and am writing full particulars of this disgusting calamity to HRH.
>
> The Prince will be terribly cut up about it . . . I felt that in writing to you I am only doing what the Prince would wish.
>
> I do not write with a view of trying to save the man. He has gone—he is beyond punishment, or rather out of reach of the law. I only want if possible not to increase the fearful disgrace which has fallen on his family.
>
> For the man, in his defence, I can only trust that he is *mad*.

The Prime Minister also wrote to the Prince of Wales, giving him the impression that he had responded favourably to Probyn's appeal, since the Prince replied to Salisbury from Sandringham on 25 October, saying he was 'glad to gather . . . that no warrant is likely to be issued against the 'unfortunate Lunatic' (I can call him nothing else), as, for the sake of the Family and Society, the less one hears of such a filthy scandal the better.'

The Prince of Wales continued in the same letter:

> I don't know whether I am asking what I have no right to ask, but, if I may ask the question, I shall feel greatly obliged by your kindly letting me know whether the man might return to England

now, or at any future date, without fear of being apprehended on this awful charge. I have no idea where he has gone, or if he would ever dare to show his face in England again even if he were free to do so, but I would like, if I may, to let the Family know if their Relative will at any time be at liberty to visit his native country.

Until I receive your reply giving me permission to speak, neither the Father, nor any of the Family shall ever know from me that I have been in correspondence with you on this painful subject.

Meanwhile Monro and Pearson at Scotland Yard continued to chafe at the delay in issuing a warrant for Somerset's arrest. The Commissioner wrote in the strongest terms both to the Public Prosecutor and to Godfrey Lushington, the Permanent Under-Secretary at the Home Office, asking for specific instructions whether charges against Somerset and Newton's clerk Taylorson were going on. 'I cannot but feel throughout this case the Police have not been fairly treated,' Monro complained to Lushington, 'and charges have been, and are still being made against them, which are absolutely groundless, and which are calculated seriously to affect their reputation. I have up to now been unsuccessful in getting any definite instructions in the case, and the result has been that the most undeserved odium has been cast upon the Police, which certainly should not be allowed to rest upon them.'

'Inaction has been publicly attributed to the Metropolitan Police in connection with this case,' Monro protested to Stephenson a few days after Somerset's flight 'and this assertion is absolutely groundless as it has been magnified into an accusation against the Police of having brought an unfounded charge against the nobleman in question. It is obvious that I cannot allow the reputation of the Police to be thus unfairly assailed, and I must press for definite information as to the action to be taken by you in the case referred to.'

Lushington informed the Home Secretary of Monro's complaint, but Matthews took no immediate action upon it. Stephenson's official reply to the Commissioner of Police was no less discouraging. 'I must repeat that the conduct of the prosecution undertaken by me by direction of the Secretary of State, and since conducted under the directions of the Attorney General,' he wrote, 'has been for some time past and is still entirely out of my hands. I am not in a position to give you any answer or any information on any of the matters on which you ask for information.'

On 26 October, the Home Secretary sent the following note to his Permanent Under-Secretary:

> The A[ttorney] G[eneral] has written to me to say that he prefers to communicate with me by word of mouth and will take the first opportunity of so doing. Meanwhile there are to be at present, he tells me, no further proceedings.
>
> I do not know when I shall have an opportunity of meeting him. Consider therefore whether it is worth while delaying the official answer to the Commissioner and the Director of Public Prosecutions.

There is no doubt that the Prime Minister was eager to oblige the Prince of Wales and to drop the contemplated prosecution, as Probyn had begged him to do, and so spare the Duke and Duchess of Beaufort the disgrace involved by the issue of a warrant for their son's arrest. Even when Salisbury realised that, in view of the statements of Allies and the other witnesses which had come out at Marlborough Street Police Court immediately prior to the committal of Veck and Newlove for trial, it would be out of the question without causing a still greater scandal by interfering with the course of justice, the Government delayed taking the action for which Monro had asked until Somerset had been given time to resign his army commission honourably and the resignation gazetted. Otherwise, in the event of a warrant for his arrest being issued, he would almost certainly have been cashiered or ignominiously discharged from the service. On 1 November, by which date the resignation was in the hands of the War Office, the Attorney General had a meeting with the Home Secretary and apparently agreed to stay proceedings until after the publication of Somerset's resignation, which took place four days later. A further week was allowed to elapse 'for some extraordinary reason not known to me,' as Monro put it to Matthews, before the warrant was finally issued on 12 November, charging Somerset with offences of gross indencency with Allies and other boys contrary to section 11 of the Criminal Law Amendment Act.

According to Labouchere, who later passed on the information to Brett, an officer in Somerset's regiment told him (Labouchere) that Somerset did not commit sodomy, 'but only indulged in gentle dalliance with the boys.' This was confirmed by the evidence of the boys at Marlborough Street, Labouchere said.

Meanwhile, the unfortunate fugitive from justice was anxiously pondering his future in Rouen. He wrote to Brett on 24 October:

> I have wandered about all day for two days trying to think what employment I am fit for and am still undecided. You see, if I got a promise of any employment, I should require a reference. To whom am I to refer? . . . My poor father and mother, it is too awful for them and I suppose I shall never see them again nor shall I see any of my many friends . . .
>
> I hope as soon as this thing is over Père Allies will kick up a devil's delight about his son being kept without any legal right whatever under what is really close arrest . . .
>
> I should like my barrack furniture stored until I know what is going to happen. I don't much fancy the idea of the Cape, as I know a lot of people out there. I think I shall make my way to Eastern Europe as soon as things are settled, but of course I must know what my financial prospects are before I go anywhere. Perhaps Drummond Woolf could get me something in Persia.[1] At this moment I know the Sultan wants a man to look after his horse breeding. I had arranged with Marcus Beresford about a man.[2] Ask him if he accepted the berth. If not, I might get it. I really could do it and the place is worth £800 a year. I don't fancy the Sultan would have any prejudice, would he? But, of course, I shall want letters before I could get the place, but I suppose no one would give me any.
>
> Another thing I thought I might do is to teach English in a

[1] Sir Henry Drummond Woolf was British envoy in Teheran where he was instrumental in establishing the Imperial Bank of Persia at this time.
[2] Lord Marcus Beresford was Somerset's brother-in-law and managed the Prince of Wales's thoroughbred stud and racehorses at Sandringham.

THE CLEVELAND STREET SCANDAL

school or to any private pupils, but it is one thing knowing English
and another to try and teach it.

. . . N[ewton] tells me that he fears it is certain that several
people will be prosecuted. In case any of those mixed up in this case
have to go abroad, I wish they would come here or I would go to
them. It would be so much less dull.

'I am very glad you think there is no warrant,' he wrote next day
after hearing from his friend. 'Has anyone been arrested? . . . You
say Salisbury will see about the warrant. Has he been approached on
the subject?' He told Brett that he would leave Rouen within a
couple of days for Boulogne, where he would be close to England
in case his solicitor or anyone else wished to see him. He added rather
pathetically that he had tried the local tramway company and also
the Commercial Union Insurance branch for employment,' presumably under the name of Arthur Short, 'but could not get any.'

His next letter was written on 26 October from Boulogne:

I write by this post to Penna [his brother Henry] asking if I may
call on him [in Monaco] on my way east. . . .My future must depend
upon what I hear from Marcus about the Sultan's place. It would
be worth anything to get that £800 a year, and employment such
as I like. But I fear the man we offered it to has accepted it. . . .

Do come over and see me either here or in Paris.

A gap which occurs in the correspondence at this point suggests
that Brett did in fact pay a flying visit either to Boulogne or Paris.
Lord Henry Somerset was then living in a villa in Monaco. Brett
probably brought the news that their sister Blanche Lady Waterford
planned to come out and meet him there at the beginning of November.
'Blanchie' Waterford had always been the closest of all the family to
her brother Arthur, and since her husband had become a cripple,
she and her brother had gone about a great deal together when she
was in London. Apparently it was her idea that she should meet
Arthur in Monaco; but, while he welcomed it, as he was anxious to
know how his parents were bearing up under the news, he was also
eager to lose no time in going after the possible job with the Sultan.

'I know not what to say to you,' was the Duke of Beaufort's

[100]

stunned reaction to his son's letter, which he received in London on the morning after Arthur's hurried departure for France. 'God help you. What will you do? I must go to Badminton tomorrow and break it to your mother.' As Arthur Somerset told his friend Brett, 'That is an awful thing to read and know one is the cause of. Poor dears, and they have always been so good to me.'

A few days later, the youngest son, Lord Edward Somerset, who was at Badminton, told Brett that the Duke dared not tell the Duchess 'as her heart is in such a weak state' and they thought the shock might kill her. 'You can't think what an awful state of suspense and misery we are all in,' he added.

Consequently it was not until 4 November, more than a fortnight later, by which date Arthur and his sister had arrived at the Villa Fleur de Lys in Monaco, that the Duke risked breaking the news to his wife. He began by telling her that Arthur was at Monaco with Henry. 'Is Henry ill?' asked the Duchess. On being told he was not, she asked, 'Then tell me, is anything the matter with Arthur?' The Duke then showed his wife Arthur's letter. Afterwards he wrote to Brett:

> Of course it did not satisfy her, and I had to tell her more than I wished because first she said, 'Of course he will face any accusation,' and then she said, 'No entanglement with a woman would oblige him to go abroad and give up his Regiment.'
>
> . . . His not facing the accusation is most fatal and that she felt, and I saw she thought it must be some dreadful thing. I thought it better that she should hear from me—so I told her we thought he had been decoyed to a House by some woman and the people of the House threatened him, and having no rebutting evidence to bring against any accusations they chose to make would not face the horrors of a trial. Poor thing, it is a terrible blow.

The Duchess wished her husband to go off to Monaco and bring back their son to face any charge that might be brought against him. The Duke's sister, Lady Kinnoul, wrote to his eldest son, Lord Worcester, in the same sense. 'It is so difficult to say, "He can't meet it",' the Duke told Brett, 'and yet that is practically what his going has done, as I explained to his lawyer. He avoids the exposé of the Police Court and all the horrors of the newspaper reports and remarks—but going like this and leaving his office and his Regiment are, with the above exceptions, as hard as being found guilty. Everybody says the same thing, he must face it. Why don't you make him?'

The Duke returned to the subject two days later in another letter to Brett:

> Many of my family write and say bring him back and make him face these charges. There are other people walking about whose names have been equally mentioned as being implicated—and he is the only one to suffer. That may be true, but it is no use coming back unless he can face a thorough and searching investigation. He must not only walk about but he must court the most thorough investigation and meet and refute the charges. He cannot otherwise retain his commission or his appointment with the Prince of Wales, and if he does not do both people will say it is because he cannot refute the charges.
>
> I never saw Mr. Newton till he came to me last Saturday fort-night 19th October. He appears a shrewd and sharp man. He declared to me that he could not successfully meet the charges as he had no rebutting evidence, otherwise I would have gone to him [Arthur] and made him, if I could, come back and meet them.
>
> Lord Salisbury's opinion expressed to Sir Dighton Probyn confirms Mr. Newton's view of the prima facie evidence against him. As I do not know what the evidence consists of, I can give no opinion and am unable to act against the strongly expressed opinions of Lord Salisbury and Mr. Newton unless I could say I can bring evidence to disprove these charges . . .
>
> My greatest comfort is that all his brother officers, those who have known him longest and most intimately, all write in the strongest terms of certainty that he is innocent.

Arthur's brother-in-law Waterford was equally incredulous 'Of this I am certain, that he was the very last man in the world to do what he is accused of,' he wrote to the Duke. 'I should about as soon as believe it about myself as about him.'

From Monaco, Lady Waterford reported progress to Brett on 14 November, at the end of her fortnight's stay:

> I meant to write to you before but have spent every moment with my dear. I keep on repeating that I never can be thankful enough that I came. We have always said everything to each other, all our lives, and although I never asked him a question on this subject he said he wished to tell me certain things, and I know and see that he could not have done differently to what he did. Miserably sad as his future prospects are, yet I think something may be found to occupy him, and I have thought of a friend of mine (in Asia we will say not to put any names or places on paper) to whom I have told the whole story and who *may* see his way to helping him. This is a second string to our bow supposing Constantinople fails.[1]
>
> We have helped each other by being here together and it was better that I should come than my mother, for the parting today would have killed them both. What it will be as it is must not be thought of. I start for home tonight and he goes east tomorrow. We settled that he shall call himself *Mr.* Arthur Somerset from now, not only on account of this trouble but to keep down expenses at hotels . . .
>
> I know how unhappy you are about this . . . Although terribly sad as this time has been, it is a comfort to me and will be to us all round. A[rthur] cannot sleep and looks 100. If that continues it will kill him—God help him. If anyone should say to him, 'Why call yourself Mr. Arthur Somerset if you are innocent?' the answer is very simple, 'Because I am not well off and it makes things cheaper.'

His brother Henry agreed that it would be better to stick to his real name. 'Short was a foolish name to take,' he told him. 'You can't look like A. Short!'

In fact, Lady Waterford postponed her journey, as just after she had sent off her letter, Arthur developed a chill complicated by fainting fits, and she stayed on at the villa for a few days to look after him until he was well enough to travel. Before he left, he heard on 16 November from Newton, who had managed to secure a copy of

[1] The friend was an Indian Maharajah.

the warrant for his arrest. 'The enclosure has puzzled me rather and frightened Penna to death,' he wrote in sending the document to Brett. 'He expects to see me dragged off by my bald head by Gendarmes. If what Newton told me was correct no one can touch me.'

Apparently the Assistant Commissioner of Police had written to Somerset in reply to his letter threatening an action for slander, since Somerset commented in the same letter: 'You never read such a letter as Pearson wrote, shilly shallying and declining any further correspondence with anyone on the subject. I sent it to Nigel Kingscote to show to Probyn.'[1]

Finally, he gave Brett this assurance:

(1) I have never admitted being at the house.
(2) I never [did] say anything except that the Police never saw me enter or leave as proved in [the committal proceedings prior to the] trial [of Veck and Newlove].

Although Somerset did not know it, the information on the strength of which the warrant for his arrest had been issued, was sworn to by Allies and his mother, also the two telegraph boys, Thickbroom and Swinscow, in addition to the police and a counter clerk at the Knightsbridge district post office named Ellen Padwick. Miss Padwick deposed that she had issued three postal orders of twenty shillings each on 20 August, bearing her signature and the corresponding date stamp, but she had no recollection of the person who purchased them. The Postmaster at Sudbury confirmed that he had cashed the postal orders for Allies on 21 August and that he had cashed other orders for Allies previously. According to Cuffe, Allies had admitted that it was Somerset who had originally sent him to Cleveland Street with a note to Hammond; furthermore the boy had been 'with Lord Arthur Somerset about every month', Somerset had given him money, he (Allies) had cashed the three postal orders at

---

[1] Colonel Robert Nigel Fitzhardinge Kingscote, a former MP for Gloucestershire, managed the Duchy of Cornwall estates for the Prince of Wales. He was doubly connected with the Somerset family, his mother being a daughter of the 6th Duke of Beaufort and his wife, Lady Emily Curzon, being the 8th Duke's sister-in-law and thus Lord Arthur Somerset's aunt.

Sudbury, and he had received about forty letters in all from Somerset which he had destroyed after receiving an anonymous communication advising him to do so. No doubt the reason why Mrs. Allies also deposed to the information was that it was thought she could afford some corroboration of the receipt of the money and letters.

'I am aware that he was in trouble about some money at the Marlborough Club, but that is the only stain on his character,' Mrs. Allies stated. 'He has been supported for the past two years by Lord Arthur Somerset, who had been in the habit of sending him postal orders on the average about every fortnight. He allowed him 15s per week. He frequently sent for the boy to go to 19 Cleveland Street, and from what the boy told me, I was under the impression that it was always for the purpose of waiting at table, as he said Mr. Charles [Hammond] used to give parties. I generally received the letters from the postmen, but I never opened one of them. I always handed them to the boy.'

In the warrant Somerset was specifically charged with (1) committing acts of gross indecency with other male persons, to wit, Allies, Swinscow and Thickbroom; (2) procuring Allies to commit similar acts with other male persons; and (3) conspiring with Hammond to procure the commission of such acts contrary to the Criminal Law Amendment Act, 1885.

Rumours had already reached Scotland Yard of the advice which was being given by the Duke of Beaufort's family that his son should come back to England and face his accusers. 'There is a report that efforts are being made to induce Lord Arthur Somerset to return and stand his trial,' Monro wrote to Cuffe on 16 November. 'Until this is definitely ascertained, it would be very unwise to allow the boy Allies—whatever may be the result of any interview with his father—to be removed from my charge. It is obvious what comment would be made, were the boy to be allowed to go and could not be got, on the accused person or persons offering to stand their trial, and I am not prepared by any action of mine to give cause for any such comments being made.'

CHAPTER III

The Trial of Ernest Parke

I

THE NEXT ACT in the Cleveland Street drama opened with the publication of a libellous paragraph in a London weekly newspaper on the same day as Somerset learned that a warrant had been issued for his arrest. On 16 November 1889, the following appeared in the *North London Press*:

THE WEST END SCANDALS

NAMES OF SOME OF THE DISTINGUISHED CRIMINALS WHO HAVE ESCAPED.

In an issue of the 28th September we stated that among the number of aristocrats who were mixed up in an indescribably loathsome scandal in Cleveland Street, Tottenham Court Road, were the heir to a duke and the younger son of a duke. The men to whom we thus referred were the Earl of Euston, eldest son of the Duke of Grafton, and Lord H. Arthur G. Somerset, a younger son of the Duke of Beaufort. The former, we believe, has departed for Peru. The latter, having resigned his commission and his office of Assistant Equerry to the Prince of Wales, has gone too.

These men have been allowed to leave the country, and thus defeat the ends of justice, because their prosecution would disclose the fact that a far more distinguished and more highly placed personage than themselves was inculpated in these disgusting crimes. The criminals in this case are to be numbered by the score. They include two or three Members of Parliament, one of them a popular Liberal.

This was the first newspaper allusion to Prince Eddy as being involved in the Cleveland Street affair, and although he was not mentioned by name, the reference was unmistakable since the Prince's alleged involvement was by this time common talk in the London clubs.

The *North London Press*, which had only been going for a few months, was a Radical journal mainly concerned with local government matters and the ventilation of grievances of such poorly paid members of the community as dockers, postmen and insurance agents. The editor was a brilliant twenty-nine-year-old journalist, who worked under the Irish Nationalist MP, T.P. ('Tay-Pay') O'Connor on *The Star* and edited the *North London Press* in his spare time. Writing in his *Memoirs* thirty years later, 'Tay-Pay' described the editor Ernest Parke as being 'a young, flossy-haired man, with a keen face, a lithe and agile body, a tremendous flair for news, and capable of twenty-four hours' work, if necessary, in a single day. He was, as he is, a singular mixture of shrewdness and ideals; an intense Radical, and at the same time a thoroughly practical journalist. He might be trusted to work up any sensational news of the day, and he helped, with 'Jack the Ripper', to make gigantic circulations hitherto unparalleled in evening journalism.'

Parke had first become interested in the Cleveland Street affair when Veck and Newlove were being prosecuted, and he inferred from the fact that they received such light sentences, as did Labouchere and Stead, that there was a conspiracy behind the scenes to hush up the goings on at 19 Cleveland Street and that both Hammond and Somerset had been 'tipped off' to escape abroad to avoid arrest. In addition to the heir of a Duke and the younger son of another Duke, Parke had also mentioned, although not by name, in the issue of 28 September, an officer holding a command in the Southern District. 'The names of these men are in our possession,' Parke added, 'and we are prepared to produce them if necessary.'

Amongst the alleged fugitives from justice he unwisely included Lord Euston, about whose conduct he had heard discreditable rumours. Through his contacts with the police, Parke later obtained some concrete information about Euston from a notorious male prostitute named John Saul, but this did not come into his possession until after Euston had begun proceedings against him and he had been committed for trial.

Saul knew a good deal about Hammond, since he had lodged with him on three occasions, including a short time in Cleveland Street, having first met him in 1879. For this reason Inspector Abberline of Scotland Yard, after Hammond's flight and Newlove's arrest, had taken two statements from Saul in August. In these statements Saul mentioned a number of well-to-do gentlemen in society who frequented the house in Cleveland Street, including Lord Euston, whom he described as 'a constant visitor at Hammond's' and identified as 'a fair looking man with a fair moustache', which broadly speaking corresponded with Euston's appearance. 'I know him well,' he added. 'He went to Hammond's with me on one occasion. He is not an actual sodomite. He likes to play with you and then "spend" on your belly.'

Saul also admitted that he had led 'a grossly immoral life' for most of the past twenty years. Indeed he had given an account of his homosexual activities to the anonymous author of *The Sins of the Cities of the Plain*, a choice example of Victorian erotica published clandestinely in 1882. He was an Irishman who first came to London about 1870, and had known the transvestite homosexuals Boulton and Park who figured in the celebrated 'drag' case along with Lord Arthur Clinton MP in the following year. Saul also seems to have been on the fringe of the notorious Dublin Castle homosexual scandals in 1884 in which the central figures were Mr. Gustavus Cornwall, the Secretary of the General Post Office, and Detective Inspector James French, the head of the CID in the Castle.[1]

Henry James Fitzroy, Earl of Euston, was a man-about-town in his early forties. On leaving Harrow, he had obtained a commission in the Rifle Brigade. But he seems to have been more interested in chorus girls than in soldiering and soon became known as something

[1] Details of these cases have been given by the present writer in *The Other Love* (1970).

[108]

of a 'stage-door Johnny'. When he was twenty-three he married a
Variety Theatre actress named Kate Cook. But the alliance did not
prosper; after seven years they separated and in 1884 were divorced.
During the legal proceedings it emerged that Kate Cook had previously gone through a form of marriage with a commercial traveller
called Smith, who was alive at the date of her marriage to Lord
Euston. That the earl was not himself prosecuted for bigamy, as he
otherwise might have been, was due to the fact that when he married
Kate Cook, Mr. Smith already had a wife living, so that his 'marriage' to the actress was invalid. After the divorce Lord Euston became interested in Freemasonry and at the time of the Cleveland
Street case was Provincial Grand Master of Northamptonshire and
Huntingdonshire.

According to the journalist Frank Harris, who boasted of his
wide experience in sexual matters, Euston was a big well-made
fellow, some six feet in height and decidedly manly looking, 'the last
person in the world to be suspected of any abnormal propensities.'
This opinion conflicted with Saul's testimony, on which Parke was
to rely when the proceedings which Euston was to institute against
him came to trial.

Under English law, libel is and for long has been both a civil
wrong and a criminal offence. Since the essence of the offence is its
tendency to cause a breach of the peace, it is sufficient if the libel is
'published', i.e. communicated, to the person libelled; it is not
necessary, as it is in civil proceedings for damages, to prove 'publication' to a third person in whose eyes the plaintiff's reputation
might be considered to have suffered injury. In the course of time it
came to be realised that, in some cases, proceeding by indictment
was the only efficient remedy open to a defamed plaintiff, since the
libeller might have no money and the plaintiff would only burden
himself with costs if he brought a civil action against, say, an un-
scrupulous editor or journalist. However, in order to protect the
respectable members of the journalistic profession, the law of libel
was amended by parliamentary statute in 1888 to provide that no
criminal prosecution could be commenced against any proprietor,

publisher or editor of a newspaper or journal without the order of a judge in chambers, who must hear what the accused had to say as well as the prosecutor. Any such order thus amounted to a judicial expression of opinion that the case was one which it was appropriate to deal with by criminal rather than civil process.

Euston lost no time in instructing his solicitor, Mr. George Lewis of the firm of Lewis & Lewis, who advised an application to a judge in chambers under the Newspaper Libel Amendment Act of 1888. The application was duly made to Mr. Justice Field on 23 November, supported by an affidavit by Lord Euston which read in part:

> The atrocious libel, that I have been guilty of an impossible and unspeakable crime, is absolutely without foundation. It is also without foundation that I have left the country and gone to Peru.

On the same morning an article appeared in the *North London Press*, which Parke had written the previous day, informing that journal's readers that he would offer no resistance to Lord Euston's application to Mr. Justice Field. The article continued:

> If the charges we preferred against Lord Euston are untrue, and were made without sufficient reason, we have no desire to escape the natural and inevitable penalty of misleading the public on so grave a matter. Nor shall we seek to lay the blame on any shoulders but our own. We have taken our position; we shall stand by it. Now that Lord Euston's case is to be made the subject of a judicial inquiry, we shall, of course, utter no syllable that can be construed into an attempt to influence public opinion against him. With regard, however, to the other persons charged by us with committing unutterable crimes, we have a word to say.
>
> And, first, it is necessary to recite a few facts as to which we challenge contradiction. The information affecting Lord Arthur Somerset, the man Hammond, and other persons, distinguished and undistinguished, was in the hands of the authorities at the end of July. In a paper dated 28 September, but issued on the 27th, we first gave the outlines of the scandal, though we mentioned no name except Hammond's. But between the 25th and the 28th of that month, the name of Lord Arthur Somerset appears among the

list of spectators of races at Newmarket. He afterwards disappeared, in obedience, as Mr. Labouchere says, to a hint from a high official at Court, and his resignation of his command and of his office of Assistant Equerry to the Prince of Wales was gazetted. When the warrant against him was issued he was safe from arrest. In the same way Hammond, the keeper of the den of infamy at Cleveland Street, had been able to put himself beyond the reach of the law. He fled to France, whence, at the suggestion of our own Foreign Office, he was expelled as a *mauvais sujet*, and he has fled, it is feared, without any prospect of his being brought to justice.

The result, therefore, of these extraordinary—these unheard of—delays in fulfilling the forms of law, and protecting the community against nameless crimes, has been that two of the chief offenders have disappeared. But that is not all. Two minor members of this vile conspiracy were committed for trial and pleaded guilty to the charge at the Old Bailey. Their cases were brought on at the end of the day's proceedings, when the spectators had left and when everybody supposed that the sitting was over. Hurried clandestinely into the dock, these guilty wretches, condemned out of their own mouths, were awarded sentences of four and nine months respectively for offences for which, at a previous Sessions, a minister at Hackney had been condemned to penal servitude for life, with the special warning from the judge that he could have no hope of a mitigation of his dreadful doom. Yet there was no trace in his case, as there is in this, of a foul and widespread plot to poison the morals of the community, and make the name of England a hissing and reproach in Christian Europe.

Now we hasten to say that we acquit Mr. Monro of any part or lot in what we solemnly declare to be a deliberate attempt to shield high-placed offenders. On the contrary, all our information is that Mr. Monro has spared neither himself nor his staff in his efforts to detect and punish. Further than that, we distinctly affirm that those efforts have been persistently thwarted by the Home Office and the Treasury, and it was not, we believe, until Mr. Monro threatened to resign his post that the matter was formally brought before the notice of the Cabinet, which has long been specially informed of the facts. What kind of action it has taken upon them may be judged from the fact that the two chief criminals have escaped, after being allowed to be at large for several weeks, so we believe, to Mr. Monro's intense chagrin and disappointment. During his tenure of Scotland Yard, the Chief Commissioner has won universal esteem as an incorruptible servant of the public, and he has fully maintained his reputation during the preliminaries of this disgraceful case.

And now a word as to our own action. It was when Lord Arthur Somerset was braving it out at Newmarket, when justice was paralyzed—to use no stronger term—by the inaction of the Home Office and the Treasury, that the *North London Press* took up the case. It is now the subject of a criminal libel. It is one small newspaper, fighting wealth, position, the ablest criminal lawyer in London, and the reluctance of those in authority to do their duty . . . If the half of what we know, and are learning from day to day, comes out in a court of law, there has been accumulating under our feet a store of moral dynamite sufficient to wreck the good name of the nation . . .

It will be for Parliament to interrogate Lord Salisbury, Mr. W. H. Smith [Leader of the House of Commons], and Mr. Matthews as to their knowledge of the nature of the charges, the date at which they were first made, the form in which they were first made, and the evidence taken in their support, the names of the incriminated persons—*be they whom they may*—and the aid the Ministry have given Mr. Monro, a zealous, a discreet, and an experienced officer, in carrying out the measures recommended by him for the detection of crime. If we have in any way contributed to that result, we shall be well repaid for the cost, the anxiety, the grave personal risk we incur in doing—and doing alone among the press—what we believe to be our solemn duty to the public. . . .

Armed with the order for trial, which the judge had signed, Euston and his counsel, Mr. Lionel Hart, immediately repaired to Bow Street Police Court where an information was laid on the prosecutor's behalf applying for Parke's arrest. On the strength of this information the magistrate issued the necessary warrant, to which Parke voluntarily surrendered at Bow Street Police Station later the same afternoon, which unfortunately for Parke was a Saturday.

'I hope I shall be allowed bail,' said the editor to the officer in

W. T. Stead
Editor of *The Pall Mall Gazette*

Henry Labouchere, MP
Editor of *Truth*
Cartoon by Carlos Pellegrini in *Vanity Fair*

James Monro, CB
Commissioner of Metropolitan Police
Cartoon by Leslie Ward in *Vanity Fair*

The Hon. Hamilton Cuffe
Assistant Director of Public Prosecutions
Cartoon by Leslie Ward in *Vanity Fair*

The Rt. Hon. Henry Matthews, QC, MP
Home Secretary
Cartoon by Leslie Ward in *Vanity Fair*

Sir Richard Webster, QC, MP
Attorney General
Cartoon by Leslie Ward in *Vanity Fair*

Lord Arthur Somerset
Cartoon by Leslie Ward in *Vanity Fair*

The Hon. Reginald Brett
From the painting by Julian Story in the
possession of Viscount Esher

charge. 'You know I have come here as soon as I knew the warrant was issued. I could have run away a week ago if I had wished.' He was thereupon charged with 'unlawfully publishing a wilful and malicious libel of and concerning the Earl of Euston', and as he was unable to get bail on a Saturday afternoon, he was obliged, since the magistrate had left the court for the week-end, to remain in custody until he was brought before the magistrate on Monday morning. By this time his solicitor had secured the services of Mr. Frank Lockwood, QC, and Mr. H. H. Asquith to appear for him. At the same time Newton sent Charles Gill a watching brief on behalf of Lord Arthur Somerset.

2

When Parke was brought up at Bow Street court on the morning of 25 November, the magistrate, Mr. James Vaughan, agreed to adjourn the hearing until the following afternoon so as to give Mr. Frank Lockwood time to study the materials for the defence. Meanwhile Parke was released on bail of two securities of £50 each. There were few spectators in court, but owing to the reports of the proceedings which appeared in the evening papers, it was crowded for the adjourned hearing next day.

After Euston's solicitor, Mr. George Lewis, had opened the case for the prosecution with a brief statement of the facts and background of the libel, the prosecutor was called into the witness-box. There was no truth in the statement that he had been guilty of the crime alleged in the *North London Press*, he said in reply to his solicitor's questions, and he knew of no warrant having been issued for his arrest. Nor was there any truth in the statement that he had left England and gone to Peru. In fact, he had not been abroad for several years.

'Will you state to the Court what you know of the house in Cleveland Street?' Lewis asked him.

'All I know is that one night I was in Piccadilly—'

'When?' the magistrate interrupted.

'At the end of May or beginning of June.'

[113]

Euston went on to say that a card was put into his hand, which he noted when he read it afterwards was headed: '*Poses plastiques*. Hammond, 19 Cleveland Street.'

'About a week afterwards did you go there?'

'Yes, about a week afterwards,' the witness replied. 'About half past ten or eleven. A man let me in and asked me for a sovereign. I gave him a sovereign.' According to Euston, he (Euston) then inquired when the *poses plastiques* were going to take place, but the man said, 'There is nothing of that sort here.'

At this point Lockwood objected to the details of this conversation, since Parke was not present on the occasion, and Lewis consequently dropped this line of questioning, contenting himself with eliciting the admission from the witness that he did not remain in the house for more than a few minutes and had never been there before or since.

In cross-examination Parke's leading counsel asked Euston whether it was true that he had previously made a statement complaining of the imputation in the libel. The witness agreed that it was, and that he had done so about the middle of October. He denied that he had made the statement either to the Home Office or the Treasury, but had made it privately to a friend.

'Is Lord Arthur Somerset a friend of yours?' Lockwood continued.

'I know him.'

'When did you see him last?'

'Last summer some time. During the season in society, I kept meeting him constantly.'

'You have not seen him since?'

'No.'

'Do you know where he is?'

To this question Euston replied that he did not.

'When this card was given to you,' Lockwood went on, 'was the man giving them promiscuously, or were you specially favoured?'

'I can't say. It was put into my hand. I was walking along sharply, as I usually walk, and I put the card into my pocket.'

'Did you see him give a card to anyone else?'

'No, it was near 12 o'clock as I was walking home'.

'I suggest to you that you had not time to stop and read it?'

'Well,' said the witness, laughing, 'I did not stop to read it under a lamp-post.'

'I do not know what there is to laugh at,' observed Lockwood.

'Well, it was a comical question,' Euston's solicitor intervened.

'Well,' said Lockwood to the witness, 'how long was it between your reading it or your going to see whether the promises on the card would be carried out?'

'Oh, at least a week,' answered Euston.

'Then you kept the card during the whole of that week?'

'Yes.'

'Did you go to the house alone?'

'Yes.'

'Take the card with you?'

'Yes.'

'And bring it back with you?'

'I took it home.'

'What did you do with it?'

'I destroyed it. I was disgusted at having found such a place.'

'You had no doubt in your mind what the character of the house was?'

'Not the slightest.'

'It is a house, as I understand you to say of your own knowledge, where crimes such as those alluded to in the libel were probably committed?'

'I should think they might be and probably were, from what was said to me.'

Re-examining his client, Lewis asked him what he had said to the man who opened the door.

'"You infernal scoundrel",' Euston replied. '"If you don't let me out I will knock you down".' Euston said that he at once left the house, and up to that moment he had no knowledge whatever of the character of the house beyond what appeared on the card.

'Or suspicion?' queried the magistrate.

'None whatever,' the witness repeated.

'You have said that you first made a statement about this house in October,' Lewis continued his re-examination. 'Was that after rumour had got about?'

Lockwood immediately jumped to his feet to object. But the magistrate in effect overruled the objection by intervening with a question of his own to the witness: 'How came you to make that statement in October?'

'Because I had heard a rumour which affected myself.'

'Did it ever occur to you to give information to the police?' Lewis went on.

'No,' replied Euston. 'I was disgusted with having entered such a place and in fact thought nothing more would come of it.'

Answering further questions from his solicitor, Euston said that he had not seen the man since. 'I heard of the prosecution at the Old Bailey,' he added, 'but it never occurred to me to ascertain whether the man [Veck] being prosecuted was the man I mean. I didn't want to be mixed up with anything of the sort.'

'Would you have taken any steps whatever but for the publication of the libel?'

'None whatever.'

'Has anyone made any accusation against you?'

'No.'

'Until the publication of the libel?'

'None'.

This concluded the case for the prosecution, whereupon Lockwood asked that the defendant might be admitted to bail.

Mr. Vaughan remarked that it was a case of 'very great gravity', and in order to secure the defendant's appearance at the trial, he should require bail in two sureties of £250 and the defendant's recognizances in £500.

The necessary bail was immediately forthcoming and Ernest Parke was committed to take his trial at the next sessions of the Central Criminal Court, pleading Not Guilty and reserving his defence.

When he was preparing his client's defence, Parke's solicitor, Mr. Minton Slater, wrote to the Home Office requesting that he should be supplied with the depositions in the case of Veck and Newlove. He was informed that the Home Secretary could not instruct the Director of Public Prosecutions in this sense, but that it was open to Parke's solicitor to subpoena the Director to produce any documents which the solicitor believed to be in his possession. The documents would then be brought into court but they could only be produced by order of the judge. But Parke's solicitor does not appear to have acted on this advice. Nor apparently did he make any attempt to secure any statements from Veck and Newlove or to subpoena them as witnesses, a curious omission, particularly as Newlove at the time of his arrest had told Inspector Abberline that both Somerset and Euston were regular visitors to the house in Cleveland Street. In fact the only witness with an intimate knowledge of the house to come forward was John Saul, and, as a male prostitute, his testimony was bound to be suspect.

Shortly afterwards it was announced that the trial judge at the Old Bailey would be Mr. Justice Hawkins, one of the best known Victorian judges from his alliterative nickname 'Hanging Hawkins', somewhat unfairly bestowed upon him from the number of murder trials at which he presided on the Bench.

'I am very glad that Hawkins tries this case,' Somerset wrote when he heard this news. 'He will I know try to keep my name quiet if possible. I am very anxious to see the result of the trial.' However, as will be seen, he had to wait a month longer than was at first thought for the result.

The next sessions opened on 16 December at the Old Bailey, and on that day Lord Euston attended before the Grand Jury, who returned a true bill against Ernest Parke for libel. Next day Euston's counsel applied that the case should not be heard before the 19th when application, he said, would be made to fix a date for the trial. Parke duly surrendered to his bail on the 19th when he repeated his plea of Not Guilty. At the same time his junior counsel put in a written plea of justification, as he was statutorily bound to do, that

the alleged libel was true in substance and in fact and that its publication was for the public benefit.

In this document Parke gave the names of five witnesses who, he
stated, were prepared to testify that Euston, knowing the character
of the house in Cleveland Street, had gone there on at least five
occasions between 1887 and 1889 'for improper purposes' in the
company of John Saul and Frank Hewitt, who according to Saul had
introduced Newlove to Hammond. The plea went on to assert that
the prosecutor, 'after he had learned of Veck's arrest and knowing
his associations with the house, left the kingdom in July 1889, and
went to foreign parts.' In the plea the specific allegation that he had
gone to Peru was withdrawn, and instead it was suggested that
Euston had travelled no further than Boulogne for the purpose of
seeing Lord Arthur Somerset.

Since the plea had only just been put in, Mr. Lionel Hart for
Euston felt justified in applying to the Recorder that the case should
not be taken this sessions so as to enable him and the counsel instructed with him, Sir Charles Russell and Mr. Willie Mathews, to
have an opportunity of considering the defence, as they might wish
to demur, i.e. to challenge it on a point of law, or to require further
particulars of the plea of justification. Asquith did not oppose the
application, although he took the opportunity to observe that his
client was 'ready and anxious to meet this charge and to support his
plea.' In these circumstances the Recorder agreed to adjourn the case
to the January sessions and he admitted the defendant to the same
bail as before.

At the same time Lord Euston publicly declared that all the
allegations about him were entirely without foundation and he was
determined to prosecute the offending editor to conviction.

'Far be it from me to say that Lord Euston is guilty of the charge
alleged by Mr. Parke against him,' Labouchere declared in the next
issue of *Truth* (26 December). He went on to inform his readers that
he had taken up the Cleveland Street scandal 'quite irrespective of
this particular allegation against an individual', and that the accusation he intended to make as soon as Parliament met was 'rather

against the authorities than against any particular person; for I am determined that a clause which I managed to get inserted in an Act shall not be used against obscure people, and people in a higher position be allowed to violate it with impunity.' However, after pointing out that the fact that Euston had elected to demand an adjournment necessarily involved additional expense to Mr. Parke, he made this appeal:

> It is to Lord Euston's advantage, as well as to that of Mr. Parke, that the case should not break down for want of funds. It is to be hoped, therefore, that those who take this view will send their subscriptions to Mr. Massingham, of the *Star* newspaper, who is the treasurer of the Parke Defence Fund.[1] If Mr. Parke has made an accusation that he cannot prove he deserves condign punishment, but it is in the interests of public morals that he should have a full opportunity to substantiate it, if he can substantiate it.

3

We must now see how Lord Arthur Somerset had been faring since he left his brother's villa in Monaco for Vienna, where he picked up the Orient Express for Constantinople. He had been quite right in supposing that the Sultan Abdul Hamid II, known as 'Abdul the Damned', did not entertain any 'prejudice' in the matter of sexual behaviour—the Sultan's harem in the palace at Yildiz housed 370 women and 127 eunuchs. On his arrival, Somerset had high hopes of landing the job he had in mind or at least some employment in the imperial stables. To his dismay, he found that it would be impossible for him to remain in the Turkish capital except at grave risk to himself. This was because of a long series of treaties between the United Kingdom and the Ottoman Empire dating from the time of Queen Elizabeth I and known as capitulations, which conferred on Britain the privilege of extra-territorial jurisdiction over British subjects in

---

[1] H. W. Massingham succeeded T. P. O'Connor as editor of *The Star* in 1890. An advanced Liberal, he later edited the *Daily Chronicle* and afterwards *The Nation*, which he created. He eventually joined the Labour Party.

Turkey. The news that he must leave before seeing the Sultan came as a bitter blow, since Somerset had already been in touch with Admiral Henry Woods (Woods Pasha), who had been seconded from the Royal Navy for service with the Imperial Ottoman Navy and was Naval ADC to the Sultan, with whom he had considerable influence owing to his work in reorganising the Turkish fleet and building up the country's coastal defences.

The bad news was repeated in a letter Somerset wrote from Constantinople to Brett on 25 November:

> I saw Woods Pasha yesterday and he was very kind and full of my getting recommendations etc from him. Late at night he came and told me the Ambassador was in an agony as he had had private letters saying there was a warrant out for my arrest and I had better leave as this town is under capitulations and I must be arrested here, put in the consular prison and shipped to England in custody if the warrant arrived, so I leave tonight.
>
> I must say, as they knew I was coming here, he might have found all this out and saved me days and nights of travelling and saved me about £50. Now what am I to do and where to go? I have not money enough to fly about the country or go on a long journey.

In the event he decided to return on the Orient Express to Budapest and see if he could get 'any horse work in Hungary'. But he was not very hopeful, since (as he told Brett) 'you see not knowing the language is so against one.' On reaching Budapest, which he did three days later, he saw Count Charles Kinsky, the famous steeplechaser and ladies' man, who promised to help. But, as will be seen, little came of this meeting.

Another idea was that he might buy horses for London dealers. 'They have great difficulty in getting honest buyers and they would of course know that I should be honest,' he told Brett, whom he asked to sound them out. 'I hardly like to write to them in case they should refuse and hawk my letter about London which might annoy my friends.' He also told Brett not to ask his father for any money. 'Of course I know all about his affairs as we were always such good friends and I know he is doing his utmost for all of us sons now.' He apparently had a letter of credit which met his living expenses for the time being. But he found the time lying heavy on his hands. 'Heavens! How long the days are! When fine I walk for miles but when it snows all day I read one Tauchnitz volume a day and the *Times* and *Figaro* and eat, drink, smoke and sleep.'

Meanwhile Somerset put up at the Reine d'Angleterre, a large hotel near the West Station in Budapest, where he continued to correspond with his friends in England. One of them was his former commanding officer, Oliver Montagu, from whom he received what he described as an unpleasant letter which he asked Brett to show to Newton. 'You can't think how that letter of Oliver's has upset me,' he told Brett.

> Trusting him as a friend I wrote a letter to thank him for his kindness to Blanchie (Waterford), and in my letter I said how curious it was that the Prince of Wales would not recommend me for employment but that he accepted my horse as a present. Oliver must have shown my letter to HRH as he (Oliver) says HRH has retained the horse. Of that I am between you and me very glad.

Apparently Somerset heard the news from his brother-in-law that the Prince had declined to give him a recommendation. 'I cannot get over Marcus Beresford after all we have done together for the Prince,' he reflected bitterly. In fact, as he subsequently admitted, Somerset did the Prince of Wales an injustice, as the Prince had actually bought his horse. But Somerset was not aware of this when he wrote, as 'no one told me and I received no money.'

'Don't let Oliver or anyone come out to me,' he urged Brett. 'If he starts, let me know and I will move. It is quite likely, I think, that he will. Let me know what you think I had better say to him but tell him nothing as it will all go to Sandringham direct. I am very sorry to give you so much trouble.'

Both Brett and Lady Waterford warned the unfortunate exile 'not to apply to Royalties again' for a testimonial. Indeed they impressed upon him that 'he should apply to no one unless certain of them beforehand . . . and he must keep his plans as private as possible.' Lady Waterford told Brett that she was 'very glad that he didn't get this appointment, poor darling, and much hope that eventually something will turn up in Hungary. Meanwhile patience and *extreme quiet* are the best things for the present . . .'

> One more thing I want to say. Podge's letters may strike you as pointing to the fact that he does not realise his awful position—but they are as different to his real self as possible. He writes in a careless way, by way of trying not to depress his friends and belongings—for a lonely man's letters must be either morbid or irrational, because he has no one to put things in a different light to him. Also he sees few English papers, and is far beyond gossip and chatter and has been away since 19 October so that he does not know the whole thing is being hawked about the streets, and that everyone invents his or her own story on top of it all. I only say this that you may not misunderstand his letters.

The text of Montagu's letter to Somerset has not survived, but he subsequently communicated its substance to Lady Waterford when he told her that he had written 'a strong letter' to her brother 'telling him I felt he could not be aware of the irreparable harm he was doing by still persisting in his silence as to the real cause of his leaving the country and insinuating that it was for the sakes of others that he had done so thereby leaving people here to draw their own inferences and drag innocent people's names through the mire.'

Somerset's explanation of his silence he gave in the letter he wrote to Brett on 10 December:

> I cannot see what good I could do Prince Eddy if I went into Court. I might do him harm because if I was asked if I had ever heard anything against him—whom from?—has any person mentioned with whom he went there etc?—the questions would be very awkward. I have never mentioned the boy's name except to Probyn, Montagu and Knollys when they were acting for me and I thought they ought to know. Had they been wise, hearing what I knew and therefore what others knew, they ought to have hushed the matter up, instead of stirring it up as they did, with all the authorities . . .
> What Oliver does not seem to see is that, if I could tell him my

reasons for not going into Court, I could not go in. Nothing will ever make me divulge anything I know even if I were arrested. But of course if certain people laid themselves out to have me arrested and succeeded, I might possibly lose my temper and annoy them.

Of course, it has very often, or may I say constantly occurred to me, that it rests with me to clear up this business, but what can I do? A great many people would never speak to me again as it is, but if I went into Court and told all I knew *no one* who called himself a man would *ever* speak to me again. Hence my infernal position. . . .

I did what I then, and still, believe was best for all concerned. If they don't mind, they will make a hash of the whole thing yet, and then I suppose they will say I did it. At all events you and Newton can bear me witness that I have sat absolutely tight in the matter and have not told my own father anything.

'That infernal letter of Oliver's set my insides going again yesterday,' he wrote again next day. 'Today I am better but still worried about it.' He went on:

You really were a prophet. You always said that if the police set this ball rolling they did not know where it would stop and I should not be the only scapegoat. It looks very much as if you were right. At all events they are in a great pother about it at Sandringham . . . I wonder when Euston's case comes on.

Somerset's curiosity was prompted by a report of the police court proceedings which appeared in the French journal *Figaro* and which he happened to pick up in a Budapest café; the report referred to the '*tendresse étrange pour les jeunes telegraphistes*' which Somerset was supposed to have shown.

An acquaintance of Brett's, the Earl of Loudoun, happened to meet a fellow peer, Lord Oxenbridge, in Manchester at this time and learned from him of Lady Waterford's visit to her brother in Monaco. According to Oxenbridge, 'Podge' had told her that 'he was perfectly innocent but that he had been driven into the wilderness in order to screen others who were amongst the highest in the land.'

'I told Oxenbridge that I was sure he had said nothing of the kind,' Lord Loudoun wrote to Brett, 'and that his (Podge's) friends, while believing that he was screening someone at his own expense, knew from him (Podge) that he did not believe a word of the reports about Prince Eddie and knew nothing of the matter himself. If Lady Waterford is going about saying this she is doing a great deal of harm which will only recoil on Podge's head.'

Lady Waterford was naturally concerned when she heard of the talk she was supposed to have been spreading and she wrote to Oliver Montagu, since she knew that he had recently visited Sandringham. 'Believe me,' Montagu reassured her, 'no one that I have heard of, and most certainly neither of the parents you allude to (T[heir] R[oyal] H[ighnesses]) have ever for one moment suggested that you should ever have hinted at your having insinuated things about Prince Eddy, though I fear there is no doubt that some female members of your family have done so, and I confess that I think it a most cruel and wicked shame on their part.' Oliver did not mention these individuals by name, but they can only have been Isabella, Lady Henry Somerset, who was separated from her husband, and her mother, Lady Somers, who were both obsessed with the subject of homosexuality.

There being apparently no chance of getting any employment in Hungary, Arthur Somerset decided to leave Budapest for Vienna, which he did on 21 December. On the day before his departure he received a short anonymous letter in disguised handwriting, which caused him considerable annoyance:

> Can it be true that you have authorised your sister to say that you are innocent and Prince Eddie. Are you determined to add treason and shameful ingratitude to bestiality. For God's sake contradict the foul calumnies of your family.

Somerset wondered whether the anonymous note which was unsigned could possibly have come from the Prince of Wales's Equerry and Private Secretary, the Hon. Harry Tyrwhitt, with the Prince's knowledge. 'Surely it is not HRH's writing on the envelope and Harry Tyrwhitt's inside,' he wrote to Brett enclosing the note. 'It seems impossible; but yet it is posted in the S.W. district (Marlborough House) by someone who knows how to address one properly. The little envelope inside is like—that is, it is made of the same paper as HRH's private note paper, and the writing inside is like H[arry] T[yrwhitt]'s or as nearly as printing can be. I suppose it is absurd and yet Prince Eddie!! That is odd. It seems incredible and yet I really cannot help thinking it especially after Oliver's letter from Sandringham. H[arry] T[yrwhitt] is in waiting!'

In the same letter Somerset asked Brett to get him a passport. 'Any name whose initials are AS except the name of the city of the Plain . . . If anyone annoyed me I should like to get away under another name, which I could do if I had a passport ready. I want to get either to Russia or even further East.' He added that he had grown quite a long beard, which had changed his appearance. 'You ask me if life is hopelessly dreary here,' he went on. 'Yes it is, although there is lots of material for making it otherwise; but they take their pleasure in a different way here to what I care for . . . I am bored at moving as I am very comfortable, but it is best. People are beginning to ask inconvenient questions.'

'I never open a paper without seeing something awful,' Somerset wrote from Vienna where he stayed at the Hotel Metropole, a large establishment with 400 bedrooms in Morzin Platz near the Danube. 'Tonight I in read *The Times* of the 19th and see that N[ewton] is in hot water . . . There never was anything like the virulence of this prosecution. I can see that they will end by dragging that name before the public that we all want to avoid.'

The disturbing news about Newton was that summonses had been applied for and granted at the Bow Street Police Court against Newton, his managing clerk, Frederick Taylorson, and Adolphe De Gallo, who was employed as interpreter at the Marlborough Street court, charging them with conspiring to defeat the course of justice 'in respect of offences alleged to have been committed by divers persons at 19 Cleveland Street, Fitzroy Square, in the County of London.'

Somerset wrote again to Brett on 23 December:

Poor Mr. N! I see he applied for a copy of the indictment.[1] I hope he will get on all right. I suppose it will be another opportunity to draw my luckless name before the public? Whom will they prosecute next? I cannot see if he remains in England how Euston can get out of prosecuting Veck and Newlove and then there will be another long trial, but I take it he has not finished with Parke yet by a long way.

Altogether the approaching winter looks stormy in England. I saw in the same *Times* that Prince Eddy will not return before the original intended time . . .

I should think they have tackled a strong and dangerous man in N. If they put him in a corner he will very likely give them a nasty one. It was to come on today I saw . . .

But something awful is sure to happen—just when one least expects it. I feel quite sure that with all this virulent prosecution of everybody they will end by having out in open court exactly what they are all trying to keep quiet. I wonder if it is really a fact or only an invention of that arch ruffian H[ammond]'s. I should be delighted if they got at him and got him 5 years. Meanwhile I trust that Abberline is seeing that A[llies] is comfortable for the rest of his life and the other youths. I am quite surprised that they have not applied to me for pensions.

The institution of proceedings against Newton was of some concern to the Duke of Beaufort, as will be seen. At the same time, the Duke took the opportunity when he was in London of seeing Probyn and Knollys on the subject of his daughter's alleged indiscretions. The two courtiers assured him that their royal master was convinced that Lady Waterford had 'nothing to do with the indiscreet rumours so detrimental to P[rince] A[lbert] V[ictor] which were being circulated by some members of his Grace's family.' Probyn afterwards wrote to the Duchess in terms which to some extent put the blame upon her third son rather than upon her daughter.

In fact, the only lady's name mentioned during our conversation was Lady Waterford's saying how kindly and well we knew she had

---

[1] The document was, properly speaking, the 'information' presented to the magistrate in order to institute criminal proceedings without a formal indictment.

behaved throughout. We feared that possibly on account of her late visit to her brother the Duke might think we perhaps referred to her, and we knew well that she had nothing to do with these cruel and unjust rumours with regard to PAV which were so painful to the Prince of Wales.

Nobody accused your son of having mentioned PAV's name, but his excuse to everybody for having to leave England is that he has been forced to do so to screen another and that his lips are closed! The only conclusion therefore people can draw from this is that he is sacrificing himself to save the young Prince. Who else is there for whom he could make such a sacrifice? Hence the false reports dragging PAV's name into the sad story.

Please, please, do not for one moment think or let dear Lady Waterford think that she is suspected of having anything to do with these abominable rumours, because she is certainly not by the Prince of Wales or by any of HRH's household.

Lady Waterford was anxious that her brother should likewise be cleared of having made the same insinuations, and she wrote in this sense to Brett:

Not only am I sure since seeing Arthur that the boy [Prince Eddy] is not to blame and has nothing to do with it, but I have told all my people so and anyone who has ever mentioned his name to me in connection with this business, and on my return I impressed upon my family—Mother, aunts, cousins and friends (Father never thought of it)—that there was no *question* about the boy, and that it was our duty to try and remove this totally wrong impression *by every means in our power*. I had Arthur's authority for writing to you, as I see you remember my having done from Monaco, to say that he knew *nothing* of the boy's comings and goings, or any single thing about him, and as you say I should have thought that was enough.

If they expect him [Arthur] to say, 'I am guilty and know the names of everyone who is so and everyone who is not,' of course he is unable to do so, as he declares and we thoroughly believe in his innocence. All that he can say is, what he has already said (and what you remember I told you), that Arthur does not the least know how or where the boy spends his time, and that he never went out with

[127]

him except twice to Jubilee fireworks and a smoking concert where
my Father was—and that nothing in the world would distress him
more than that his going away should throw the smallest doubt
upon the boy.

I am *most* anxious that Arthur should be cleared of ever having
insinuated such things, as such a thing can never have been in his
thoughts and is absolutely untrue.

'I do so want to clear my Podgie,' she wrote again a few days
later. 'Do you think he could write to Sir Dighton Probyn or some
one to explain he believes the boy to be perfectly innocent, but that
the man [Hammond] threatened to chantage him as a stronger inducement to extract hush money from Arthur? But you will know
what it is best he *should* write. Only I do think something ought to be
written, as the boy should be cleared at all risks.'

Something indeed was written, though not by Lord Arthur
Somerset. December 1889 marked the height of the rumours about
Prince Eddy and his involvement in the Cleveland Street affair, and
it led to the announcement in the English press, to which Somerset
alluded in one of his letters to Brett, that there was no intention of
curtailing the Prince's Indian tour. Although the Prince's name was
never mentioned by any English newspaper in the Cleveland Street
context, it did appear in an American journal. This prompted a
correspondent to address a letter on the subject to the reputable
New York Herald. The letter, which occupied three columns,
appeared in the issue of 22 December over the signature 'A Member
of Parliament'. It was almost certainly written by Mr. Charles Hall,
Queen's Counsel and Attorney General to the Prince of Wales, who
was attending an international conference in Washington at this time.

The letter, which was headlined 'The Policy of Hushing Up,'
began as follows:

> The authorised announcement which has appeared in the papers
> concerning Prince Albert Victor will not be misinterpreted by any-
> one who is familiar with the kind of talk which has been afloat for
> several weeks past. Over and over again it has been whispered about
> that 'Prince Eddie' would shortly be recalled from India under

circumstances peculiarly painful to himself and his family. It was impossible either to trace these reports to their source or to check them. It may, however, put some slight restraint upon the gossip-mongers to be informed in a semi-official manner that the arrangements in connection with the young Prince's visit to India will not be altered in any way, and that he will return at the time originally fixed, and not before.

The issue of this notice was, no doubt, the subject of careful consideration beforehand, and it was wise. There are some people who will believe anything, and there is never any telling how far slander may spread. I have heard, though I have not actually seen the paper, that a New York journal recently published an article on certain abominable scandals, with a portrait of Prince Albert Victor in the midst of it. If this be so, a more atrocious or a more dastardly outrage was never perpetrated in the Press.

Speaking with some knowledge of the charges in question, and of the persons who are really compromised by them, I assert that there is not, and never was, the slightest excuse for mentioning the name of Prince Albert Victor in association with them. A feeling of delicacy can alone have prevented this statement appearing in a form to command universal credence, but now that there are libellers who do not hesitate to assail the young Prince—at a safe distance—it is a mistake for the English Press to maintain absolute silence on the subject. It is much to be wished that the editor or proprietor of the New York paper to which I refer could be reached by the law which he has violated. Meanwhile, wherever his action is known, it is spoken of with the utmost detestation. Whatever may be the motive which inspires such attacks as these, they can only have the effect of injuring the reputation of the Press, and of strengthening the attachment which the English people are proud of entertaining for their Sovereign and her family.

After developing the principal theme of his letter that it was becoming more apparent every day that the persons responsible for the Cleveland Street scandal should be brought to justice, the writer went on:

The solicitor whose prosecution begins tomorrow, Mr. Newton, was the legal adviser of Lord Arthur Somerset, and he is accused of aiding and abetting in the flight of the miscreant who kept the house in Cleveland Street. This man, Hammond by name, knew most of his customers and had kept a list of them. That list is now in the possession of the police, unless it has mysteriously disappeared with certain other papers which passed between police headquarters and the Treasury. When Hammond found out that the game was up, he demanded a certain sum of money from his 'noble' (and other) supporters to enable him to fly to America. It is alleged that Mr. Newton acted as the go-between in this business. Hammond got his money, and made himself scarce. It is very certain that Mr. Newton's client disappeared at about the same time. But of all these transactions, except the retirement from the army and from his country of Lord Arthur Somerset, Mr. Newton alleges that he has a satisfactory explanation.

The writer's conclusion was that if the trials of the culprits proceeded freely, none of the threatened attacks in Parliament by Labouchere and others might be made.

What is quite clear is that the authorities are now determined to go on, and that sooner or later the real culprits will stand revealed to the public eye, even if they manage to escape the hands of justice. This may perhaps allay the irritation which has undoubtedly been created by the belief that the Government was shielding offenders on account of their rank or influence. It may, therefore, happen that the threatened attacks in Parliament will never be made. It is needless to say that if they come from Mr. Labouchere's party only, they will produce no effect on the public mind, and do no injury to the Government or anybody else. They will be attributed to political animosities, and to a desire to upset the Ministry by any means, fair or foul. There is nothing that the public resent so much as that. In the present case, the circumstances alluded to at the beginning of this letter would add heavily to the condemnation that would fall on all who gave cause for the suspicion that they were dabbling in loathsome slanders for the purpose of bringing discredit upon the Ministry. There would be a tremendous reaction of feeling against the politicians who were caught in any such manoeuvre. It behoves the assailants, therefore, to be very circumspect, and to take care that the engineer is not hoist with his own petard.

The Prince of Wales, who received a copy of the paper with the letter at the earliest possible moment, asked Knollys to send it on to Lord Salisbury, describing it as 'a very good article' which he felt that the Prime Minister 'may perhaps like to glance at.' Lord Salisbury did so and afterwards filed the paper away carefully.

4

The unfortunate Somerset spent a cold and lonely Christmas in Vienna. 'All last night and all today it has been and is snowing,' he wrote to Brett on Christmas Day. 'The awful melancholy, when one has no one to speak to and nothing to do, and when one cannot even walk about and get exercise, is not to be told.' Someone had sent him a cutting from an Irish paper which said that the police had got hold of Hammond's wife and that 'they had gleaned a deal of information from her.' Meanwhile he wondered how Newton was getting on, as well as Euston. 'I suppose the authorities will not want me any more on account of Newton's case, will they?' He now thought of going to Gardone on Lake Garda. 'It is between that and Africa or Asia to my mind. In many ways I should prefer the latter as life is too utterly hopeless as it is.' He also wrote to his mother complaining about the Viennese climate, which prompted the Duke to ask Brett: 'Is there no place near Mentone, quiet where he could go and get warm and he could then run up sometimes to Henry at Monaco or Henry could run down to him and he would have someone to speak to?'

'I am so sorry,' his mother had written when he left Budapest, 'for he was comfortably lodged and was occupying himself in learning languages. Now he will be a wretched wanderer again. It may be that he has heard of some employment—would that it might be so. But it is all so hopeless and miserable, my poor dear child!' Unfortunately nothing came of his approach to Count Kinsky. 'Kinsky's plan is quite a castle in the air,' he told Brett. 'In twelve months he would get his cousin to let me live in his country house which he never uses and let me manage his estate! Fancy! so likely! An utter stranger knowing nothing of the markets or anything.' But Lady Waterford would hear nothing against the Hungarian. 'I am sure Count K behaved like an angel, as he is,' she wrote at the time, 'and I do believe we may always count on him as a real good friend, bless him!'

Somerset's next tribulation was to be harassed by the local police. It began on Boxing Day. 'The Vienna police have made a fox of me for two whole days,' he wrote on the evening of 27 December. 'I cannot move but I am pursued by armies of plain clothes police aided and abetted by small boys. At all events I have given them some exercise and I don't suppose they have any right to touch me. But of course they might embroil me in some row and I suppose they are like their English compères. What one lies all the rest swear to, so I must clear out of this.'

Next day he wrote again:

> The very moment I have shown my nose outside my room door I have been pursued by boys and detectives, positive relays of them, in the passages, on the stairs, at the front door, and then they started off and pursued me all over the town, into the telegraph office, wherever I went. When we got into the darker smaller streets I thought there was a disposition to hustle me evidently with a view to making me lose my temper so that they might have some pretext for arresting me.
>
> It got so bad that when I came home tonight I asked to see the manager of the hotel and I told him that of course I did not know whether he wished people who came to his hotel to be persecuted and chased all over the place both in and out of the house, but I was being so hunted and I told him that I had already written to London saying what was taking place in case the police succeeded in embroiling me in any way. I told him I had lived in London 20 years and had never been in any police court bother and did not mean to begin. He appeared very much astonished and said there must be some mistake, to which I replied that I had made no mistake and that if I was embroiled in any way I should subpoena him as a witness to say that I had declared all to him. Since then, 7.30 p.m., I have had no peace . . .

Nevertheless he continued to be hunted. 'The Vienna detectives must have very little to do,' he told Brett the following day. 'Every street holds one and a small urchin for my benefit.' He added that he thought of going to Pressburg (Bratislava) for the week-end, before taking the night train to Paris on the 30th. One time capital of Hungary, Pressburg, which was some forty miles east of Vienna, then belonged to Austria and was mainly inhabited by Hungarians, Czechs and Slovaks. However Somerset seems to have changed his mind about visiting the historic town, thinking he might be pursued there by the police if he went. 'I always thought our London detectives pretty bad, but they are artists compared to these fools,' he wrote to Brett on Sunday the 29th. 'If the police behave fairly well tomorrow, perhaps I shall leave here. If they are troublesome I shall stay to show them they may go to hell for all I care.'

Something the head waiter said to him at lunchtime that day put him more than ever on his guard:

> I cannot help fancying they have a plant for me at a concert tonight. There is one at the Musik-Verein I believe it is called close to the Hotel Imperial. The head waiter announced it to me: and as he has never told me anything before I am a little suspicious. You see I never go out after 6.30 p.m. so as not to give them a chance of embroiling me in any way. It makes the evening very long and dull as I never speak to anyone; but it is safer while this is going on. So I shall not attend the concert tonight.

'I *have* had a time of it here I tell you,' he wrote on the day he eventually left. 'They tried getting boys to insult me in the street today. But as I don't understand the language that had very little effect. I have fairly tested them though. Of course it has played the deuce with one's nerves and I shall feel the reaction more than the event.'

> I suppose they will telegraph my departure for Paris to the police there. D—— them. It is nearly 3 and my train goes at 5. I have not yet asked for my bill or said I am going, so the streets thank God are teeming with half frozen detectives and boys with red noses.

They certainly tried me with every description. All sizes from 12 to 25 and all colours and grades in society, and I think with a boy in woman's clothes. If not, then with a woman with very ugly feet. Of course I dared not look very much as I knew they wanted to pick a quarrel with me . . .

I do hope I shall get someone to speak to before long. I must get a paid companion if this life is to go on, or I shall go mad. You see if one had someone to walk and feed with they could not play one of these tricks. There would be no excuse for them.

Somerset did not know Paris at all well and he asked Brett's advice as to where to stay. 'For a few days a hotel does very well,' the exile told his friend. 'But as no one stays more than two or three days it would be best to get rooms somewhere in that city . . . I don't know the place at all. But if I could get an airy room in the suburbs (like Hampstead or Fulham) I should be comfortable and my *friends* might come and see *me* sometimes, if they would.' His sister Blanche agreed and likewise wrote to Brett:

All these next few months must be full of misery, and I should think it would be such a good thing for my mother to go off and stay with Arthur at Versailles, or somewhere near Paris, to take her out of it all—but I shall say nothing to her till I hear if Arthur wishes it. Perhaps he would rather wait till these trials are over.

As far as the general world is concerned, nothing matters much, and God will pull us through it all, somehow.

After a few days in a hotel, thanks to an introduction provided by Brett, Somerset found a quiet pension in Passy, 40 Rue Copernic. 'This house is full of Americans and children but I never speak to any of them,' he wrote on 11 January 1890 after moving in, 'and there are two old Spanish ladies.'

Shortly after his arrival in Passy he heard from his father, to whom he had also written an account of his unpleasant experiences in Vienna. 'I regret you did not let me know before you left Pest that you meant going to Vienna for I would have stopped you,' wrote the Duke to his son. 'I don't believe for a moment that Scotland Yard communicated with them. They are the most meddlesome police in the world and they hunt every stranger that stays more than a couple of days there unless he can give a reference to a well known Banker or to an Embassy that he is a man of means and respectable.'

'I do not know by whom the Vienna police were inspired,' Somerset commented, 'but that they knew me of course I am certain by their conduct and hunting me with boys and saying insolent things—Austrian boys saying insolent things in French when they found I did not understand German. There is a French word beginning with P which is unmistakable.'

There were now two trials pending in which Somerset was deeply interested, that of Newton and his clerk and the interpreter for obstructing the course of justice and that of Parke on the prosecution of Lord Euston for criminal libel. 'Very glad you think so well of N[ewton]'s case,' Somerset wrote to Brett on learning that the latter had had a long meeting with the solicitor. 'Wish him luck from me when you see him. I think he could nob Dick Pearson and Cranbrook for jabbering. I have Pearson's letter to me if it would be any use but I suppose not. I should be glad if the other case could be compromised on honourable terms. His Grace is sure to stick to N.'

5

The trial of Ernest Parke for criminally libelling the Earl of Euston opened at the Old Bailey before Mr. Justice Hawkins and a jury on 15 January 1890. Sir Charles Russell, QC, MP, led Mr. Willie Mathews, later Director of Public Prosecutions, and Mr. Lionel Hart for the prosecution. Parke was defended by Mr. Frank Lockwood, QC, MP, later Solicitor-General, and Mr. H. H. Asquith, later Home Secretary and afterwards Prime Minister. At the outset the defendant surrendered to his bail, took his place in the dock and repeated his plea of Not Guilty.

In opening the case for Lord Euston, who sat beside his solicitor at the solicitors' table, Sir Charles Russell began by drawing the jury's attention to the recent Law of Libel Amendment Act which had extended, as he conceived very properly, considerable protection to those responsible for the contents of newspapers. That this was a case of a serious character could not be doubted, the libel being of a very serious nature, counsel said; but it was made still more serious and required all the more anxious attention of the jury because of the fact that the defendant Parke had thought proper not only to plead Not Guilty of writing and publishing the libel, but he had also added a plea of justification that the libel itself was true. There might be some technical objections to the form of the plea, but Lord Euston did not propose to take advantage of them but rather, as he had done at the preliminary hearing in the magistrate's court when Parke was committed for trial, to meet the alleged justification 'openly and uprightly'. It was now 'unhappily the notorious fact' that for some time past the house at 19 Cleveland Street had been used 'for purposes of the most nefarious kind', and the alleged libel, which he later read out to the jury, associated Lord Euston's name with the house and 'the practices there carried on'.

Counsel went on to detail the circumstances in which the prosecutor received the card advertising the house and its attractions, and how, after keeping it for a week on the table or chimney-piece of his dressing-room, 'prompted it might be by prurient curiosity which did him no credit', he did unquestionably go to the house in Cleveland Street. The mode of enticing visitors to the house might have been for the purpose of what the French called *chantage*, or blackmailing—'that is to say, extorting money from persons who have been weak enough to resort to that place'. In any event, said counsel, that was the beginning and the end of Lord Euston's connection with the house. Later in the year the prosecutor heard his name mentioned in connection with Cleveland Street and he 'straightaway did what any honourable man would do'—he took the best advice he could, and after consulting his solicitor he began proceedings against the editor of the *North London Press*.

It was implied in the offending editorial, headed 'The West End Scandals', Russell continued, that Lord Euston had left the country in order to escape from a warrant issued or about to be issued against him by the authorities, and had gone to Peru. There was not a single word of truth in that statement. It was not true that any charge had been made against Lord Euston, and no warrant had ever been issued or applied for. Nor was it true that Lord Euston had left the country impelled by the desire to escape or any other reason. Except in 1882, when he visited a sick relative in Biarritz, Lord Euston had not been out of England for eight or nine years. So far as the defendant's written plea of justification went, counsel said that his client emphatically denied its allegations; indeed he never heard of John Saul or Frank Hewitt, in whose company he was supposed to have been. Nor had he left the country after the arrest of Veck and Newlove. The defence had 'vaguely and without particularity made certain charges', and in these circumstances counsel informed the court that he proposed 'to follow the course pursued in leading cases of a similar kind'—that was to call Lord Euston as a witness by way of rebuttal after the defence had attempted to show what were the grounds for putting forward Parke's most serious plea of justification. In other words, Lord Euston's counsel would first prove the publication of the libel and would then call upon the defence to justify it, after which Russell would put his client in the witness-box, where the latter would tell his story and be cross-examined, unless the judge expressed any contrary opinion.

After the judge had remarked that he did not think he ought to express any opinion, Russell called his formal witnesses. The first of these was a friend of Lord Euston's, a solicitor named Edward Bedford, who deposed that he had bought a copy of the *North London Press* with the libellous article on the day of publication and showed it shortly afterwards to Lord Euston, who after having seen Mr. George Lewis, instructed him to begin criminal proceedings against the defendant. The two other formal witnesses were the printers of the offending journal, of which it appeared that 4,500 copies containing the libel had come off the presses.

Lockwood then opened the case for the defence. He began with a sharp criticism of Russell's tactics in not immediately calling his client to give evidence. In his own experience, 'which of course was not so prolonged as that of Sir Charles Russell', Parke's counsel declared that he had never known a case of this kind where a person had come into court and had complained that his reputation had been attacked and had deliberately shrunk from tendering himself for cross-examination. The client preferred to trust rather to the prowess and skill of his counsel and the attack which the latter would make on the defence testimony, Lockwood went on, and 'knowing well in establishing a case of this kind a great deal of the evidence would necessarily be tainted, the courage of Lord Euston might increase as the credibility of the witnesses against him was weakened.' Lockwood then commented that Sir Charles Russell was not in a position to give any undertaking as to whether or not his client would be put into the box, since that was entirely in the option of Lord Euston. Meanwhile he (Lockwood) would call witnesses to show that Lord Euston had visited the Cleveland Street house on the dates mentioned in the plea of justification. There was another class of testimony which would be offered—testimony which was capable of being treated as tainted, and on which the jury might have some hesitation in relying. Two names had been mentioned in the plea, one of whom, Saul, would be called as a witness, while the other, Hewitt, was out of the country, though Saul would speak also with regard to him.

Lockwood concluded his opening speech to the jury as follows:

It is necessary in a defence of this description to satisfy you, gentlemen of the jury, not merely of the truth of the charges made, but it is incumbent upon the defence to show that the publication is for the public benefit. Now I doubt whether there will be any argument on that point. In July last, two persons (Veck and Newlove) were convicted in this court of a criminal offence with regard to this particular house. They were persons in a humble position of life, and their conviction caused little comment. The inquiry, so far as they were concerned, was conducted with an extraordinary amount of secrecy, for certainly very few people are aware that that conviction had taken place. If with those persons of humble origin persons of position have been associated, such as those mentioned in connection with the infamies of this house, I should be surprised to hear any argument suggesting that it is not in the interest of the public that names such as those should be published.

The first witness for the defence was John O'Loughlin, who was examined by Asquith. He said he was a coal-dealer and greengrocer, working in Tottenham Street. He knew Cleveland Street and the house at No. 19, which was only twenty-seven yards from his door. Some time last summer, about May 20, he said, he was standing between seven and eight o'clock in the evening at the corner of Cleveland Street, talking to a Mr. Smith, when he saw a gentleman get out of a carriage, and Smith called his attention to him. The gentleman knocked or rang the bell at No. 19 and witness saw him go in. The witness added that he had seen the gentleman since then—first at Hyde Park Corner six weeks ago and next outside the court that morning.

At Asquith's request, Lord Euston stood up in court, and O'Loughlin said he would like to see him walk. Lord Euston obligingly took a few steps across the court, and later, in cross-examination, the witness raised a laugh when he admitted that Lord Euston's walk reminded him of a policeman 'who had done twenty years' walking on the stones—it was not a smart or nimble walk.'

Russell, who cross-examined this witness, had little difficulty in demolishing his evidence-in-chief. He did not know whether the carriage in which the gentleman arrived at Cleveland Street was a private carriage or not. Nor did he notice whether there was one horse or two in the carriage. 'I know more about coal-barrows than carriages,' he said. O'Loughlin admitted that he suffered from bad eyesight and that it was getting worse every day. Consequently he might easily have been mistaken in his identification of Lord Euston as the man he had seen entering Cleveland Street. After his visit to Hyde Park Corner with a man whose name he did not know—he was a private detective employed by Parke—the man showed the witness a photograph of a man and asked whether he thought he would recognise him. The witness said he thought he would, but he did not think it was the same as the man he saw in Cleveland

Street, being fuller in the face. The man who went into Cleveland Street was 5 ft. 9 in. or 5 ft. 10 in. in height, and dressed in light grey with a high hat; he was good looking and looked healthy. Another man also showed him a different photograph of the same man, and the witness managed to raise a further laugh when he told the court that he had been informed that one of the private detectives who showed him the photographs had been employed by *The Times* in Ireland 'to get up evidence against Mr. Parnell'. (The letters allegedly written by Parnell indicating complicity in the Phoenix Park murders and published in *The Times* had recently been proved to be forgeries as the result of Russell's devastating cross-examination of the forger before the official commission of inquiry.)

The next witness gave his name as John Smith and said he was a porter. Answering Lockwood, he confirmed that he had been in Cleveland Street with O'Loughlin one evening in the previous May, but he gave the time as nine o'clock or a little later, instead of seven or eight. He remembered seeing a gentleman get out of a carriage which stopped next door to No. 19, and the gentleman knocked at the door and went into the house. The witness said he had not seen the gentleman since, to his recollection, but he had seen him about a week before the occasion on which he saw him with O'Loughlin, when the gentleman walked up to the door of No. 19 and went inside. The witness then proceeded to identify Lord Euston as the gentleman in question. He said he believed that he had seen him altogether on six or seven occasions, but he admitted that he might be mistaken as to the exact number, owing to its being at night. He noticed in particular that the gentleman wore very loose trousers.

In cross-examination, Smith did not agree with the previous witness about the colour of the gentleman's clothes. He was dressed in a dark coat and striped trousers, 'not exactly light'. It was a private carriage that the gentleman drove up in on the night that he (the witness) was with O'Loughlin, and the gentleman opened the door of it himself. He went on to say that he never thought anything more of the incident until he was reminded of it by O'Loughlin, who told him that he had seen a private detective named Captain Webb who was making inquiries about Cleveland Street and whom he (the witness) had also met, although he had had 'no particular conversation with him'. Smith too had been shown a photograph, but he said he was not told who it was nor asked to identify the subject. Questioned further about the gentleman who got out of the carriage, the witness said he was about his own height, 5 ft. 8 in. or a little taller, and he remembered him by the looseness of his trousers. He added that he recognised Lord Euston as the same man by his moustache, 'which however, was not so curled today as on the previous occasion.' Asked by the judge how many times he had seen the person in Cleveland Street, Smith replied that he had done so five or six times altogether, spread over a period of nine months.

The porter was followed in the witness-box by O'Loughlin's son Michael, who said that he lived with his father in Tottenham Street and was an unemployed barman. He said he remembered going to Ascot Races two years before on Hunt Cup day and Lord Euston was then pointed out to him by name. Since then he had seen the gentleman in Cleveland Street, going in and coming out of No. 19, more precisely about three times at the end of May and beginning of June. The first time the witness saw him, he (the witness) was coming along Cleveland Street on the same side as No. 19, when he saw Lord Euston coming out. Five weeks later he saw him going into the same house, and two or three days after that, he saw him coming out. Asked in cross-examination where Lord Euston was pointed out to him at Ascot, young O'Loughlin said it was near the paddock. He also said that he had been asked to give evidence by Captain Webb, who had told him that Lord Euston lived in Grosvenor Place, from which he understood that he was to go there and identify him. He too was shown several photographs, and he had recognised one of them as that of Lord Euston.

Russell tried to fix the witness by dates that he last saw the gentleman some time about the 7th, 8th or 9th of July. It was about then, said Michael O'Loughlin, but he could not be certain.

'Don't you know that the house was closed and Hammond had gone away on the 5th July?'

The witness looked uncomfortable and admitted he might have been mistaken. In fact, he knew a great deal more about the house than appeared from his evidence, since his name appeared in the rate books as the nominal occupant of the house between midsummer 1888 and midsummer 1889, although Hammond actually occupied it, since it probably suited him to have a man-of-straw as a ratepayer. But this fact was apparently unknown to the prosecution, since it was not brought out.

At this point the court adjourned for luncheon. So far it could not be said that the defence witnesses had made a particularly good impression on the jury, as Lord Euston was 6 ft. 4 in. in height, and was thus considerably taller than the gentleman they swore they had seen visiting Cleveland Street.

6

On the reassembling of the court, a woman named Ann Elizabeth Morgan was called and examined by Lockwood. She stated she had lived for about twelve months at 22 Cleveland Street, which was immediately opposite No. 19. She had noticed as many as fifty or sixty persons, possibly more, going into and coming out of this house on various occasions, she said. She went on positively to identify Lord Euston in court as one of these persons. She could not give the precise date when she saw his Lordship going into and coming out of the house, but she thought it might be three or four months before the house was shut up. She had sometimes seen him between twelve and one o'clock midday, and she thought once in the evening. He came sometimes in a hansom and sometimes in a four-wheeled cab.

Cross-examined by Russell, the witness was forced to admit that of the many people she saw in Cleveland Street, the only one she could identify was Lord Euston. He was a tall man, she said. Sometimes he had on a black coat and a grey suit, she said, but on the first occasion she saw him, he was wearing a blue pilot top-coat with a velvet collar. About three weeks before the case came on, she had been driven by 'a little dark gentleman', one of the private detectives employed by Parke, to Grosvenor Place. While the cab was standing by St. George's Hospital, she saw a tall gentleman come out of 4 Grosvenor Place, whom she identified as the gentleman she had previously recognised in a photograph as one of the frequenters of 19 Cleveland Street. Up to the time the photograph was placed in her hands and the name told her, she went on, she had in no way connected Lord Euston's name with Cleveland Street. Asked by the judge how she recognised the photograph, she said that she did so by the face. She added that she had never seen Lord Euston sitting down or without his hat. She thought he wore his hat well over his forehead.

The next defence witness was another barman named Frederick Grant, who lived nearby and was at one time in the same employment as Michael O'Loughlin. He remembered going with young O'Loughlin to a music hall at the end of May or beginning of June, 1889. Afterwards they walked home together, and as they passed along Cleveland Street he noticed a gentleman coming out of No. 19, the time then being about 11.30 p.m. 'I have seen the gentleman since and I see him now,' said Grant, pointing towards Lord Euston in court. Answering Russell in cross-examination, this witness admitted that young O'Loughlin had told him that the man they saw coming out of the house was Lord Euston. He had never seen him before, except in a photograph, he went on, until that day in court, thus contradicting what he said in his evidence-in-chief. He added that O'Loughlin had told him of the bad character of the house as they were passing.

The final defence witness was John Saul, the male prostitute and pimp, who as Parke's leading counsel had indicated in his opening speech, had something more to speak to than having seen Lord Euston go in and out of the house in Cleveland Street. He answered Lockwood's questions in his examination-in-chief in an effeminate tone of voice and manner.

'I have known Charles Hammond since May 1879,' he said. 'He

[143]

was then living at 25 Oxenden Street, Haymarket, and two weeks afterwards I went to lodge with him there. We both earned our livelihood as sodomites. I used to give him all the money I earned, often £8 a week.'

The witness went on to say that he lived with Hammond at various other addresses before going to Ireland and returning to London, which he did after the Dublin Castle scandals. He remembered Hammond moving to Cleveland Street just before Christmas 1885. About fifteen months later he went to live with Hammond again in March 1887, for seven or eight weeks. 'During the time I there,' he added, 'I remember many persons visiting the house, and many I brought home myself.'

'Do you see any person in this court you have ever seen in Hammond's house in Cleveland Street?' Lockwood asked him.

'The gentleman there with the moustache,' answered Saul, pointing to Lord Euston.

'Was that the first time he had been there?'

'Yes, I believe.'

'When was that?'

'Some time in April or May 1887.'

'Where did you meet this person?'

'In Piccadilly, between Albany courtyard and Sackville Street. He laughed at me and I winked at him. He turned sharp into Sackville Street.'

'Who did?' the judge asked.

'The Duke, as we used to call him,' replied Saul.

'Go on,' said Lockwood, 'and tell me what happened.'

'The Duke, as we called him, came near me, and asked me where I was going,' said the witness. 'I said "Home" and he said "What sort is your place?" "Very comfortable", I replied. He said, "Is it very quiet there?" I said yes it was, and then we took a hansom cab there. We got out by the Middlesex Hospital, and I took the gentleman to 19 Cleveland Street, letting him in with my latchkey.'

'I was not long in there, in the back parlour or reception room,' he added, 'before Hammond came and knocked and asked if we wanted any champagne or drinks of any sort, which he was in the habit of doing.'

At this point some one in court laughed and, on Lockwood protesting, the judge observed that such levity was brutal and disgusting and he trusted it would not occur again.

Saul then proceeded to relate what passed between him and Lord Euston in language which *The Times* reporter described as unfit for publication. The witness added that Lord Euston gave him a sovereign, leaving it on the chest of drawers in the room.

'Did you see Lord Euston at this house again?' Lockwood continued his questions.

'Once, and I did not forget it,' said Saul. Frank Hewitt, who had, he believed, been sent abroad, and Henry Newlove were both present on this occasion, he said. 'I complained to Hammond of his allowing boys of good position in the Post Office to be in the house,' he went on, 'while I had to go and walk the streets for what is in my face, and that is my shame.' With this remark Saul turned his head away from the counsel with a theatrical gesture.

Saul concluded his evidence-in-chief by stating that he quarrelled with Hammond at the end of May 1887 'through taking his mother's part'. He then left the house and did not return.

There was tense silence in court when Sir Charles Russell rose to begin his cross-examination of this witness. 'Where are you living now?' was his first question.

'With some very respectable people in Brixton,' Saul replied, giving their name and address. Asked how he existed, he said that he was receiving ten shillings a week pocket money from Captain Webb's detective agency, because he had to send something to his mother 'who was very poor in Ireland'.

'When did you first give your evidence?'

'The first statement I made was at the Criminal Investigation Office to Inspector Abberline.'

This answer produced quite a sensation, since observers in court naturally asked themselves why the police had not taken some action at the time as the result of Saul's statements.

He had been taken to Brixton, the witness went on to say, after he had been to Scotland Yard. He knew Newlove and Frank Hewitt, but none of the other boys such as Wright and Allies, whose names Sir Charles enumerated. He was very sorry for Newlove, Saul said. But he repeated that he knew none of the Post Office boys, adding that 'Hammond was getting a very good collection of them at the time he left.'

Before he went to Hammond's with Lord Euston in a cab, Saul continued, he had no idea who he was. 'I picked him up just as I might have picked up any other gentleman,' he admitted callously.

'When did you first learn Lord Euston's name?'

'About a fortnight or three weeks after the first occasion on which Lord Euston visited 19 Cleveland Street.'

'Who told you?'

'A friend of mine in the street.' On being pressed, Saul admitted that his friend's name was Carrington. He was known as 'Lively Poll'.

On the second occasion, when Lord Euston came to the house and was let in by Hammond, the witness stated that he saw him but had no conversation with him. According to Saul, when they parted on the first occasion, Lord Euston said to him, 'Be sure, if you see me, don't speak to me in the street.' Consequently he had never spoken to him, although he often saw him in Piccadilly and elsewhere.

Questioned by Russell about his mode of living, Saul admitted that he had led the same kind of immoral life in London as he had previously done in Dublin.

'Did you do anything to earn your living?'

'Not much.'

'What?' asked counsel.

'I worked hard at cleaning the houses of the gay people,' he replied. The 'gay people' it appeared were not homosexuals like himself but 'the gay ladies on the beat'. He had also done some casual work in two theatres, but he had not earned much.

Asked about his quarrel with Hammond, Saul said that one of

[146]

the reasons was that Hammond charged him too much money and kept him hungry when he did not earn much. The witness further admitted 'practising criminality in other houses', but he denied living with a prostitute in the neighbourhood of Leicester Square. But he had lived in Nassau Street, near the Middlesex Hospital, where 'vicious practices were carried on'.

'Did you live with a woman known as Queen Anne in Church Street, Soho?'

'No, it is a man. Perhaps you will see him later on.'

'Is he in attendance here, then?' asked Russell, looking round the courtroom.

'Yes, sir,' replied Saul. 'He is a young fellow who knows a lot of the aristocracy.' Saul added that his name was Andrew Grant and he knew Hammond well.

'Did you live with this man Grant?' Russell repeated his question.

'No,' said Saul saucily. 'He lived with me.'

'And were you hunted out by the police?'

'No, they have never interfered,' was the astonishing answer. Saul added that the police had always behaved kindly to him whilst he was taking his walks at night.

'Do you mean they have deliberately shut their eyes to your infamous practices?' asked Russell in a shocked tone of voice.

'They have had to shut their eyes to more than me,' Saul replied blithely.

It then transpired that Saul had offered himself as a witness in the Dublin Castle scandal trials, but his evidence was considered to be 'too old'. He denied that he had been told that his word was 'not worthy of credit on oath'.

He was first approached in connection with the present case by a young man in Captain Webb's office, Saul went on in reply to further questions. That was after Parke had been committed for trial. No one had seen him before then, because he was employed in a show at Drury Lane Theatre. He swore that before consenting to give evidence he had not seen the announcement that a considerable sum of money had been subscribed for Parke's defence.

He did not know Mr. Parke at all, he said, and he only came forward as a witness because he thought that Mr. Parke was being 'acted very unfairly to'.

Finally, Russell handed the witness a photograph of Lord Euston. 'Do you recognise it?' asked Sir Charles.

'Yes,' answered Saul. 'You could tell him by his big white teeth and his moustache.'

After Euston's leading counsel had resumed his seat, Lockwood rose to re-examine the witness. However, he only asked one or two questions to establish the fact that when Saul went to Scotland Yard his statement was made not to Inspector Abberline himself but to his clerk. Lockwood then announced that this concluded the case for the defence.

Thereupon Russell called Lord Euston into the witness-box to tell his story under oath.

7

After describing the circumstances in which he had come to institute the prosecution, Euston recalled being in Piccadilly one night about the end of May or beginning of June in the previous year, when a card was handed to him with Hammond's name and address and the words '*Poses plastiques*' written at the top. On reaching home he read the card and put it on his table. About a week afterwards, after dining one night at his club, he called a hansom and drove to Cleveland Street. The door was opened by a man of medium height, rather stout in the face, clean shaven, dark moustache, and hair getting rather thin on the top. This was evidently Hammond, who then took him into a ground-floor room and made the 'improper proposals', as already mentioned, after he had asked for and was given a sovereign and Euston had inquired where the *poses plastiques* were going to take place. 'I asked him what he meant by saying a thing like that to me,' said Euston, 'and told him that if he would not let me out of the house at once, I would knock him down. The man then opened the door and let me out and I went away.' At that time he did not mention the occurrence to anyone.

[148]

'What height are you?' asked Russell.

'Six feet four,' replied Euston.

Except on the occasion he had described, Euston swore that he was never in Cleveland Street in his life. It was utterly untrue, he said, that in May 1889 he went there in company with a man called John Saul, whom he had never seen in the whole course of his life until that afternoon in the witness-box. Nor did he know of Saul's existence until he saw his name in the defendant's plea of justification. Nor was it true that he went to Cleveland Street for improper purposes on any other occasion. Neither did he know the name of Frank Hewitt until he read it in the plea. Nor was it true that he left the country in July and went to Peru, or to any other place out of the jurisdiction of the English courts. Indeed he had not been out of England since May 1882, when he went to see his sister in Biarritz. It was not true, he continued, that any charge had been made against him or warrant issued against him for any offence whatever. As for the blue pilot coat with the velvet collar which the witness Morgan said she had seen him wearing, he did not possess a coat of that description. He never visited Cleveland Street in a private carriage. In fact, he did not own a private carriage, although he occasionally borrowed his father's. His sole visit to Cleveland Street had been in a public conveyance, namely a hansom cab.

Replying to Lockwood, who cross-examined him, Lord Euston said that it was not until he heard of the proceedings against Newlove and Veck the previous summer that it came to his mind that the house with which they were concerned was the one he had gone to on the sole occasion. Some weeks later he heard that his name was being coupled with the house in Cleveland Street, when he told his solicitor friend, Mr. Bedford, and afterwards another friend, Lord Dungarvan, and they agreed to take the advice of a senior peer, Lord Dorchester, as being an older man and one whose judgment they thoroughly respected. Up to that time he had told no one about his experience, because he was 'thoroughly disgusted at being trapped into a place or caught in a place like that and was not going to talk about his own folly.'

[149]

'Did you consider or not that the card you were given referred to some filthy exhibition?' asked Lockwood.

'I knew what *poses plastiques* were,' answered Euston. 'I have seen some *poses plastiques* that you could not call filthy.'

'Did you consider that the card referred to some kind of exhibition that you would be ashamed for it to be known amongst your friends that you had visited?'

'No, sir, I do not think I should have been so ashamed amongst my friends for that!'

Questioned further about his compromising visit to Cleveland Street, Euston said he thought he was in the house for under five minutes. It did not occur to him that he was induced to go there in order to be blackmailed. He thought nothing about it at the time as he was only too glad to get out of the place. Afterwards he tore up the card and for the time being thought no more about it. Asked about Lord Arthur Somerset, he said he did not know when he left England. Nor had he visited Lord Arthur in Boulogne or anywhere else in that neighbourhood. On the other hand, he did admit going to Ascot races every year for several years past and generally staying with friends there during race week.

This concluded the evidence, and counsel then addressed the jury. Since the prosecutor called no evidence other than himself apart from the formal testimony as to publication of the libel, this meant that his counsel had the last word with the jury, and Russell took full advantage of this. He declared with characteristic vigour that the defendant's statement in the libel was unsupported by his plea and his plea was unsupported by the evidence, and he asked the jury to come to the conclusion that the evidence for the defendant, such as it was and as far as it went, was not worthy of the implicit credence of twelve honest gentlemen who desired to arrive at a decision in accordance with what they believed the truth in this matter.

Since it was now growing late, the judge said he would postpone his summing up until the following morning, and the court adjourned.

8

Mr. Justice Hawkins began his summing up of the evidence to the jury in a crowded court by saying that the publication they had to consider was a libel of a very atrocious character if it was not justifiable. 'The libel imputed to Lord Euston heinous crimes revolting to one's notions of all that was decent in human nature,' he said. No one could doubt that it was a very serious libel and that the defendant was responsible for it unless he proved the justification he had undertaken to prove. The question of privilege did not arise on this occasion. He then stated the law on the matter.

> No man even in a civil court, when an action is brought to recover damages against the publisher for libel—no man can justify a libel so as to exonerate himself from the consequences which attach to the publication of a libel on an individual unless he is prepared to prove the truth of that which he alleges. If he is not prepared to prove that which he alleges, the law says that he has no justification. He must prove, therefore, the truth of what he alleges in order to justify himself.
>
> In the interests of the public, in a criminal prosecution for libel, there is a further matter which must be proved, and that is, not only must it be proved that the libel is true in fact, but that the facts published in the libel are such as in the public interest should be made known. You must be satisfied not only that the libel is true, but that it is for the public benefit that it should be made known.

The judge went on to point out that at the preliminary hearing before the magistrate, Lord Euston had submitted himself for cross-examination, but no question was put to him then on any of the matters subsequently given in evidence at the trial, and Lord Euston had himself repeated his evidence at the trial. Consequently on the question of his counsel's not calling him until the defendant's evidence had been concluded, the judge said he thought Sir Charles Russell was absolutely right. 'Down to the time when Parke's written plea of justification had been put in, Lord Euston had no intimation of what witnesses were to be called by the defence or what they would say, and when his counsel came into court at the outset of the trial, they were in absolute ignorance of who were to be called for the defence.' Indeed the judge emphasised that he thought the discretion exercised by Euston's counsel was rightly exercised, and if he (the judge) had been in the position of Sir Charles Russell, he should have done the same thing.

Turning to the plea of justification, Mr. Justice Hawkins remarked that there had not been any attempt to prove that Lord Euston had departed for Peru, and with regard to the allegation in the plea that he had left the kingdom there was not one particle of evidence. If that was introduced for the purpose of prejudice, it was a cruel allegation and one which ought not to have been introduced. It was stated in the libel that Lord Euston had gone to Peru, and when it was found that this was not true, it was then suggested in the plea that he had gone to foreign parts, and the way in which it was suggested that that could be proved was the question put to Lord Euston when he was cross-examined as to whether he had not gone over to Boulogne for the purpose of seeing Lord Arthur Somerset. But Lord Euston had replied that he was not there and had not been out of the country since 1882, when he went to visit his sister in Biarritz. 'There is no proof that he left the country,' said the judge. 'There is not a particle of foundation for saying that Lord Euston went abroad for the purpose of avoiding process, and that part of the plea must consequently be treated not only as not proved, but as disproved.'

The judge then commented on the evidence given in support of the defendant's plea, and indicated its contradictory character. For instance, in regard to the dress of the gentleman whom John O'Loughlin and Smith said they saw going into the house in Cleveland Street, O'Loughlin said he was dressed in a light grey suit, while Smith stated that he wore a black coat and striped trousers. Again the height of the gentleman was stated to be 5 ft. 8 in. or 9 in., whereas Lord Euston's height was 6 ft. 4 in. The judge also referred to the fact that photographs of Lord Euston, showing him with his head uncovered, had been shown to the witnesses, but all the witnesses had testified that they saw the gentleman with his hat on. 'A man looks different with a hat on to what he does when it is off.' As to the witness Saul, 'a more melancholy spectacle or a more loathsome object', the judge said, he could not imagine. He hoped for the honour of the police of the metropolis that what this witness had sworn to was not true, namely, that the police had behaved kindly to him whilst he was taking his walks at night for the purpose of procuring male prostitutes for homosexual gentlemen or acting as such himself.

What the jury now had to ask themselves was whether Saul's story about seeing Lord Euston on two occasions in the male brothel and what he did there was true. 'Lord Euston says it is as foul a perjury as a man can commit,' the judge reminded them. 'Of course, you only have the oath of Lord Euston against the oath of this man. It is necessary for me to speak out, and you will have to ask your-selves which oath you prefer—the oath of a man who, according to his own account, if he has spoken the truth, is liable to be prosecuted and sent to penal servitude, or the oath of the prosecutor.' So far, continued the judge, he marvelled that nobody had suggested that the man should be prosecuted. If it were true that Saul told Inspector Abberline his story in August, the judge said he would like to know, as one of the public—and he dared say that the jury would like to know—why it was that, if the police inspector knew the story in August, he held his peace, said nothing, and did nothing up to the present hour. 'It should be the first duty of those who are the guardians of peace and public morality, if they have evidence of crime like this, to bring the criminal to light—no duty can be more obligatory. On the other hand, if Saul did not tell Abberline, or, if he did and Abberline could not believe the story or could get no corroboration of it, I do not wonder at no proceedings being taken, because I should think it the height of cruelty to make a charge of an abominable crime against a gentleman unless there is in the command of those instituting the prosecution evidence that it was right and reasonable to submit to a jury.'

After commenting on the fact that neither Newlove nor any of the frequenters of the house had been called to give evidence in support of Saul's testimony, the judge repeated the questions which the jury had to decide—first, whether a libel had been published by the defendant reflecting on Lord Euston's character; and, secondly, if so, whether the libel was justified by the facts.

The jury then retired to consider their verdict. After an absence of three-quarters of an hour they returned to court and the foreman announced that they had found the defendant 'guilty of libel without justification'.

Immediately after this announcement, Mr. Willie Mathews for Lord Euston rose to call the judge's attention to the issue of the *North London Press* of 23 November, in which the defendant stated that 'if the charges he had preferred against Lord Euston were not true, and were made without sufficient reason, he had no desire to escape the natural and inevitable consequences of misleading the public on so grave a matter.' Again, in the issue of a week later, Parke, although he had been committed for trial on the 26th, published in his paper three portraits, the first being of Lord Euston, the second of Hammond, and the third of Lord Arthur Somerset.

'No one would recognise Lord Euston,' the judge observed after studying the portraits.

'That may not have been the intention of the defendant,' said Mathews, who went on to submit that there were matters of aggravation. He also pointed out that on November 16, when the libel was published, Parke was not in possession of a single fact upon which he could rely as proof of the justification he had pleaded.

The judge, who throughout had done his best to be fair to the defendant, then offered to postpone sentence until the following day if Parke desired to communicate with his counsel or to submit anything himself. However, his counsel said that his client did not wish to have it postponed. Asked by the judge whether he had anything to add to this, Parke replied that he only desired to say that he had acted in perfect good faith, and that what he had published he had published simply in what he believed to be the public interest. 'I did not, as had just been said by counsel appearing against me,' he went on, 'publish the libel without what I believed to be—and have since found not to be—adequate evidence. What that evidence is I cannot state. Of course, I have been misled.'

'Only mentioning it is not evidence,' replied the judge. 'The libel is, I think I may say—I do not mind telling you—exceedingly bad, but if you would like to have until tomorrow to give me any information which you think would alter my view of the matter, you shall. But at present, as the evidence stands, I see none that was in your possession at the time the libel was published.'

'I can only say that I had evidence at that time.'

'I really must have more than that,' said Mr. Justice Hawkins. 'I will not argue with you except that I was going to say that it is a very, very serious thing to publish in a paper, having a circulation of 4,000 or 5,000 in number, and circulate through the country imputations of this horrible character. No man could live under them.'

Parke continued his exchange with the bench a little longer before sentence was finally passed. 'With regard to the two points now mentioned by Mr. Mathews as instances of aggravation, I undoubtedly have to take the consequences of the error into which I have fallen,' he said. 'With regard to the second, the portrait of Lord Euston was published in that paper for precisely the same reasons, and for none other whatever, for which it appeared in many other papers which publish illustrations. May I add that I had, among other evidence, Saul's statement.'

'I do not wish to invite you to say anything except that which you think may assist you and be in your favour,' the judge now told the convicted journalist. 'Do not suppose that in giving me any information that I desire to have it unless it is of a character to assist you. I only tell you that at the present moment I fail to see any evidence at all to justify—to justify morally—the publication of the libel which appears in this paper, and of which the jury have just found you guilty. It is for that reason that I desire to give you, if you like to avail yourself of it—it is entirely for you and not for me—an opportunity of putting before me any matter which will in any way palliate or mitigate your guilt in this matter. You shall have till tomorrow morning if you like to think it over, or have any communication with your counsel about it.'

To this Parke's counsel responded, 'I think it would be better for all parties under the circumstances if your Lordship would give the sentence now.'

'Very well,' said the judge, adding as he turned towards the defendant in the dock, 'And you think so too?'

'Yes, my Lord,' said Parke. 'I cannot give you the other evidence without a breach of faith.'[1]

'Then I must say that I think that a more atrocious libel than that of which you have been guilty has never been published by any man in circumstances than those in which you have published this libel. You had before you in November nothing more than the idlest rumours, suggesting to you that among other persons Lord Euston had been guilty of an abominable crime. You suggested to me that you had the evidence of Saul.'

'And of others also, my Lord,' the defendant broke in.

'I cannot credit you on that,' said Mr. Justice Hawkins.

> If you had had other evidence, you should have produced it. If it had been creditable, you should have produced it, and your abstaining from producing it shows that you did not place any reliance upon it. The plea that you could not produce this evidence without violating a confidence is one that I myself will never tolerate. If a man chooses to take the responsibility of publication in his newspaper, as you said that you were willing to do, he must take that responsibility. The man who would recklessly, and I think wickedly, publish of another person a libel which he has no evidence to prove has been guilty of an offence which deserves the most condign punishment.

> I have expressed myself as strongly as any man could on the character of the libel. I absolutely and entirely agree with the verdict of the jury. I do not believe that it would have been possible to have found in England twelve men who, conscientiously and care-

---

[1] It was rumoured at the time in Fleet Street that the source of this evidence, which Parke had promised not to divulge, was an Inspector from Scotland Yard, probably Abberline.

fully and honestly looking at the evidence which they had put before them, could have come to any other conclusion than that this was a wicked libel, published without any justification whatever and endeavoured to be supported by testimony absolutely unworthy of real credence. In all the circumstances I feel it to be my duty to pass upon you a sentence which I hope, besides being a punishment to you, will be a warning to others not to publish atrocious libels upon others without justification.

The judge then sentenced the defendant Parke to twelve months' imprisonment without hard labour.

'So *thankful* poor Lord Euston has won his trial, and only *wish* it were poor Arthur,' wrote Lady Waterford on reading the news of the result next day. 'However it is a mercy that somebody is made happy.'

9

Twelve months without hard labour could not in all the circumstances of the time be called a particularly severe sentence, since no more horrible libel could be imagined then than charging a man with being involved in 'an indescribably loathsome scandal' concerning a male brothel and then being allowed to leave the country and thus defeat the ends of justice. With two notable exceptions the press generally did not consider the sentence passed upon Ernest Parke excessive. These were Frank Harris, then editing the *Fortnightly Review*, and the editor of *Reynold's Newspaper*, a Labour Sunday paper which could usually be relied upon to take a strong anti-Establishment line in any matter affecting the upper strata of English society. Both Harris and the editor of *Reynold's* denounced the sentence as vindictive. Harris knew Euston and Parke, and Euston had told Harris, when the rumours about his visit to Cleveland Street first began to circulate, that he would 'make it hot' for anyone who repeated them in print. It was certainly an unlucky moment for Ernest Parke when he did so in the *North London Press*. After his release from prison, Parke, whom Harris described as 'a convinced Radical and a man of high character', complained to

Harris that really all he had done was to reproduce the substance of a statement made to a police inspector, which apparently in his and Harris's view should have made it privileged. On the contrary, no question of privilege arose, and the fact that Parke chose to publish a grossly defamatory statement supported by, if not originally based on, statements by a male prostitute like Saul, afforded the editor no protection unless he could justify their contents. This, despite the fact that Saul gave evidence for the defence, Parke manifestly failed to do to the satisfaction of the jury. In a letter which he wrote to a left-wing French journal, *La Lanterne*, before the trial but not published until afterwards (19 January), Parke attributed his 'ruin' to the fact that Euston had succeeded in having the trial adjourned for a month and that certain witnesses who had agreed to give evidence for him became alarmed for their own safety and went abroad before the adjourned hearing came on. Why he did not call Newlove and Veck, who were still in custody, in support of Saul's testimony, an omission adversely commented upon by the trial judge in his summing up, remains a mystery. One can only infer that they would not have borne out Saul's version.

In an editorial which appeared in *Truth* on 30 January 1890, Labouchere wrote:

> The Public Prosecutor, apparently has made up his mind not to prosecute the creature Saul for perjury. If this be so a more scandalous decision was never taken. A jury has declared the 'creature' committed one of the most horrible perjuries on record—a perjury for which the longest sentence permitted by the law would not be sufficient. An eminent judge has endorsed the opinion of the jury. And the Public Prosecutor takes no action! Why? He must not be surprised at persons asking this question.

In the same editorial Labouchere referred to the case of a poor woman who had passed twenty-two years in prison for having stolen provisions worth ten shillings. 'To say that a poor woman was justly punished in this cruel fashion for a petty larceny,' Labouchere commented characteristically, 'and that a wretch like Saul is to be allowed to swear away the honour and good name of a person with impunity, without any action on the part of the Public Prosecutor, is an insult to law and justice.'

Labby had guessed correctly. On the day after his editorial appeared, Stephenson wrote to the Attorney General with a request to consider prosecuting Saul. Webster replied on 3 February:

> No proceedings should at present be instituted against Saul.
>
> As regards *perjury* I see no means by which sufficient evidence can be adduced to prove the arraignment of perjury.
>
> As regards *sodomy* it would be both impossible and in my opinion improper to put Saul on his trial for the offence. The only evidence against him is his confession contained in his Statement. That Statement is in my judgment utterly unworthy of credit. It could not be used without inflicting irreparable damage upon other persons against whom there is no trustworthy evidence whatever. . . . Taken by itself the statement of such a man is utterly unworthy of credit.

The Attorney General added that it was up to the police to take any further action against Saul and that depended upon whether they could get any independent evidence.

The editor of *Reynold's Newspaper*, on the other hand, was not prepared to accept the evidence given by Lord Euston at Parke's trial at its face value. On the Sunday after the trial he wrote in a leading article:

LORD EUSTON'S CASE

Another incident concerning the abominable institution frequented by aristocrats and others moving in fashionable circles has passed away, and only clouded the whole affair in further mystery, so far as the general public is concerned. The trial of Mr. Parke for libelling Lord Euston, heir to the duchy of Grafton, has ended as we fully expected it would end. It certainly appears strange that the singular statement made by his lordship should be accepted by judge and jury as eminently satisfactory and fully substantiated. He told a somewhat cock-and-bull story about receiving a card as he was walking in Piccadilly, indicating where a display of naked females was on view. It seems odd that a person like Hammond should allow tickets, indicating where a criminal exhibition was on view, to be indiscriminately distributed in the public thoroughfares, where, amongst other, the passengers might comprise plain-clothes detectives. So much for the explanation of how he got to Cleveland Street. What followed is simply and solely his lordship's utterly uncorroborated statement, the whole of which we are asked to accept on his *ipse dixit*! The evidence of the witnesses who testified to having seen him several times was ridiculed by Sir C. Russell as being that of persons in a very low grade of life. Surely he did not expect that the Archbishop of Canterbury would appear in the box and testify to having met the Earl coming to or from that den of infamy.

Saul is unquestionably a filthy, loathsome, detestable beast, but he has evidently played no inconsiderable part in the abominable orgies of Cleveland Street. Judge Hawkins seems to us to have committed a grave error at first stating, when he evidently intended the jury to believe that Lord Euston's statement of how he got there, and what transpired when there, although utterly and entirely unsubstantiated, was a plain, unvarnished truthful statement. And in his summing up the judge to our thinking, did not dwell sufficiently on the very extenuating circumstance that Lord Euston *had*, according to his own admission, once visited the infamous Cleveland Street inferno. However, as judge and jury have exculpated and whitewashed the future Duke, it is to be hoped his ardour for witnessing exhibitions of nude females will be somewhat cooled by recent circumstances.

The editor of *Reynold's* returned to the subject in the following Sunday's issue of the paper when he wrote under the heading 'The Horrible National Scandal':

As we expected would be the case, the result of the trial of the young journalist, Parke, for publishing a libel on the Earl of Euston has raised a storm of indignation not only at home, but abroad. The whole affair is considered part and parcel of the plan intended to whitewash the police and Government from all participation in the frightful miscarriage of justice that has taken place. We do not mean to assert or contend that Lord Euston was a frequenter of the odious den in Cleveland Street, or that his story of what occurred when he paid, according to himself, the one and only visit to the place was inaccurate. But in his virulent address to the jury, and when passing what we can but consider *a most vindictive sentence* on the accused, Judge Hawkins emphatically declared that the libel was one of the grossest ever published without a single extenuating circumstance. Now we contend that the circumstance of a person knocking at the door, or ringing the bell at any particular house, being instantly admitted, remaining there, never mind how short a time, and then coming out and walking away, might naturally, and, indeed, would obviously lead to the conclusion in the mind of anybody who witnessed all this, that he was a frequenter of the place into which he had so readily gained admission. But Hawkins refused to recognise any extenuating circumstance in the case, and Mr. Parke's was made an example to others who dare tamper with the name of our virtuous and noble aristocracy.

What, then, is the conclusion come to? Why, that the authorities are more anxious to conceal the names of those who patronised the horrible den of vice, than punish the principal patrons of the hideous place. And we much fear that their project will be partially, if not wholly successful.

Why were the wretched telegraph boys taken to the Old Bailey . . . whilst Lord Arthur Somerset, being duly warned of what had occurred, made his escape, and is now living in clover abroad? All this requires, but we suspect will not obtain, satisfactory explanation. A Parliamentary inquiry cannot open the mouths of those who are determined to keep them closed.

The editorial concluded by denouncing the prosecution of Newton, his clerk and the interpreter, as 'a feeble effort on the part of the Government to bamboozle the public into the belief that it is acting with energy and resolution in the matter.'

To the circumstances of this prosecution we must now turn.

CHAPTER IV

The Trial of Arthur Newton
and Frederick Taylorson

I

ON 16 DECEMBER 1889, Sir Augustus Stephenson, the Public Prosecutor, accompanied by the Hon. Hamilton Cuffe and other officials from the Treasury, the Post Office and Scotland Yard, including Inspector Abberline, met Mr. James Vaughan, the magistrate, in his room at Bow Street Police Court. The result was that the magistrate issued summonses against Arthur Newton, his clerk, Frederick Taylorson, and Adolphe de Gallo, the interpreter at the Marlborough Street court, charging them that on the 25th September, 'and at divers times between that and the 12th day of December, 1889' they

> did unlawfully conspire, combine, confederate, and agree together to obstruct, pervert, and defeat the due course of law and justice in certain proceedings then pending at the Marlborough Street Police Court and in the Central Criminal Court in respect of offences alleged to have been committed by divers persons at 19, Cleveland Street, Fitzroy Square, in the County of London, and to obstruct, prevent, and defeat the due course of law and justice in respect of the said offences.

The summonses were duly served upon the three defendants, who were directed to answer to them at the Bow Street court a week later.

[162]

'I see by the newspapers,' Brett wrote to Newton on 21 December, 'that there is an attempt being made to prove that you have interfered with the course of justice. I presume that the charge is false and has been put forward by the police to screen their effeteness and has been adopted by the Government who finding themselves attacked require a scapegoat after the manner of governments. It seems to me a very mean affair.' Brett went on to invite the solicitor to meet him at his London house next day and discuss the matter, in which he felt he might be of some use to Newton.

Brett asked his friend John Oswald, who was an experienced précis-writer in the Foreign Office, to be present and make a memorandum of what passed at the meeting. This Mr. Oswald did, stating at the beginning of this document that they wished to see Newton so as 'to form our own opinion as to whether in defence of his client he had outstepped the limits which a solicitor may legitimately employ.'

Newton began by informing them that there were two charges preferred against him in the information which he had been allowed to see the previous day. The first was that on 25 September he had endeavoured through his clerk to procure an interview with the witness Allies. Secondly, that about 10 December he collected three of the other witnesses who had been released from police control (Wright, Swinscow and Perkins) and that he sent them to some lodging-house 'with the object of getting them to leave the country in order to remove evidence against two individuals against whom warrants had been issued and never executed', namely, Charles Hammond and Lord Arthur Somerset.

In answer to the first charge, Newton told Brett and Oswald that his clerk had met Allies 'accidentally' in September in the street and had had a few moments' casual conversation with him as to his treatment by the police. Before many moments had passed, a police inspector appeared and accused the clerk of endeavouring to tamper with a police witness, and the inspector added: 'We shall have your Mr. Newton in the dock.' The clerk then left and travelled down to Newton's house in the country and informed him of what the inspector had said. But in the charge, it was represented that Newton was in the street at the same time as this casual meeting and watching what occurred.

In answer to the second charge, Newton stated that the Duke of Beaufort was anxious to see the witnesses in order to form an opinion personally as to the nature of the evidence against his son, whom he had not seen since he had first heard of the case. The Duke, said Newton, naturally believed that the case against his son was partly owing to a conspiracy on the part of the witnesses and partly owing to blundering on the part of the police. He was anxious to interrogate the boys himself and instructed him (Newton) to assemble them together for that purpose. 'His belief was that the boys had been terrorised by the police, and having made depositions with the object of clearing themselves, would as long as they were in police control repeat like parrots what they had said, and if he saw them alone without this fear constantly before them, they would probably tell him the complete truth and enable him to form his own opinion as to the truth or falsity of the charges brought by the police against his son.'

Newton went on to explain that he thought the only way to get the boys away was to employ a ruse and tell them that some clients of his would perhaps be able to give them a new start in life far away from the scene of their recent occupation, since they had been suspended from duty and it was certain that they would be dismissed from the Post Office. He therefore took steps to collect these boys and sent them to spend a night in a lodging-house, since if they went to their respective homes it would take time to collect them together, so as to allow the Duke to interrogate them separately and collectively.

However, on reflection the Duke decided that he ought not to see them until the boys had been home to their parents and had become 'amenable to their lawful guardians'. Accordingly next day Newton caused the boys to be informed that his clients could not act without the consent of their parents and the best thing they could do would be to go home and await a further communication. Shortly afterwards he heard that 'this action of his had been represented as an intention to defeat the ends of justice by procuring the removal of the witnesses as aforesaid.'

Oswald's memorandum of the meeting continued:

> This explanation being perfectly satisfactory to us that he had no intention of conspiring to defeat the ends of justice and that he was justified in employing a ruse to give a bereaved father an opportunity of forming his own opinion on the evidence which owing to his son's departure might never be sifted in a court of law, we proceeded to discuss reasons which could have induced the police to take the action referred to. Mr. Newton pointed out that all through the case till that moment the Government had acted with him in endeavouring to minimise the scandal. In court he had suggested that it was unnecessary to mention names in connection with the case and the Treasury officials had concurred and cautioned the witnesses against doing so.
>
> The only conclusion that we could come to therefore was that the Government, alarmed at the attacks which were being made on them for the miscarriage of justice which was alleged to have taken place, had determined to make a scapegoat of Mr. Newton by suggesting they had done their best to obtain evidence that they found Mr. Newton against them at every turn.
>
> It appeared that more than one police officer had boasted that they would get Mr. Newton struck off the rolls and that Mr. Abberline was reported to have spoken most vindictively against him.
>
> Putting all this together we could only conclude that this action was vindictive on the part of the police. We then felt ourselves authorised to offer Mr. Newton our sympathy and our assurance that in our opinion he had not outstepped his duty in conducting the case of his client who was our friend's son.

Their advice to Newton was to consult George Lewis, that most experienced and knowledgeable solicitor, who had been instructed by Lord Euston in the prosecution of Ernest Parke. But if Newton preferred to conduct his case himself, they urged him to bring out the points that the Government had acted up to a certain point entirely in unison with him 'in an endeavour to keep the matter secret', and if there was any technical offence in what he had done, the highest members of the Cabinet ought to be defendants with him in this matter. 'We thought that, if he could bring this out clearly, public opinion must be on his side, as it showed clearly the change of attitude on the part of the police coincided with the attack which Mr. Labouchere threatened in Parliament. It would thus be clear that he was made a victim to screen the action of the Government.'

The following morning, the Duke of Beaufort called on Brett and corroborated Newton's statement. According to Brett, the Duke said that 'he was prepared to go into the witness-box and swear that Mr. Newton was acting on his instructions in endeavouring to ascertain from these boys the nature of the evidence against his son and to arrange an interview between him and them once they were beyond the influence of the police.' The Duke added that he knew nothing of the charges against his son nor had he ever heard a whisper of them until after his son's disappearance. He assured Brett that he had never seen his son since he heard of these charges nor did he know the nature of the evidence which the authorities were said to possess.

2

While Brett and the Duke of Beaufort were conversing in Brett's house in Tilney Street on the morning of 23 December, the case against Newton and his two co-defendants was being opened by Mr. Horace Avory, the Treasury counsel, on behalf of the Director of Public Prosecutions, before the magistrate, Mr. Vaughan, at Bow Street Police Court. At this preliminary hearing, Newton was represented by Mr. Charles Gill, who had defended Veck, while Mr. St. John Wontner appeared for Taylorson and De Gallo.

Avory's opening speech occupied the whole morning and part of the afternoon, since he felt it necessary as background to the charges to relate in considerable detail the whole story of the Cleveland Street affair from the time the first inquiries were made in the Post

Office and the flight of Hammond early in July followed by the arrest and conviction of Newlove and Veck more than two months later. As regards Taylorson's meeting with Allies on 25 September, this was far from an accidental encounter in the street, as Newton had told Brett and Oswald, but a deliberately appointed meeting consequent upon Taylorson having gone down to Sudbury on Newton's instructions and obtained the boy's address, after which he called at the coffee-house in Houndsditch where Allies was lodging under police protection and made the arrangement to meet him later that day, Allies having got in touch with Inspector Abberline in the meantime and been told to keep the appointment while the police kept watch, with the result which has already been described.

Avory went on to refer to Newton's correspondence with the Treasury on the subject of Allies allegedly being held under duress, stating that Newton had been warned that any persons who were parties to sending the lad out of the country with a view to preventing him from giving evidence would render themselves liable to criminal proceedings. 'From what was said to Allies on the 25th September,' said Avory, 'it did not appear that the money which had been offered to him should he leave the country was coming from his father, who is a coachman in service, and it was therefore not difficult to arrive at the inference that the funds were to be furnished by some interested party,' especially when Allies had apparently been advised to burn any compromising letters he might have received. 'Matters remained in this position for a few days,' Avory continued, 'and then things became known to the authorities which led them to suppose that Mr. Newton's efforts were being made, not in the name of the boy's father, but really in the interests of Lord Arthur Somerset, whose name had come to light during the investigation of the case, and against whom on the 12th of November a warrant had been issued from the Marlborough Street Police Court for offences alleged to have been committed by him in the house in Cleveland Street.'

Almost immediately after that warrant had been obtained, said Avory, negotiations were resumed by Mr. Newton with the Treasury with a view to obtaining an interview with the boy Allies, and on 19 November an interview was arranged to take place between young Allies and his father.

At this point, Newton's counsel, apparently at his client's suggestion, interrupted to ask the magistrate that Inspector Abberline, whom he would have to cross-examine severely as the chief police officer engaged in the case, and against whom he would have to make some imputations, should be ordered to leave the court. The magistrate acceded to this request and Abberline was directed to withdraw.

Resuming his speech, Avory stated that about 17 November Newton wrote to Allies's father, telling him to come up to London. The father replied that he was only a poor man and could not afford the journey from Suffolk, whereupon the solicitor sent him a postal order for £1. However, the boy eventually declined to see his father, as he had done previously.

On 6 December, the warrants at that time being still out against Hammond and Lord Arthur Somerset, the boys Wright, Perkins, Swinscow and Thickbroom were finally dismissed from the Post Office, Avory continued, and this seemed to have come to Mr. Newton's knowledge, for either the same day or the following day communications were made to Perkins and Thickbroom. As a result these boys went next morning to the corner of Poland Street, off Oxford Street, where they met Newton who entered into conversation with them.

First of all, according to Avory, Newton reminded them that he was the person who had cross-examined them at the police court when Veck and Newlove were committed for trial. He then told them that he knew someone who was prepared to do them a considerable amount of good. If they were willing to go to Australia, they could have a complete outfit, a sum of £20 down and £1 a week for three years when they were there. He added, 'Two or three have gone away and are doing well,' apparently referring to two or three boys who had or might have given evidence about the house in Cleveland Street. In this context Newton also mentioned Allies and said, 'This boy Allies has made a great fool of himself,' no doubt meaning by not going away.

Finally, Newton asked them whether they could get Wright, Swinscow and Barber to meet him with them at the same place next day. Perkins agreed to do this, but as he did not have Wright's address, Newton told him he would get his clerk to send it to him. This was duly done, Perkins at the same time being given ten shillings as his fare from his home to Wright's home in the East End of London. In the event only Wright, Swinscow and Perkins kept the appointment, since Barber was away from home and Thickbroom was prevented from coming by his father being ill.

On arrival at Poland Street on 10 December, the boys were met not by Newton but by De Gallo, who told them he knew what they had come for and that they were to start that very night for Marseilles. When they embarked on the Dover-Calais ferry, they would see someone they knew on board.

'Would it be Mr. Newton?' one of the boys asked.

'Never mind,' said De Gallo. 'You will know who it is when you see him.'

De Gallo, who had taken the boys to a nearby pub, then suggested that they should write to their mothers, saying that they would not be returning home but not to worry about them. This Perkins and Swinscow did, giving the letters to De Gallo, who evidently posted them, as they were received next morning.

Apparently De Gallo told the boys he must leave them for a short time to telegraph about the boat. He later returned and told them that the boat had gone. He then took them to a coffee-house in the Edgware Road, where they were given rooms for the night, De Gallo suggesting they should use false names. De Gallo also gave them a sovereign for their food, and told them he would come next day to see them off. When he did so, about one o'clock in the afternoon, Thickbroom had not turned up as expected, and after keeping the boys hanging about for several hours, De Gallo told them they had better go home as 'there was some difficulty about their parents' consent.'

What was the real reason was at present a matter of conjecture, said Avory, but some light was thrown upon it by the circumstance that Swinscow's parents, having received their son's letter, immediately communicated with the police, who had already begun to make inquiries as to what had happened to the boys. 'Probably the defendants altered their plans on this becoming known; also it was obvious, from what Newton had said on the Monday [9 December], his object was to get the five boys together and pack them all out of the country. When they found they did not succeed in getting more than three, it might have been that that made them change their minds.'

On these facts, which the prosecution was prepared to prove, Avory concluded, he would ask the magistrate to come to the conclusion that he found the three defendants 'acting—it is true independently of each other—but all acting with one object, which was to get several boys out of the jurisdiction of the law.' He suggested that the object was 'to prevent them giving evidence either against Hammond or against Lord Arthur Somerset or against other persons who might afterwards be proceeded against.' If three persons were found acting apparently with the same object, he would ask that the inference should be drawn, and in the event of the magistrate committing the three defendants for trial, the jury would be asked to draw the conclusion that a conspiracy existed.

Finally, on Avory indicating that he proposed to call as many witnesses as time allowed that day, Gill for Newton asked for an adjournment, since (he said) he would have to cross-examine some of the witnesses severely, particularly Inspector Abberline, and he thought it desirable that the examination-in-chief and cross-examination should proceed as far as possible consecutively. After some discussion the magistrate agreed to adjourn the hearing until 6 January and as many succeeding days as would be required to complete the evidence for the Crown.

In thanking the magistrate, Newton's counsel expressed the hope 'that the Press and the public would withhold their judgment for the present, as the defendants maintained they had a complete answer to the charges.' He asked this, he said, in consequence of an announcement in some journals that his client had been a party to Hammond's disappearance, 'whereas this was not suggested by the prosecution, but was shown that he had left when inquiries were made.'

Labouchere for one did not withhold his judgment, but it was one with which Newton's counsel could hardly disagree. Writing in *Truth* on 2 January 1890, Labby remarked:

> I would suggest to the Public Prosecutor that he should at once issue a summons against Lord Salisbury and Mr. Matthews for seeking to defeat the ends of justice in the matter of the Cleveland Street scandal. As to whether Mr. A. Newton, the solicitor, be guilty or not, it is not for me to express an opinion, as the case is *sub judice*; but the proceedings look very much to me like a noisy attempt to close the stable door after the steeds have been allowed to issue from the stable.

3

The resumed hearing of the charges against Newton, Taylorson and De Gallo began before Mr. Vaughan at Bow Street on Monday 6 January 1890 and lasted for the rest of the week. The first witness for the prosecution was Algernon Allies. He was examined by Horace Avory and his evidence occupied the greater part of the first day.

Answering Avory's questions, Allies said he was now twenty years of age and that he had previously lived with his parents at 16 Gregory Street, Sudbury. He recalled Police Constable Hanks coming to Sudbury about 23 August and taking a statement from him. The statement was in writing.

'About the house, 19 Cleveland Street?'

'Yes, sir.'

'Had you received anything before Hanks went to Sudbury?'

'Yes, one or two days before Hanks came down I received an anonymous letter.'

'What did you do with it?'

'I destroyed it.'

'Did you do anything in consequence of it?'

'Yes. I destroyed other letters.'

'Which were in your possession?'

'Yes.'

'From whom were those other letters?'

'Lord Arthur Somerset.'

'At the police court did you in your evidence speak of a person known as Mr. Brown at 19 Cleveland Street?'

'Yes, sir.'

'And did you describe his personal appearance?'

'Yes, sir.'

'Who was that?'

'Lord Arthur Somerset.'

Avory then took the witness through the incident of the call he received from Taylorson, Newton's clerk, when he was living in Houndsditch on 25 September and the attempt to persuade him to go to America.

'How long before that had you seen your father and mother?'

'I had not seen them since I left Sudbury.'

To the further question whether anything was said about them, Allies replied that Taylorson said he had been to see them the previous day, and that they were quite willing that the witness should go. According to Allies, Taylorson added that if he liked he could go and see his friends that afternoon.

'At Sudbury?' interposed the magistrate.

'Yes.'

'What did you do and where did you go?' asked Avory.

'I went to Scotland Yard and saw Inspector Abberline about half an hour afterwards.'

'And did you, after seeing Inspector Abberline, act under his directions?'

'Yes.'

'What did you do and where did you go?'

'Mr. Abberline took me to the Treasury that same afternoon, and I made a statement.'

This concluded Avory's examination-in-chief, and Gill now began his cross-examination with several pertinent questions.

'Before you saw Hanks at your father's house, had you been living at home?'

'Yes.'

'How long?'

'I should say six or eight months.'

'Since you left Cleveland Street?'

'Yes.'

'Your father and mother had always treated you well?'

'Yes, pretty well.'

'Had they or not?'

'Yes.'

'There was no reason why you should be afraid of your father?'

'No.'

'Or be afraid to see your mother?'

'No.'

'When did you go to reside on the premises at Cleveland Street?'

'I cannot say. It was before Christmas 1888.'

'And, as I understand, you remained some months?'

'Yes.'

'Before that had you been convicted?'

'Yes.'

'And let off without imprisonment?'

'Yes.'

'Convicted of stealing?'

'Yes.'

'When you were convicted of stealing, was Lord Arthur Somerset surety for you or did he get someone else?'

'I think so.'

'So it was that you did not get imprisonment. Did he not become surety?'

'I knew some time afterwards that he did.'

'You knew Lord Arthur Somerset', Gill went on, 'by being employed at some club?'

'Yes,' Allies agreed, 'where I was employed and where I was charged with stealing from.'

Gill now asked the witness about his meeting with P.C. Hanks at Sudbury. 'Did you know he was a police officer?'

'No.'

'Did he say he was going to question you?'

'Yes.'

'Did he frighten you?' Gill reminded Allies of what he had previously sworn to on this point.

'He frightened me just at first.'

'You thought you were going to be imprisoned?'

'Yes.'

'Before he questioned you?' the magistrate asked.

'When he began to question me,' Allies replied.

Asked by Gill whether he knew Newlove was in custody at this time, the witness said he did not.

'You knew some steps were being taken for the purpose of punishing persons in connection with Cleveland Street?' Gill continued.

'Yes.'

'Knowing you had been there three months, did you think the sooner you made some sort of statement the better?'

'Yes.'

'A statement that might save you?'

'Yes.'

'Up to the 23rd August you had no reason to be fond of the police. Did you tell Hanks you would like to be a witness?'

'I was glad when he said I should be a witness.'

'You were ready and willing to give evidence against anybody?'

'Yes.'

'Do you know that you were bound over to give evidence against Newlove and Veck?'

'Yes.' Allies added that he did not go before the Grand Jury and give evidence, as they pleaded Guilty.

'After that were you under any recognizance to give evidence?'

'I had a subpoena to appear at the Old Bailey.'

'Up to that time,' Gill went on, 'were you unwilling to see your father and mother?'

'I did not particularly want to see them,' Allies answered. 'I thought they knew of the case. That was the reason I did not want to see them.' In answer to a further question he added that the police never told him not to see them.

Gill now produced a letter from Allies to his parents dated 25 September 1889 and headed, 'All letters to be addressed "Care of Inspector Abberline".' It contained the following passage which Gill put to the witness together with the heading:

> Some person called on me today, all through you giving my address. Am all right under the care of the Treasury, so do not wish any such people to know where I am. I shall return home as soon as I have dispensed my services.

'Did you write that of your own free will?' asked Gill.

'Yes,' Allies replied. 'I meant it as an intimation that their letters should be addressed through the police.'

Counsel then produced another letter, which was handed up to the witness-box. 'Do you recognise that?'

'Yes,' said Allies. 'It is my letter, dated 10th October 1889.'

'You say it is your own letter?'

'Yes, it was addressed to my father.'

'I suggest to you that every word was dictated to you or that you copied it word for word?'

'No.'

'Was it out of your own head?' asked the magistrate.

'Yes, the wording is mine,' the witness declared. 'It is not Hanks's.'

'Was Hanks present at the time it was written?' Gill went on.

'No.'

'Where did you write it?'

'I decline to say.'

Pressed to answer, Allies agreed that it was written from his present address in Houndsditch as the result of a letter he had received from his brother Ernest saying that it was Hanks who had spread a report about him in Sudbury. He had not shown Hanks the letter. In fact Hanks, who handed it to him unopened, thought that it came from Mr. Newton. Afterwards he destroyed the letter.

'Did Hanks tell you that there had been an inquiry as to Mr. Newton's conduct at Scotland Yard?'

'No, sir.'

Gill then asked the magistrate to compare the style of the two letters. The second letter read as follows:

> I can only say that, under the circumstances, it is much better that we should not meet, as I am fully convinced you have been misled by some person who is only seeking his own ends, and not your interests or mine.
>
> With regard to your statement that a rumour concerning me was circulated in Sudbury by Hanks, I can only tell you you are wrong. If you are right, how is it that nothing was heard until weeks after we left the place, when your so-called friend visited you there? I know for a fact that he, and not Hanks, is the author of the scandal.
>
> You are also wrong in saying that I wrote my last letter at the dictation of the police, for I can assure you I am not under their influence. My position stands thus: I am staying here of my own free good will, and I propose to do that which I consider to be just; and as I am old enough to think for myself, I shall not be advised by anyone in the matter. When you know the truth, you will be glad I have acted as I have done.
>
> Hoping that you and mother are quite well,
>
> I remain your affectionate son,
>
> A. ALLIES
>
> Remembrance to all.

'You say that was not dictated?' Gill queried in amazement.

'No, it was not,' the witness repeated.

'Your brother said in his letter that you were a mere puppet in the hands of the police, who were dictating what you were doing and saying?'

The witness answered that this was so.

[176]

Arthur Newton
Solicitor of the Supreme Court
Cartoon by Leslie Ward in *Vanity Fair*

Sir Thomas Chambers
Recorder of London
Cartoon by Leslie Ward in *Vanity Fair*

Horace Avory

Harry Poland, QC

Sir Charles Russell, QC, MP

Frank Lockwood, QC, MP

Cartoons by Leslie Ward and 'Quiz' in *Vanity Fair*

The Marquess of Salisbury
Prime Minister and Foreign Secretary

Lord Halsbury
Lord Chancellor

The Duke and Duchess of Beaufort
Parents of Lord Arthur Somerset

Badminton House, North Front

The Hon. Oliver Montagu
Colonel of the Royal Horse Guards
From a photograph in the possession of
Mr. Victor Montagu

The Marchioness of Waterford
Sister of Lord Arthur Somerset

The Prince and Princess of Wales with their Family at Marlborough House in
1889
Standing left to right : Prince Albert Victor, Princess Maud, Princess of Wales,
Princess Louise, Prince of Wales
Sitting : Prince George, Princess Victoria

Sir Dighton Probyn, VC
Comptroller and Treasurer to the
Prince of Wales

Sir Francis Knollys
Private Secretary to the Prince of Wales

'Did your brother also say in his letter they would like to have an opportunity of your being seen at Sudbury, so that people should see that you were not in prison?'

'No.' But on being pressed, he admitted that his brother said his father and mother would be glad to see him if he could come home, as there were rumours that he was locked up.

'Did your brother tell you the rumours were so serious that in consequence your father had lost his employment?'

'Yes, sir—.' The witness then corrected himself. 'No,' he said. 'Not my brother in his letter. My mother told me when she came up.'

'If there were such rumours, you knew it was important you should be seen?'

'Yes, sir.'

'And yet you swear it was of your own free will you refused to go, in order to stay and do what you thought right and just?'

'Yes,' Allies agreed.

'What do you know of what is right and just?' A note of contempt was in Gill's voice as he put this question.

'I thought what I was doing was proper,' Allies answered uneasily. 'I thought at the time my father and mother would not be my best friends.'

'Did Taylorson tell you this matter was affecting your mother's health?'

'No, sir. He said he would go down with me that afternoon, if I liked to go to Sudbury to see my people. I said it would not be convenient for me to go, as Abberline or Hanks might call.'

'Did Taylorson tell you that neither Abberline nor Hanks had the slightest power to prevent your going, and that you need not have the slightest fear if you went with him that afternoon to Sudbury?'

'Yes, sir.'

'Did he also tell you that you need not be afraid of their locking you up, as you had already given your evidence?'

'I don't remember that. He said they couldn't lock me up. He also said, "You are practically living here as a prisoner".'

'Did he say your father and mother were the best friends you could have?'

'No, sir.'

In answer to further questions, Allies denied that Taylorson had told him that he need have no fear of his parents, as they would forgive him for anything he had done. He also denied that he had told Taylorson that Inspector Abberline had told him to say he wanted to stay where he was as he was happy and comfortable there.

'Did Taylorson say it was not true that you were happy and comfortable?'

'No, sir.'

'Did you say you knew it was not true, and that you wished you were out of it.'

'I said I wished I was out of it,' Allies agreed. 'I meant the case altogether. I said I should not like to go and live in Sudbury any more because I knew Taylorson must have told my mother about the circumstances.'

'Was it not because your sweetheart had written to you about the rumours of the case?'

'I could almost swear I did not say any such thing.' However, Allies did agree that he had a girlfriend in Sudbury and that she had written to him. But he denied telling Taylorson that he had written to her to say that the allegation about him was untrue. 'But I did write a letter telling her not to believe it.'

'From the time of your conviction had Lord Arthur Somerset given you money?'

'Yes.'

'Did you ask Taylorson whether Lord Arthur Somerset was willing to help you?'

'No.'

'Did you mention his name?'

'I don't think so.' Then after a moment's pause, Allies corrected himself. 'Oh, yes, I did. I said, "I suppose it is Lord Arthur's wish."'

'What was Lord Arthur Somerset's wish?'

'To go abroad.'

'What made you say that?' the magistrate interjected.

'I supposed that was who Taylorson meant by saying, "You know who is to give you a new start in life."'

'In July and August, before you saw Hanks,' Gill continued his cross-examination, 'had you been trying to get money from Veck?'

'Yes,' Allies agreed. 'I wrote him one or two letters.'

As proof of this admission, Gill had copies of the letters which had been originally put in at Marlborough Street Police Court, and Avory did not object to their being read out and put to the witness.

'Did the police tell you there was a warrant out against Lord Arthur Somerset?' Gill now asked Allies. The witness admitted that this was so.

'Did they tell you he had left the country before the information was sworn against him?'

'No, sir.'

In reply to further questions, Allies confirmed that he went to the Treasury and was told by Sir Augustus Stephenson that he had received a letter from the defendant Newton asking for an interview between the witness and his father. Allies refused to see his father, he said, and never expressed his willingness to go to Sudbury.

'I wish to ask you,' was Gill's final question, 'if Inspector Abberline did not tell you that if he mentioned anybody else's name he would get into trouble?'

'No, I cannot allow that,' said the magistrate.

'Very well,' said Gill, as he resumed his seat. 'I must ask the other witnesses.'

4

Allies was followed in the witness-box by Charles Thickbroom, who along with William Perkins had met Newton on 9 December at the corner of Poland Street and Oxford Street. After he had told his story and how he had been asked to get hold of three of the other boys, Thickbroom was cross-examined by Gill.

'Had anything been said to you about Inspector Abberline?' Gill asked him.

'Yes,' the witness replied. 'Mr. Newton said it would take a lot more than Abberline to frighten him.'

Thickbroom confirmed that he did not keep the appointment on 10 December since his father was ill. Next day he communicated with the police and on the following day swore an information against Newton at Marlborough Street Police Court.

Asked whom he thought he was going to meet on an earlier occasion, Thickbroom replied that he thought he was going to meet Lord Arthur Somerset's father.

'Who was it suggested to you that you might meet Lord Arthur Somerset's father?'

'Two constables.'

'Do you know their names?'

'I know one.'

'What is his name?'

'Sladden.'

The mention of P.C. Sladden's name by Thickbroom gave an additional interest to the case, since it was Sladden who had been detailed to watch Hammond's house in Cleveland Street after the brothel-keeper's disappearance. 'They did not say I should see Lord Arthur Somerset's father,' Thickbroom added, 'but they spoke like it.'

'That was your guess, then?' the magistrate queried.

'Yes.'

'Were you going about during these days trying to speak to anybody you could about your position?' asked Gill, continuing his cross-examination.

'No,' answered Thickbroom, who went on to say that he had met Sladden by appointment outside Sladden's house on Saturday 7 December and so did Perkins. According to the witness, he and Perkins and Sladden walked together towards the Tottenham Court Road police station, after which they followed a rank of policemen until Sladden fell out on his beat. They then informed him that they had been dismissed from the Post Office, and Sladden said, 'Go on, you aren't, are you? I never thought they would do that dirty trick.'

Sladden was said by the witness to have continued: 'I know somebody who wants to know when you are dismissed, and who asked me
to tell him. I'll go and do so and let you know.' Shortly afterwards
another constable came up, whose name the witness did not know.
According to Thickbroom, this constable said to them: 'You leave it
to these toffs, and you will be all right. I know myself there's a
thousand pounds down for you when you start.' Nothing further was
said and the two boys went away soon afterwards.

Thickbroom's statement was later taken down by Abberline at
Scotland Yard in the form of the information he swore against
Newton on 12 December.[1] According to Thickbroom, he told
Abberline at the time that he did not wish to mention Sladden's
name, not wishing to get him into trouble. Abberline remarked on
'Sladden's stupidity in having anything to do with the matter', but
he did not tell the witness he need not say anything about Sladden.

In re-examination, Avory endeavoured to have the best possible
construction put on Sladden's conduct. 'Sladden said he did not
know what the proposal was,' said Thickbroom, 'but if we did not
like it we need not listen to it. This was said on the Saturday night
before the other constable came up.'

'Had anything been said by Sladden which led you to go to him?'

'He said we might let him know how we were getting on.'

'Did Sladden ever say anything to you with regard to speaking to
other people about the case?'

'No. He merely said he did not want to be mixed up further in the
case, or to have anything further to do with it.'

Two officials from the Old Bailey and Marlborough Street Police
Court gave formal evidence as to the indictment of Veck and
Newlove and the particulars of the warrant which was issued for
Somerset's arrest on 12 November. Besides Allies, Swinscow and
Thickbroom, as we have seen, the deponents to the information on
the basis of which the warrant was issued were Abberline, Sladden
and Hanks of the police, Allies's mother and Ellen Padwick, the

---

[1] Thickbroom was described by Abberline as 'a very important witness in the
case'. His statement is in the Home Office Papers (HO 144/477/X24 427a).

counter-clerk at Knightsbridge district post office. Avory tried to stop all the names being mentioned, but the magistrate saw no reason for excluding them after Gill had stated that, although the information was not sworn until 12 November, 'every word of it was in the possession of the authorities months before.'

William Perkins was called to confirm Thickbroom's evidence particularly as to the meetings with Sladden and Newton.

'You were annoyed that the promises to send you away had not been carried out?' Gill asked this witness in cross-examination.

'Yes.'

'The others were annoyed, too, weren't they?'

'I suppose they were,' Swinscow remarked, 'I thought somehow we shouldn't go.'

Perkins added that he was himself doubtful about his going abroad as Thickbroom had not appeared and clothes had not been supplied as promised. 'We suspected that we were being made fools of.'

'After the trial of Veck and Newlove, did you go about with the police?'

The witness admitted that he went with Sladden to the St. James's Club every evening, presumably to watch Somerset's movements. 'Wright was sometimes with us and sometimes Thickbroom', he said.

'Who told you to go with Sladden?'

'I think I had a telegram from Hanks telling me to do so.' He added that they used to see Inspector Abberline 'nearly every evening'.

He was anxious to go away, said Perkins, and this admission supported Gill's line of cross-examination that the suggestion about going abroad came from the boys and that the interview with them was sought by De Gallo in order to extract information concerning the case of Veck and Newlove for Newton's client, Lord Arthur Somerset. However, in re-examination Perkins declared that 'from first to last' Newton and De Gallo had never asked him for any information about the Cleveland Street case.

On the third day of the hearing the evidence took a sensational

turn when prosecuting counsel sprang upon the defence three witnesses from Belgium who identified Newton and Taylorson as having
assisted in Hammond's escape to America. The first was a Brussels
jobmaster, who testified that he had driven them to the station to
meet Hammond and the boy who was with him, afterwards taking
them to a hotel and then, at Newton's request, driving Hammond and
the boys to Vilvorde to catch the train for Antwerp. The other two
witnesses were employees of the Red Star shipping office in Antwerp
who deposed to supplying sailing tickets for Taylorson, Hammond
and the boy, which had been done at the instigation of Newton, the
berths on the *Pennland* being reserved in Taylorson's name.

The last of the telegraph boys to give evidence were Wright and
Swinscow, who confirmed the meeting with De Gallo and the suggestion of going to Australia. Under cross-examination Swinscow's
testimony was considerably shaken when he admitted that his
original statement to P.C. Hanks on 4 July, to which he had subsequently sworn in Great Marlborough Street Police Court, was false
in an important particular. He had told Hanks that he had only been
to Cleveland Street twice. That was a lie, he admitted. He had been
there five times. He had told the lie, he said, as he did not think
there would be any bother about it. But when he came to swear the
information, he knew that there would be bother since he had sworn
falsely, as he had told Abberline at the time. He had not previously
said anything to Abberline about it, he added, but Thickbroom knew
the story was false.

Further questioned by Gill, the witness confirmed that he and
Thickbroom had been with the police in Piccadilly and had pointed
out Lord Arthur Somerset as the man who had been with them in
Cleveland Street, although when they did so, they did not know his
name.

Re-examined by Avory, Swinscow declared that he had been
anxious that an assumed name should be given for him at the coffee-
house in the Edgware Road where he was taken by De Gallo, not
because of what he thought might happen to him there but because
if his real name were recognised when he got abroad, he might not

get any work. At least this was what the witness appeared to say, although Gill objected that Avory had mis-interpreted what he said, maintaining that he ought to have the exact words of the answer. 'It is a lamentable thing that a prosecution should be started on such evidence,' he commented. To which Avory rejoined that Gill's remark 'might explain why earlier proceedings were not taken in the matter.'

The fourth day's proceedings closed with formal evidence of identification by the manager of the coffee-house where De Gallo had taken the boys; also with the production by Ernest Parke under subpoena of Hammond's letters which he had published in the *North London Press*, together with other letters, cards and photographs. Asked if there was any objection to the defence inspecting these documents which were put in, Parke replied, 'Certainly not.' Since Parke's trial for libel had not yet come on, no further questions were put to him.

The earlier part of the fifth day was taken up with the evidence of three of the boys' mothers, and in the case of Allies, his brother and father as well. Mrs. Swinscow told the court that she had received a letter from her son saying that he was not coming home on the night of 10 December. No one had asked her consent to her son's going abroad. Similar evidence was given by Mrs. Perkins, who added in answer to Gill that her son had been at home from July to September and could have been found by anyone wishing to obtain his evidence during that time. When Mrs. Allies went into the witness-box, she was asked to identify the person who had called at her house in Sudbury in September to make inquiries about her son and obtain his address. She pointed out several persons in court as being the right man, and finally selected one of the reporters in the press seats. She absolutely repudiated the idea that it was Taylorson, after he had been asked to stand up for identification.

In reply to Gill's questions, she said that since her son had been under the care of the police in connection with the Cleveland Street case, she had never been allowed to see him alone. She thought he was being frightened and coerced by the police, she said, and she

also thought that the letters which he wrote home must have been
suggested or dictated to him. She had asked that Algernon might be
allowed to return home if only for a day or two, and the fact that he
was being kept away from her was making her ill. However, when
re-examined by Avory, she stated that she did not wish her son to go
abroad, as both she and her husband were getting old, and her husband was older than she was.

Mrs. Allies's inability to identify Taylorson was immediately
corrected both by her other son Ernest and by her husband William,
who had no doubts about the matter. Ernest said that it was he who
had given Taylorson Algernon's address. William Allies also deposed
to seeing Taylorson, 'who had said that he had come from London,
as some persons wished to do his son some good and to help him to
retrieve his character.' The elder Allies was inclined to assent, he
said, in consequence of the disgraceful talk there was at Sudbury.
He also wanted his son to come home to disprove the rumours that
he was in prison.

In cross-examination Gill asked him about the letter Algernon had
written to the effect that he was old enough to act on his own responsibility and was not acting under the influence of the police.
'Had you the slightest doubt that that letter was concocted by the
police?'

'Not the slightest,' the witness replied emphatically. He added
that he had complained to the Director of Public Prosecutions and
he was given to understand that his son utterly refused to see him.

'When Taylorson left you, you wished him to see your son?'

'Yes.'

'You gave him full authority?'

'Yes. I wished him to do whatever he thought proper. He was to
do anything that was necessary to get my son home.'

5

Inspector Abberline was the next witness to be called. He was
examined at length by Avory as to events since he obtained a warrant

for the arrest of Hammond and Newlove. He stated that he arrested Newlove on 7 July and then found that Hammond had disappeared. 'I afterwards traced him abroad, and with the assistance of the foreign police, kept observation upon him—as far as possible.' Answering Gill in cross-examination, Abberline said that after he arrested Veck he found certain documents on him which led him to send down to Sudbury and cause the boy Allies to be brought to London.

'As far as you know, has this boy Allies while living in London been threatened by the police?' Gill asked him.

'Certainly not,' Abberline replied. Nor was it true that Allies had been ordered not to leave the place where he was staying or been told what to say in his letters to his father. 'He has never been dictated to in any way, as far as I know.' Also, far from keeping him without adequate clothing, the detective swore he had given him money to fit him out with what he needed.

'Is there any truth that Allies was told that if he went away he would be locked up?'

'Certainly not. He appeared only too pleased to remain.' As for Mrs. Allies, according to this police witness, she had seen her son twice, once when Veck and Newlove were being committed for trial, and again when she deposed to the information resulting in the issue of the warrant for Somerset's arrest. 'On that occasion the mother saw the boy in a passage in the court when we were all together.' But on neither occasion had any obstacle been placed in her way to seeing him without the detective being present.

Abberline's evidence was completed on the sixth and final day of the hearing, when he was questioned about the information he had obtained as the result of his investigation of the Cleveland Street affair.

'Were you cognizant of the different steps being taken by the authorities in regard to the case?' asked Gill.

'Yes,' Abberline replied.

'Was it your cognizance that the case had been before the Foreign Office authorities?'

'Yes. That was in regard to Hammond.'

'From whom did you learn that?'

'I saw a copy of the reply from the Foreign Office.'

'It was a reply?' the magistrate queried.

'Yes. It was the reply sent to the Commissioner's office.'

'What became of that reply?' Gill went on.

'It is among the documents in the possession of the police. There is a large number of documents in our hands.'

'This was after you had obtained a warrant for Hammond's arrest?'

'Yes,' Abberline proceeded to explain. 'It was a question whether the matter came within the Extradition Treaty or not.'

'From whom did you take your instructions?'

'From the Commissioner and the Assistant Commissioner.'

'And from the Treasury?'

'Yes. I frequently took instructions from the Hon. Mr. Cuffe, and also from Sir Augustus Stephenson. All the information I had I gave to the authorities—all the names mentioned by any of the boys, all the statements they made, and all the documents that came into my possession.'

Answering further questions from Gill, the witness said that he did not know that the boys were to be discharged from the Post Office, and it was a surprise to him to learn that they had been discharged. 'It is very possible,' he added, 'that I told the boys I would see what I could do for them.'

In his re-examination by Avory, Abberline declared that he had never seen Newton or Taylorson after 25 September, and neither of them ever approached him to know whether the prosecution was to be dropped or not. 'I never suggested that it was to be dropped.'

'I never suggested that Mr. Abberline did,' Gill interjected. 'He had no more control over it than I had.'

'Is there any ground for the suggestion that you wished more publicity should be given to the case?' Avory went on to ask the witness.

'Certainly not,' replied Abberline. 'Nor did I say anything of the kind.'

'Was the nature of the case disclosed by the information before the magistrate?'

'Yes.'

'Was Newlove's confession part of the information?'

Abberline agreed that it was, adding that he applied for a remand on 7 July so that further inquiries could be made.

'Were subpoenas served on all the boys?'

'Yes.'

'At that time did you know where Hammond was?'

'Yes.'

'There was at one time a question as to whether this offence came under the Extradition Treaty with France?'

'Yes, we thought it did.'

Gill immediately rose to object to this line of questioning. It was a matter to be settled by the Foreign Office, said Gill, and he strongly objected to an inspector of police being asked his views about an Extradition Treaty.

'I am only asking the fact,' said Avory.

'If Mr. Abberline is to answer questions on this subject,' Gill rejoined, 'I shall be entitled to ask about other matters which came within his knowledge—*whether the highest authorities expressed the opinion that the prosecution should not be proceeded with.*'

The magistrate intervened at this point and suggested that Avory should not press the question. However, he added that his own impression of the Treaty was that the offence with which Hammond was charged was mentioned in it.

'No, your worship,' Avory corrected him. 'In the original Treaty in French, only assaults with violence are mentioned.'

Finally, the witness was asked about what he had heard from Swinscow about his visits to Cleveland Street. 'I remember Swinscow telling me that he had made a false statement in the information he had sworn as to the number of offences he had committed,' Abberline replied. 'We were coming away from the court at the time, after the information had been sworn. I told Swinscow that it

[188]

was very wrong for him not to have told the truth and that he must correct his statement on the first opportunity.'

At this Mr. Vaughan put a pertinent question of his own from the Bench to the witness. 'Why did you not take the boy at once before the magistrate, so as to have the correction made there and then?'

'I knew that he would have to appear again,' Abberline answered, 'and I did not think the difference as to the number of offences was of sufficient importance to make it necessary to go back to the magistrate at once.' And with this explanation the court appeared content.

The last witness for the prosecution was Constable Luke Hanks, the policeman attached to the Post Office who took the original statements from the boys. He recounted the course of his relations with Allies from the time he went to Sudbury and brought him up to London on Abberline's instructions to the incident of the meeting with Taylorson and the boy at the Marlborough Head public house, after which he took Allies to his lodgings.

'Have you ever threatened the boy, or told him what to say when he wrote to his father?' Avory asked this witness.

'No,' he replied.

'You were a party to the information against the present defendants?' Gill asked him in cross-examination. Hanks agreed that he was.

'You swore to seeing Mr. Newton on the night of 25 September?'

'Yes.'

'Did you see De Gallo at the door of the public house talking to another man?'

'There was another man with him.'

'Are you sure it was not the landlord?'

'In my own mind I am certain it was not.'

'You knew Mr. Newton by sight?'

'Yes.'

'He had cross-examined you at the police court?'

'Yes.'

'And you did not like him?' Gill went on.

[189]

'Yes, I had a great respect for him,' Hanks replied to this question, adding after a slight pause, 'at one time.'

'Did you recognise him at once?'

'Not immediately. I followed him in order that I might be positive it was Mr. Newton.'

'What time was this?'

'After nine o'clock.'

'Did you go up to him?'

'Mr. Newton and the gentleman with him crossed the road, and I ran after them. I went sufficiently near to satisfy myself that it was Mr. Newton. I was no more than two or three yards from him and, after I recognised him, I went back to the public house where I saw Inspector Abberline, Taylorson and Allies standing in the doorway. De Gallo was standing outside on the pavement.' Hanks went on to say that Abberline told him to take charge of the boy, which he did, and he made a report the following morning.

'Did you notice anything particular about Mr. Newton? Did he do anything suspicious?'

'I thought his movements were suspicious,' the witness replied. 'He recognised Mr. Abberline, or at least appeared to do so.'

'Describe the other man.'

'He was taller than Mr. Newton and fair.' Hanks added that to his knowledge he had never seen him before and he did not know who he was.

'Inspector Abberline has sworn that he did not dictate any letters for Allies,' Gill continued. 'I suppose you will swear the same?'

'Yes.'

'Did you know the contents of Allies's letters?'

'No. Certainly not.'

'Did the boy complain that you had spread a report of his having been sentenced to eighteen months' imprisonment?'

'I had no complaint from him,' Hanks answered, 'but he showed me a letter from his mother to that effect. He also told me that his father and brother complained that his letters were dictated by the police.' The witness agreed with Gill that he might in conversation with Allies have suggested the phrase in the second letter about 'some person who was only seeking his own ends in spreading the report of his imprisonment'.

'You treated him as a perfectly free agent?'

'Yes, and I told him that he must know whether he was under any influence.'

'You have had large experience in interviewing people likely to be charged?' Gill continued.

'You know as much about that as I do,' Hanks remarked.

'Yes,' said Gill. 'Is it not the fact that most people you interview plead Guilty?'

'Frequently,' replied the witness, whose answer caused some laughter in court.

'The letter is a very good one. Even if you did not write it, you could hardly write a better?'

'Perhaps not.'

'The boy received his education very quickly, then?'

'I cannot say.'

'Did you advise Allies not to see his father?' asked Gill, concluding his cross-examination of this police witness.

'On the contrary, I advised him to do so,' Hanks answered, 'and he said that he was determined not to do so.'

'Were all the boy's statements voluntarily made?'

'Yes.'

'No moral pressure?'

'No.'

In re-examination Hanks confirmed that he had never at any time suggested to Allies that he should not see his father. An interview had been arranged to take place between Allies and his father at the Treasury on 19 November, but at the last moment Allies declined to see his father.

'Did you ever hear of any complaint from the parents until after you had taken the boy to the Treasury on November 19th?' asked Avory.

'No.'

'That is the case for the prosecution,' said the Treasury counsel as soon as Hanks had stepped down from the witness-box.

Gill now asked the magistrate to adjourn the hearing for a reasonable period so as to enable him, as he put it, to consider and consult, if necessary, with more experienced counsel than himself what course he should adopt for the defence, 'as far as this court is concerned'—in other words, whether the defendants should plead Not Guilty and reserve their defence or whether to submit, in the light of the facts, that they had no case to answer, since the prosecution had failed to establish that they had committed any offence in law.

Accordingly the magistrate adjourned the case until the following Thursday week, 23 January.

6

Meanwhile Newton had applied to the Duke of Beaufort for substantial financial help with the costs of his defence. On 9 January, while the proceedings at Bow Street were going on, the Duke wrote to his son, who was then in Paris:

> I both hope and think that Newton will get out of the mess he has got into—I must say I think rather foolishly, tho' I don't think he has done anything contrary to law in what he has done. If Mr. Vaughan dismisses the case, it will be a very good thing for him. If he does not, he will have to retain the most expensive counsel, Sir Charles Russell for himself and some other Radical who will enjoy abusing the Government for his clerk's. He makes out it will be very expensive—very much more so than I am sure it really will be.
>
> I have told him that I will help him, but as he certainly did not see the boy [Allies] on the 25th September or Hammond on the 4th October at my instigation, for I was not aware of their existence then, I have declined to send him £3000 for his defence [for which he asked]. On the 19th October he told me it was too late to do anything for you—he also told me there were several people implicated. I said to him, 'Let them bear their share and I will help you,

but only to a share, and you must stir up these people to whom it is more important than it is to me.' The mischief is done in your own (yours Arthur I mean) case, and I will not pay for the consequence of acts in which I had no voice and no part and was in absolute ignorance of, and which were done at the instance of others and for their benefit. £3000 is a very large demand.

Somerset agreed that this demand was indeed a heavy one for his father to meet. 'After all,' as he told Brett, 'Newton has already received £3,100 from me and that with what his Grace promises him ought to be enough. You see nothing can help me. I am clean done. There are others whom he has saved upon whom I suppose he will call for help.' In the event the Duke of Beaufort sent Newton £1,000, and this enabled him, as the Duke had anticipated, to retain Sir Charles Russell to lead Gill when the case was eventually sent for trial.

At the conference between Gill and Newton during the period of the adjourned hearing at Bow Street, it was agreed that counsel should open the defence with a submission to the magistrate that his client had no case to answer. This he did, when the hearing was resumed on 23 January, with a powerful speech in which he castigated the police, particularly Inspector Abberline, whom he blamed for allowing Hammond to leave the country in July. 'It may not have been thought desirable to institute a prosecution on the evidence of the telegraph boys,' Gill said; 'but it also did not seem to have occurred to Abberline to have Hammond watched. Abberline simply strolled up on the afternoon of July 6th—forty-eight hours after the statements were made by the boys—and then for the first time asked for a warrant against Hammond.' On the next day came the arrest of Newlove, Gill continued, Newlove not being in a position, as Hammond was, to leave the country. It was later shown in evidence at the police court that Hammond only left the house a little earlier the same day, but he was not arrested. 'A more remarkable introduction to a prosecution, in which it is suggested that the course of justice has been perverted, cannot be imagined.'

Next, the Treasury was communicated with, counsel went on,

and the case was bandied about between the police and the Treasury. Newton, whom he described as 'being now offered as a sacrifice', had in the meantime been instructed for the defence of Newlove, and although he asked the magistrate that the case against his client should be speedily dealt with, Newlove was repeatedly remanded. At the same time every opportunity was given to Hammond's confederate Veck to get away, and the authorities waited for six weeks before arresting him on 20 August. All this time Hammond was out of the country and could not be extradited for any conspiracy except conspiracy to mutiny. No sane person could expect under these circumstances that Hammond—who like the man Saul, who recently gave evidence in Lord Euston's case—would say that the police had been very kind to him; that Hammond, having fled from justice, would return to a country where he could be prosecuted. 'I do not suppose for one moment that it was suggested that he was going to be a police witness,' Gill commented sarcastically. 'Yet after the committal of Veck and Newlove, the solemn farce was gone through of having the name of Hammond placed on the indictment—in fact it was impossible to prove the conspiracy charge in the indictment without having that name on it.'

As for the use made by the police of the telegraph boys who had been subpoenaed, Gill was most scathing. 'Anything more deplorable and scandalous than the proceedings of the police in taking these boys to Pall Mall and waiting outside clubs with them on the lookout for anyone they might pretend to identify, I cannot conceive,' he said. 'It is infamous that the names of persons should be whispered away by boys of such character, egged on by police officers desirous of promotion.' It was well known that many names had been given to the police in connection with these scandals, Gill went on, but in spite of this, no further proceedings were taken, and in consequence his client assumed, as he was entitled to assume, that after the time which had elapsed the matter had been dropped. Being engaged to act for certain persons who had complained that their characters had been traduced by the evidence given at the police court proceedings which led to Veck and Newlove being committed for trial, Newton naturally took an interest in the boy Allies, whom he knew had lied at the police court when he said he was then living with his parents at Sudbury. He had therefore sent Taylorson, his clerk, to Sudbury, where he had an interview with the boy's parents and his brother, who expressed the opinion that he was acting under compulsion and not of his own free will. The parents also complained that they were suffering from the rumours and scandalous stories which were being spread around about their son, and Taylorson was ultimately empowered by the father to find his son, induce him to come home, if only for a little while, and to disabuse his mind of the idea that the police or anybody else had a right to keep him under control.

Referring to the meeting between Taylorson and Allies at the Marlborough Head public house on 25 September, counsel said he would show that the statement by Hanks that he had seen his client and another gentleman outside the pub was an absolute falsehood. Mr. Newton lived at New Malden in Surrey and on the day in question left his office in Marlborough Street at seven in the evening and went home, where, besides some relations who were staying with him, he entertained several friends at dinner. It would also be shown that Taylorson, who was so upset at the manner in which Inspector Abberline had spoken to him in the public house, went down to New Malden the same evening to complain to his employer. These facts would be 'absolutely fixed' and would, in counsel's opinion, 'throw a great deal of light on the sort of fictitious colours it had been sought to throw upon Mr. Newton's conduct.'

In conclusion, counsel asked how his client could possibly be accused of conspiracy to defeat the course of justice by visiting Hammond on the Continent, where he was out of the jurisdiction and within which he was not likely to return—or even by providing young men with money to go to America. Upon the facts connected with the charges of conspiracy which had been brought against his client and the other two defendants, Gill formally submitted that there was no evidence of conspiracy, and he asked the magistrate whether there was any need to send the case for trial, but rather that the whole proceedings should be ended by dismissing the summons.

After Gill's speech, which had occupied most of the morning, the court adjourned for luncheon. When it resumed, Mr. St. John Wonter addressed the magistrate on behalf of Taylorson and De Gallo very briefly, in view of the whole ground having already been covered at length. He simply stressed that there never had been any communication between Taylorson and De Gallo and that all they did individually was done under the instructions of their principal and relying on his judgment.

Gill then called six witnesses, three guests who had been at dinner in Newton's house on the night of 25 September, besides the cook, parlourmaid and groom employed in the Newton household, to swear that the solicitor had been at home all evening until his clerk called about ten o'clock and Newton returned to London with him. Incidentally it is an interesting reflection on how the middle classes lived at that time that Newton, who had only been in practice for five years, was able to live in a commodious detached house in what today would be called the commuter belt, with an indoor staff of two, a groom and horses, and no doubt a gardener as well. In addition to Newton and his wife, the party included an accountant named Samuelson and his wife, who lived at Putney, a Miss Bedford who came from Marlow and was staying with the Samuelsons, a Miss Crosby who was a cousin of Mrs. Newton's, and Mrs. Newton's grandmother.

Mr. Samuelson, who said he had known Newton for about ten years, described Newton's arrival home about eight o'clock, the journey from London taking about an hour. For the next two hours Newton did not go out of the house. Then about ten o'clock a servant came into the drawing-room and told Newton that Taylorson wished to speak to him. This was confirmed by the parlour maid, who had waited at dinner and later opened the door to Taylorson. And it was corroborated by the other witnesses, although there was one discrepancy which does not appear to have been commented upon by the magistrate. Samuelson stated that about ten minutes after Taylorson appeared in the house, he and his wife walked to New Malden Station with their host and his clerk, boarded the train together, and got out at Wimbledon, leaving the other two in the train. On the other hand, Newton's groom swore that he had driven them all to the station.

In giving his decision on Gill's submission, the magistrate began by expressing his regret that Mr. Newton, who had practised before him, and whose conduct had met with his approval on several occasions, should have laid himself open to a charge of conspiracy. However, while agreeing with much of what Newton's counsel had said, Mr. Vaughan could not bring himself to agree with the opinion that there was no evidence before him in support of the charge. 'Conspiracy is one of those offences which need not be proved by evidence of any direct combination,' he remarked. 'It is sufficient to prove that persons were acting with a common object, and that their actions converged to one common point. In my opinion the evidence tends to show that all the defendants were acting together for the accomplishment of a definite object.' That object, as he put it, was 'to abduct certain boys from the jurisdiction of the courts and to remove them to distant parts, so that their evidence could not be available against persons who might be prosecuted.' The letters Newton wrote to the Treasury, the magistrate went on, were 'to say the least of it, untruthful' and, as far as Hammond was concerned, the magistrate believed that Newton thought his offence was extraditable. 'I would have been glad to come to some other conclusion with regard to the whole case,' he concluded, 'but I cannot but think that it has prima facie been established.' The three defendants would therefore be committed for trial at the next Old Bailey sessions.

Asked by the magistrate if he had anything to say, Newton declared that he was guiltless of any intention of doing wrong. All through he had acted under the best legal advice, he said, doing what he considered, and still believed to be, right and proper. After Newton had sat down, Taylorson rose and pointed out that he had only acted under his employer's instructions. He added that many of Allies's statements were untrue. Finally, De Gallo said he was employed by Mr. Newton to make inquiries, and he only acted under his orders. He had no intention to interfere with the due course of justice.

On Gill's application, the magistrate allowed bail for each defendant in one surety of £100.

7

During the next few days Newton considered his position very carefully. He discussed it among others with Brett and also with Henry Labouchere after Brett had brought them together in the hope that they might be able to help each other, since Labby was busy collecting material for the attack he intended to make on the Government for its handling of the Cleveland Street affair when Parliament met in February.

Labby thought that Gill had made a mistake in trying to prove that Newton's clients were actuated alone by a fatherly interest in the telegraph boys. 'It was clear as day that he wanted to get them out of the way and not to withdraw them from the police,' he wrote to Brett after his talk with Newton. 'Presumably he acted on instructions, though how Lord Arthur Somerset would have benefited by the action I fail to see.' Apparently Labouchere was not told about the Duke of Beaufort's desire to meet the boys and find out what evidence they had against his son, and the ruse which Newton had employed to get the boys together for this purpose.

The tactics Labby proposed he developed in his letter to Brett:

> He [Newton] can only fight by showing that the Government sought to hush up the affair and that consequently he had a full right to suppose that there was no bona fide intention to prosecute Lord Arthur Somerset. This would be shown
> (1) by the bargain in regard to Veck and Newlove at the Old Bailey;
> (2) by the police having aided and abetted in his getting Hammond to America;
> (3) in the action of the police towards Lord Arthur Somerset.
> They had full evidence against him equal in force to that on which

they prosecuted Veck. They had no fresh evidence when they issued the warrant. Lord Salisbury did state that a warrant was to be issued and because of this statement Lord Arthur Somerset bolted. Then and only then they issued the warrant.

No sane human being can doubt that they sought to defeat the ends of justice. It is with this that I propose to charge them and to point out that assuming Mr. Newton to be guilty the prosecution is nothing but one criminal turning Queen's evidence against the other. If he is to be tried, so should Lord Salisbury, Matthews and Cranbrook. Mr. Newton will, therefore, I think see that the stronger my case against them is, the stronger is his vindication; but all turns upon my facts being quite correct.

'Personally I think their behaviour scandalous,' Brett wrote back. 'Had they stuck to their original determination to hush the thing up, I think they would have been right. As it is, they have acted meanly and foolishly.' Unfortunately for Labouchere, however, his allegations were by no means all capable of being substantiated, as was to be shown when the Attorney General effectively refuted them in the House of Commons.

Eventually Newton came to the conclusion that he and the other two defendants would secure a more satisfactory trial if, in the event of the grand jury returning a true bill, the case were to be tried by a High Court judge in the Law Courts instead of by the Recorder at the Old Bailey. In certain circumstances it was possible to do this by a motion for the issue of a writ of *certiorari* to remove any indictment which might be found at the Central Criminal Court to the High Court for trial there. The motion was usually supported by an affidavit setting out the reasons for the change of venue. In the present case it was prepared by Newton with counsel's help and read out by Sir Charles Russell when he moved for the issue of the writ before Mr. Baron Pollock and Mr. Justice Hawkins in the Queen's Bench Division on 31 January.

There were two reasons which were urged in the affidavit. The first was that questions of law of more than unusual difficulty and importance would arise at the trial, such as whether there could be any conspiracy between Newton and two others who were acting under his instructions, whether it was an offence to prevent a person from being available as a witness in the event of a charge being made at some future time, whether it was an offence to communicate with a person against whom a warrant was in existence in this country but who was beyond the jurisdiction of the courts in any country from which he could not be extradited, or to pay money to such a person with a view to preventing him from blackmailing persons in this country, and whether acts done abroad and outside the jurisdiction of the English courts could properly form part of a conspiracy charge. The second reason given for the desirability of having the trial in the Queen's Bench Division was that it could be with a special jury which was not possible at the Old Bailey, where all cases came before common juries. A special jury consisted of householders of substance who 'from their position', as Russell remarked in moving for the writ, 'might be presumed to be men of independence and intelligence'.

In making his application Russell relied solely on the second reason, since so far as questions of law went the case could always be put into the judges' list at the Old Bailey and tried there by a High Court Judge, as the Attorney General pointed out in opposing the application. However, in spite of Webster's argument that the removal of a case for the purpose of a special jury could not be allowed on the ground of 'complexity' unless there was a danger of prejudice, which was not apparent in this case, the judges decided to grant the application. There were cases of a novel character in which a special jury was required, said Mr. Baron Pollock, and the legislature had recognised the difference between the two kinds of juries. The present was certainly 'a new and peculiar kind of case'— he remembered only one like it—and 'very nice questions might arise as to the applicability of evidence to the different parties, and in a branch of law with which the courts were not very familiar.' Mr. Baron Pollock thought therefore that the present case was 'eminently one in which the application should be granted', an opinion in which his fellow judge concurred.

Four days later, on 3 February, the three defendants attended Bow Street Police Court and formally entered into recognizances to appear in the Queen's Bench Division. Later the same day the grand jury at the Old Bailey, having considered the depositions of the prosecution witnesses, returned true bills against Newton and Taylorson, but threw out the bill against De Gallo, who was accordingly discharged.

There was a delay of more than two months before the case eventually came to trial in the Queen's Bench Division, partly because there were such arrears of business in the Law Courts and partly, it appears, because the Government took so long to decide whether or not to continue the prosecution. Meanwhile Labouchere continued to belabour the Government, both in the pages of *Truth* and from the floor of the House of Commons, with particular reference to Somerset's flight and his visit to Constantinople when, 'showing, as he was able to do,' as Labby put it in the House, 'that he had been allowed to honourably resign his position in the Army, that he was a magistrate for two counties in England, he asked for some official position in the Court of the Sultan.'

> By this time public attention had been drawn to a certain extent to what was going on, and Ministers began to think they were getting into a mess. They were a little frightened at what might happen, and so they looked round for a Jonah, and they found him in the person of Mr. Newton, solicitor to Lord Arthur Somerset, and they prosecuted him for getting witnesses out of the way.

'I do not blame Mr. Newton,' Labby went on; 'so far as I know he only aided Lord Salisbury in defeating justice, but it seems to me that if Mr. Newton is prosecuted, Lord Salisbury and several other gentlemen ought also to be prosecuted and charged under the same indictment.'

Early in May Labouchere was asked whether he would make trouble in the event of the Government dropping the prosecution. 'You can tell Newton that in all probability the Government will not go on with his case' he wrote to Brett on 8 May. 'I have been privately approached to know whether, if it is dropped, I shall make a point of showing the *mala fides* of the whole matter and have promised not to express an opinion in regard to it.'

Brett immediately passed on this news to Newton and advised him and his clerk to be very discreet in anything they might say about it. Newton replied on 12 May:

> Your *most* kind note just to hand. I hope you will understand how warmly I appreciate the trouble and efforts you have taken with regard to this unfortunate matter—the case is fixed for Friday next. Russell and the other counsel have had their briefs about a week ago. I do not think there will be any indiscretion as we are really doing nothing except waiting for the day to come on.
>
> We have a second consultation with Russell tomorrow. Shall I tell him that I understand that a persuasive rather than a hostile attitude towards the authorities might result in the matter not being gone into?

There were six counts in the indictment to which Newton and Taylorson had pleaded Not Guilty. The sixth count specifically charged that Newton, knowing that certain offences against the Criminal Law Amendment Act had been committed 'by divers male persons', and believing that a prosecution would take place, conspired with Taylorson and others to prevent their prosecution. A second leader, Arthur Jelf, QC, had been briefed besides Russell, and at the consultation in the latter's chambers, Russell told his clients that if they pleaded Guilty to the last count he thought he could persuade the Attorney General to accept the pleas of Not Guilty in respect of the other five counts, and in respect of the sixth to assure the judge, after he (Russell) had done likewise, that the defendants had acted in an excess of zeal. In this event Russell felt sure that the judge would simply bind over both defendants to be of good behaviour. To this course Newton intimated that he was quite agreeable, but not so his clerk, who refused to plead Guilty to any of the counts. Russell did not press the matter further with Taylorson, feeling that the clerk would be amenable to his suggestion when they saw the Attorney General before going into court.

On the morning of the trial all the counsel had a consultation in the Law Courts with the two defendants, when Webster intimated that Russell's proposal was quite acceptable to the prosecution. However, Taylorson emphatically refused to be a party to it. As Avory's clerk who was present put it, Russell talked to him 'in the manner of a stern parent', and Webster 'gently advised him not to be so foolish', but Taylorson was adamant. At last Russell lost his temper.

'Damn it, sir, do as I tell you!' he shouted.

'Damn it, sir, I will not plead Guilty,' Taylorson retorted, and he was to prove as good as his word.

8

The presiding judge was Mr. Justice Cave, an unfortunate choice for Newton as it turned out, since he had little experience of the criminal law, except in relation to bankruptcy cases, in which he mainly adjudicated. In the barristers' seats were what was usually described in the press as a distinguished array of counsel, of which no less than four appeared for the prosecution. These were the Attorney General, the Solicitor General (Sir Edward Clarke), and two Treasury juniors, Horace Avory and Robert Wright. The latter had written a learned work on 'the law of conspiracies and agreements' and no doubt was retained as the leading expert on the subject. The fact that both Law Officers of the Crown appeared was some indication of the importance which the authorities attached to the case. Newton was defended by Sir Charles Russell, Arthur Jelf and Charles Gill.

After the special jury had been sworn and the clerk of the court had read the indictment, Newton asked leave to withdraw his plea of Not Guilty as to the sixth and last count, and this was done. However, Taylorson when asked to plead gave a vigorous 'Not Guilty' to all the counts. Russell then addressed the court in what, so far as Newton was concerned, was really a plea in mitigation of the sentence. But he felt he was on fairly sure ground, since he knew that the Attorney General would agree generally with what he had to say, besides accepting Newton's pleas.

Russell began by referring to the magistrate's testimonial to Newton's reputation as a young solicitor at the police court when Mr. Vaughan said that he had formed a high opinion of him in his professional character and he had had occasion to commend him more than once for the manner in which he had conducted his professional business. For obvious reasons, Russell went on, he would not trouble the judge with the details of the Cleveland Street case. ('It would serve no useful purpose whatever, but would have the reverse effect.') Nevertheless he felt obliged to give some of the background in the context of his client's actions, which he did in these words:

> It is unhappily a notorious fact that there was a house of infamous character kept by a man named Hammond in Cleveland Street, to which it has been alleged—and there cannot be any doubt that there was truth in the allegation—that persons of the male sex resorted for criminal purposes. In the autumn of last year the police were taking steps in relation to it. One immediate result was that Hammond left the country before any legal process could be or was obtained against him, and was residing out of the jurisdiction of the court—namely in Belgium.

Russell felt sure, he said, that the Attorney General would agree that, for such an offence as Hammond could alone have been charged with, there was no means by which, under the existing extradition arrangements, he could have been taken into custody and handed over for the purpose of justice to the authorities in England. He described Hammond as 'living by infamous traffic and living perhaps less by any filthy payments made to him than by blackmailing operations'. It would not be right, he added, even if pertinent to the case, that he should mention names of people who had attended at Hammond's house for the purpose of the commission of criminal acts. 'Of those persons, two or three were clients of Mr. Newton's, and they protested that an attempt was being made to blackmail them and that they were innocent.'

> It is probable that Mr. Newton, believing in the protestations of his clients, thought that in what he did he was rather shielding men from infamous charges, dictated by infamous motives, than doing anything that would impede the actual course of justice. That was illustrated in this way. The man Hammond, being in Belgium and unquestionably threatening to make charges and use his position for the purpose of blackmailing, it is true that Mr. Newton did exert himself in the interests of his clients, and in the relief of those clients from infamous charges, and did take active steps and actively intervened to get Hammond to leave Belgium and go to America, from which point his attempts at blackmailing, whether rightly or wrongly, were thought to be less effective.

Nobody would for an instant suggest that in the course Mr. Newton took in procuring Hammond to go to America he was acting in the interests of Hammond, Russell continued. 'Mr. Newton had no interest in protecting Hammond from a court of justice.' However wrong and improper was Mr. Newton's intervention—and his counsel conceded it to have been both—Russell emphasised that it was 'clearly not an intervention in the interests of Hammond, or to shield him from any charge that might be brought against him.' As regards any other charges against anybody else, at that time there was no definite charge formulated by warrant or by summons against any other person. 'Amongst the persons who were making these charges, true or false, were some who had been guilty of taking part in these criminal offences. At a later stage one person left the country'—Russell did not allude to Lord Arthur Somerset by name—'but at that time no charge had been made against him. On the 12th of November a warrant was issued against him, but at that time he was out of the jurisdiction of the court, and he had not, so far as it was known, been within the jurisdiction since. In that state of the case Mr. Newton did see some of the people who were supposed to be witnesses, but it was for the purpose of getting to know what were the allegations made against his clients.'

However, taking the whole of the circumstances into account, Russell admitted that there was 'certainly a technical breach of the law'; but the charge which was founded upon that breach was of a class which was very rare, and in regard to which Baron Pollock said, when the motion for a writ of *certiorari* was made, that it was a branch of the law upon which even the judges of the High Court had but comparatively little knowledge. 'I hope I will have the assent of the Attorney General when I say that, admitting the impropriety on the part of Mr. Newton in some particulars, the offence amounts to no more than an indiscreet act of a zealous man acting in the interests of those whose honour was confided to his charge, and whose characters had been attacked at the instance of a few persons whose testimony is unworthy of credence. It is not a case in which a solicitor deliberately lent himself to a violation of the law.'

Russell concluded by appealing to the judge to bind Newton over:

> Under all the circumstances of the case, looking to the fact of the moral torture, the pain and anxiety, to say nothing of the cost of the proceedings inflicted upon the defendant, I would respectfully ask your Lordship to allow Mr. Newton to stand out to come up for judgment when called upon. Of course, if any circumstances come to your Lordship's knowledge hereafter, you can call upon Mr. Newton to come up to receive judgment.

'Have I to pass sentence?' asked the judge.

'Yes, my Lord, according to the existing law you have,' said Russell. 'As regards the other prisoner, Taylorson, I have the intimation of the Attorney General that he does not propose to offer any evidence, and a verdict of Not Guilty will have to be returned in his case.'

This was confirmed by the Attorney General when he replied to Russell's speech in mitigation, which he did immediately Russell sat down. 'In regard to Taylorson, it would not be right for me to offer any evidence, because I must admit that from the beginning to the end of the proceedings in the police court, Mr. Newton has said honestly that what has been done by Taylorson has been done under his instructions.' This produced the curious result that, while

Taylorson was found Not Guilty of conspiring with Newton to obstruct the course of justice, Newton was convicted of conspiring with him to do just that.

For the rest Webster associated himself with Russell's plea. He admitted that there was no evidence before him of personal motive or of any inducement to Newton to act as he had done, and accepting, as he wished to accept, what Russell had said that Newton was acting for some persons who were accused by vague rumours which had been floating about, he agreed that Newton 'might have been led away by his zeal for his clients into acts which he ought to have considered more carefully, and for the consequences of which he must be held responsible.' It was suggested on Newton's behalf that he was endeavouring to shield persons from blackmailing. 'I feel it right to say,' the Attorney General declared, 'that there is nothing in my instructions to negative that view.' Nor was there anything in the evidence inconsistent with it. Webster also drew the judge's attention to the fact that there was no communication with the telegraph boys until *after* the issue of the warrant against Lord Arthur Somerset, and it was clear that they were sent to Newton by police constables and that he did not seek them out. It was also perfectly true—and this might have had some effect on the legal view—that 'no extradition was possible against either of the persons for whom warrants were out, while the other persons against whom warrants were obtained were brought to justice and convicted, the convictions being before any of the acts complained of in the present indictment.'

Finally, the Attorney General referred to the magistrate's expressed opinion of 'the previous high character of Mr. Newton', and he hoped the judge would be able to accept Russell's statement. 'I do not feel it is my duty to press any other view against Mr. Newton than that which my learned friend has submitted,' he concluded. Accordingly the Attorney-General accepted Newton's plea of Guilty on the last count and he did not offer any evidence on the earlier counts, adding that it was 'with great satisfaction' that he found it unnecessary for him in public to go into the case, 'because the mischief done by discussion of such matters cannot be over-exaggerated.' The verdicts in respect of both defendants were then formally returned by the jury.

Everybody in court now prepared to leave under the impression that the judge would simply bind over Newton with a few admonitory words. There was therefore a buzz of surprise when Mr. Justice Cave said he would take the opportunity of reading the depositions and would pass sentence in Newton's case next Tuesday morning.

Sensing that there were some doubts in the judge's mind, Russell asked, 'Would your Lordship like to have an affidavit from Mr. Newton verifying the facts I have stated?'

'No,' replied the judge, 'unless you wish to add additional matter.'

Newton's bail was thereupon renewed until Tuesday 20 May when he would have to come up for judgment.

9

As Mr. Justice Cave took his place on the bench in Queen's Bench Court VIII in the Law Courts four days later, he looked stern. A bundle of the depositions which he had devoted the week end to reading lay near to hand. Newton immediately stood up to hear what the judge had to say to him.

'Your counsel, who addressed me with much eloquence,' the judge said, after briefly reviewing the facts, 'made an appeal on your behalf founded on statements you made to him and certain facts which had come out in the course of litigation, and he appealed to me to take a lenient view of your case on the ground that you thought you were shielding a man from certain infamous charges, made from infamous motives, rather than doing anything to impede the course of justice, and that your offence was rather to be ascribed to the indiscreet zeal of a solicitor on behalf of an accused party than to any design or intention on your part to impede the course of justice.' The judge went on to refer to a remark of the Attorney General on that subject 'of which he had some difficulty in appreciating the force.' This was that there was nothing in his instructions to negative

Sir Augustus Stephenson
Director of Public Prosecutions

One of three postal orders for £1 which were bought by Lord Arthur
Somerset at Knightsbridge Post Office in London on 20 August 1889 and
made payable by him to Algernon Allies at Sudbury. The order was issued
by a clerk in the office named Ellen Padwick, who later identified it under
oath. It was signed by Allies when he cashed it at Sudbury on the following
day.
  From the original in the Public Record Office

THE WEST-END SCANDALS.

COMMITTAL OF THE EDITOR OF THE "PRESS" FOR TRIAL.

A DEFENCE FUND OPENED.

Lord Euston emphatically denies the libellous statement, and explains the circumstances under which he once visited the house in Cleveland-street.

The editor of this paper has been committed to take his trial at the sessions of the Central Criminal Court, which open on Monday, 16 December. The proceedings were initiated last Saturday morning, when on the application of Mr. Lionel Hart, instructed by Messrs. Lewis & Lewis, Justice Field granted his fiat for the commencement of criminal proceedings against Mr. Ernest Parke, whose solicitor, Mr. Minton Slater, offered no opposition. At Bow-street Police Court the same afternoon, Mr. George Lewis obtained from Mr. Vaughan a warrant for

LORD EUSTON.

Mr. Parke's arrest, the Earl of Euston supporting the application by testifying to the truth of the affidavit he had made denying the libellous statements complained of. Sergeant Partridge was sent with the warrant to the *Star* office, but being by inadvertence informed that Mr. Parke had left, went to his place of residence at Clapham. Meanwhile, however, Mr. Parke heard of the issue of the warrant, and at once went to Bow-street

TO SURRENDER HIMSELF,

accompanied by gentlemen who offered bail to the amount of £1,500. The magistrate had, however, left, the hour being half-past five, and Detective-Inspector Conquest—who was in charge —had no authority to accept bail. The Chief Commissioner Mr. Monro was consulted, but finally at 10.30 Mr. Parke and his friends were informed that the ordinary course could not be departed from and he must be detained in the cells till Monday morning. Everything was done for his comfort that the police regulations permitted, every officer from Mr. Conquest downwards treating him with all the considera-

regarded as the disgrace and opprobrium of modern civilisation." The paragraph concluded by warning Mr. Matthews, the Home Secretary, that if he did not take action before Parliament met he would have a heavy reckoning to settle. Mr. Lewis continued that the accusation was a very atrocious one, and he should ask that the defendant be committed for trial. The circumstances, so far as Lord Euston was concerned, were these. He had never committed any crime of any sort or kind. That statement was

ABSOLUTELY WITHOUT ANY FOUNDATION

so far as he was concerned. He had never left the country, and there had been no warrant issued so far as he knew for his apprehension. If there was any warrant out, Lord Euston was present that day to be apprehended ; but it was perfectly untrue that such a warrant had issued. All that he knew about the case was simply this. One evening at the end of May or the beginning of June Lord Euston was walking in Piccadilly at about 12 o'clock at night when a man put into his hand a card on which were the words "Poses Plas-

HAMMOND.

tiques.—Hammond, 19, Cleveland-street." About a week later

LORD EUSTON WENT TO THE HOUSE,

between 10.30 and 11 at night. A man opened the door to him and asked him for a sovereign, which Lord Euston gave him. Lord Euston asked about the poses plastiques, when the man made an indecent proposal to him, on which Lord Euston called him an infernal scoundrel, and threatened to knock him down if he did not at once allow him to leave the house. The door was then opened and Lord Euston at once left the house. That was all he knew of the matter.

Formal evidence was then given of the publication of the libel and of the connection of Mr. Parke with the paper, but Mr. Lockwood observed that the evidence was hardly necessary as the responsibility of the defendant was not disputed.

The Earl of Euston was then examined by Mr. Lewis. He said—My name is Henry James, Earl of Euston. When in London I reside at

4, GROSVENOR-PLACE.

When not in London I reside at Euston Lodge, Thetford, or Wakefield Lodge, Stoney Stratford, my father's place.

You have seen the copy of the paper of the 16th of November, *The North London Press*?—I have. I at once gave instructions for a criminal prosecution for libel in respect of the matter contained in that paper.

Is there any truth Lord Euston, in the state-

You say the statement was first made in the month of October ?—Yes.

Have you made a statement at the Home Office about it ?—No.

Or at the Treasury ?—No.

You made no statement to any official ?—None whatever.

Just wait and hear my question. You made no statement to any official at all either at the Treasury or the Home Office ?—I have had no communication of any sort or kind either with the Treasury or the Home Office.

That you swear ?—That I swear.

You said you first made your statement in October. That I take it meant to some friends ?—Yes, privately.

IS LORD ARTHUR SOMERSET

a friend of yours ?—I know him.

When did you see him last ?—Last summer some time during the season. That is as near as I can remember. I was in London during May June, and July. I saw him in society. I was in the habit of meeting him constantly.

Did you meet him in society ?—Yes.

You have not seen him since ?—No.

Do you know where he is ?—No.

Now just tell me with regard to this occurrence in May or June, you say you afterwards read the card. How long afterwards ?—When I got home I think. I don't remember particularly. I think when I got home and took my coat off. I did not read it in the street. I just shoved it in my pocket and looked at it when I got home.

Just tell me what it was that was on the card ; was it a printed or a lithographed card ?—It was a lithographed card, but the words *poses plastiques* at the top were in writing.

Was the gentleman giving out these cards promiscuously, or

WERE YOU PARTICULARLY FAVOURED ?

—Witness (laughing): I cannot tell you. He shoved one into my hand, and I put it in my pocket.

Was he giving them away to other people ? —I really cannot tell you. I was walking along pretty smart home. I do not walk slowly as a rule.

Did you see him give a card to anyone else ?— No. It was near 12 o'clock as I was walking home.

I suggest to you that you had not time to stop and read it ?—Well (laughing), I did not stop to read it under a lamppost.

Mr. Lockwood—I do not know what there is to laugh at.

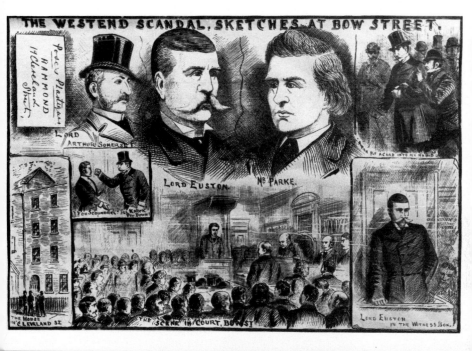

THE WEST END SCANDAL, SKETCHES AT BOW STREET.

Percy Plantagenet HAMMOND 19 Cleveland Street.

LORD ARTHUR SOMERSET

LORD EUSTON

MR PARKE

"YOU SCOUNDREL! I'LL KNOCK YOU DOWN!"

THE HOUSE IN CLEVELAND ST.

THE SCENE IN COURT, BOW ST.

LORD EUSTON IN THE WITNESS BOX.

WEST-END SCANDAL CASE.

SEVERE SENTENCE ON MR PARKE.

THE BOYS GIVING INFORMATION SCOTLAND YD

MR PARKES INTERVIEW WITH HIS WIFE

PICCADILLY VULTURES.

THE HOUSE IN CLEVELAND ST, A DEN OF INFAMY.

MR PARKE IN JAIL.

(Above)
Mr. Justice Hawkins
T. P. O'Connor, MP
Editor of *The Star*
Cartoon by Leslie Ward in *Vanity Fair*

Ernest Parke
Editor of *The North London Express* and
Assistant Editor of *The Star*

THE BOY WITNESS

SWINSCOW.

THICKBROOM.

ALLEYS

WESTEND SCANDAL CASE.S

(Far left)
Mr. Justice Cave
Cartoon by Leslie Ward in *Vanity Fair*

(Centre)
James Vaughan
Magistrate at Bow Street Police Court

(Right)
Charles Gill
Junior Treasury Counsel
Cartoons by Leslie Ward in *Vanity Fair*

(Left)
Some of the prosecution witnesses in the
trial of Arthur Newton

Lord Arthur Somerset's Grave, in the
'English section' of the Town Cemetery at
Hyères in the South of France

the view that Newton was shielding persons from blackmailing and that he accepted this as one of the motives which had influenced Newton in what he did, since there was nothing in the evidence inconsistent with it.

'Now I am bound to act on my own view of the facts, and the responsibility of the sentence will be mine,' Mr. Justice Cave continued. 'And I am sorry to say that I find myself unable to accept that view. I have stated the facts, and they hardly seem to me to justify any conclusion of that kind, nor do I see in the evidence given before the magistrate, or any statement you made before the magistrate, anything which would lead me to come to the conclusion that your real motive for the acts which you committed was that suggested—that is, that Hammond had been not only a party to permitting practices of a criminal nature to take place in his house, but afterwards made use of his position to levy blackmail on some who were, and some who were not, guilty of such practices.'

The judge proceeded to say what he thought of Newton's conduct with regard to Allies and Hammond and the other boys.

> In the case of Allies, however, at the time when you sent to induce him to leave the country Hammond had absconded, and he [Hammond] was charged with a criminal offence, and everything he would say under those circumstances would be received with the utmost suspicion. Allies, on the other hand was under the care of the police; and there is nothing to lead me to suppose that he was conspiring with Hammond or taking measures of that kind.
>
> I can see in your attempt to remove Allies out of the jurisdiction nothing but a desire to get rid, in the course of the inquiries which it was known were being made, of a witness who might give evidence which would be inconvenient. And so I am unable to see in your conduct with regard to Hammond the excuse suggested on your behalf. He, it was alleged, was pursuing the calling of a blackmailer, and yet at the time when he was out of the jurisdiction, in a country not very far removed from this, you assisted him with money, and also by sending your clerk with him to remove himself still further from this country into a country where he would be not less amenable to English justice than he would be in Belgium.

I say nothing—for I can place but little reliance upon what took place—as to the other boys, because it is admitted that they were put in your way by the police; and secondly, because there was, beyond proposals not carried out and which the boys thought were not intended to be acted on, nothing to show that you had intended to remove them out of the jurisdiction. The consequences of such a step would in all probability have been so serious that I am glad to be able to accept the view put forward on your behalf that the object of your interview was rather to ascertain what evidence they were going to give. At the same time, your conduct was fraught with suspicion, and I must regard that along with the other matters which I have to consider.

In passing sentence there were two points in Newton's favour which the judge particularly mentioned. The first was that the charge of conspiracy to which he had pleaded Guilty had not in fact succeeded and consequently the course of justice had not been impeded by it. 'It is true that at the time Allies was not removed out of the jurisdiction, though the suggestion was made to him to go, and that when Hammond was sent from Belgium to America he was not more out of the reach of the courts than he had been in Belgium, and therefore I do accept that as a palliative consideration. We have always in courts of law been accustomed to look to the attempt as not so grievous where it has not succeeded, and to that extent you will have the benefit of a more favourable consideration of your case.'

The second point in Newton's favour had already been stressed by Russell, and Mr. Justice Cave appreciated it. 'You were admitted a solicitor only in 1884, and are, therefore, still but young in your profession,' he told the defendant, 'and something may be set down to the zeal and indiscretion of youth. You have also the advantage of what Mr. Vaughan stated in your favour, that he had known you in your professional character.' Nevertheless, the judge went on to observe, 'it must be regretted that one for whom a magistrate could express a favourable opinion should have placed himself in the position in which you stand. I cannot regard this as other than a serious offence, and I cannot adopt the suggestion thrown out by your counsel to allow you to come up for judgment when called upon. The punishment for such an offence is fine or imprisonment, at the discretion of the court.'

Those in court, and no doubt they included Newton and his counsel, who thought that he would get off with a fine were mistaken, when they heard the judge's next words. 'This, however, is one of those cases in which a fine would be no punishment.' The judge went on to give his reasons:

> Your offence has been committed for the purpose of securing the absence of these persons from England in the interests of wealthy clients, and to impose a fine, therefore, would only in all probability result in their paying the fine for you. I must, therefore, pass a sentence of imprisonment.
>
> It is quite impossible that I should overlook the case in the way suggested and leave you to come up on your own recognizances. The case is too serious for that course. An attempt to defeat the law is a matter which throws too much scandal on the administration of justice, and which, if it were successful, would have such a bad influence that I must pass upon you a sentence of imprisonment, and that is imprisonment for six weeks.

Fortunately for Newton, Mr. Justice Cave did not add the words 'with hard labour' to the sentence, which he might have done. Before the judge left the bench, Newton's counsel, Arthur Jelf, asked that he might be treated as a first class misdemeanant, which meant that he could wear his own clothes in prison and enjoy other privileges, such as having such books and newspapers as he wished. The judge said he would consider that. Later the same day Mr. Jelf submitted an application, supported by medical evidence, that the prisoner should be so treated, but the judge ruled that 'the matter must remain in abeyance and at present he saw no reason for departing from the ordinary course.' Newton greatly resented this decision, particularly as W. T. Stead had been treated apparently on medical grounds as a first-class misdemeanant during his imprisonment for an offence which was no less heinous than Newton's.

Newton's sentence was served in Holloway, then a male prison, where as an ordinary convict he had to wear the rough prison clothing with its distinctive broad arrow marks and to brush and clean his cell and utensils every morning, the dust from which, he said, affected his eyes. He complained that he had been unable to do any writing or read any books and had been strictly confined to his cell for the whole day except for the daily hour's exercise, and after the first three weeks for light labour out of doors in the afternoons when the weather permitted. He further complained of lassitude, depression and acute diarrhoea, the latter being a frequent complaint due to the coarse food served to prisoners in those days. As a result the prison medical officer prescribed an extra two pints of cocoa and twenty-four ounces of white bread a day. In addition he was, from the time of his admission, given a mattress to sleep on instead of the usual plank-bed, but this concession did not relieve the insomnia from which he likewise suffered. His prison labour was described by the medical officer at the time as 'needlework (repairing clothes).'

During the six weeks he spent in Holloway, Newton addressed two petitions to the Home Secretary, praying for a reduction of his sentence on medical grounds or alternatively that he should be treated as a first-class misdemeanant. If he were in the latter category, his office clerks could visit him, he pointed out, and he could thus keep an eye on his professional work. Also he had a young wife who was expecting a baby, and he naturally wished to have regular news of her progress. In a letter supporting the first petition, his solicitor, Mr. St. John Wontner, who was the official police solicitor, stated that his client was 'thrown amongst the lowest criminal classes, some of whom he has professionally acted for and contact with whom is a torture to him.'

Certainly the feeling at the time in the profession generally was that in the light of all the circumstances of his case, Newton should have been bound over and not sent to prison. As a result a 'memorial' was got up among the leading London solicitors and sent to the Home Secretary, asking that Newton should be treated as a first-class misdemeanant, and this document bore the signatures of no less than 250 firms, headed by Lewis and Lewis, a remarkable tribute showing the high regard in which Arthur Newton was held among his professional colleagues at the time.

But none of these representations had any positive effect. It was the policy of the Home Office to regard the matter of a prisoner's category as one for the court, and in this Mr. Justice Cave was inflexible. After the prisoner had been in Holloway for a fortnight, the medical officer's report was sent to the judge, and on 12 June Mr. Justice Cave gave his opinion that 'prognostications of injury to his health have not been verified and there seems no reason to apprehend any serious effect upon his mental and physical condition.' Consequently, the judge added, 'unless the medical officer should report a change for the worse, I see no reason for altering the sentence.'

Apparently the papers in this matter did not reach the Home Secretary's desk until 26 June, and Matthews merely initialled the file, since Newton was due for release a few days later. Nor did his incarceration have any adverse effects upon his health. Indeed he gained two pounds in weight, which at the time of his admission was 160 lbs.

More serious for Newton than being deprived of his liberty for six weeks, however unpleasant he found the conditions in Holloway, was that his conviction would be reported to the committee of the Law Society, which regulated the professional conduct of solicitors, and that there was a possibility of his being suspended from practice for a period or even struck off the rolls altogether. However, the committee on reviewing the case decided to take no action of any kind. This 'very important and critical news' was conveyed by the solicitor's father in a letter he wrote to Brett on 7 June. 'I was assured beforehand of the very strong personal sympathy with myself of many leading members,' the elder Newton added.

On his release from prison Newton applied to the Duke of Beaufort for some further financial help to meet the costs of his case. But the Duke, 'after mature consideration', came to the conclusion that the £1,000 he gave towards his defence was 'all that he justly and rightly ought to do', and therefore formally declined to do 'anything' further. 'This is a very great blow to me and at the same time a great surprise,' Newton told Brett. 'Meanwhile I am so to speak at a standstill. Can you suggest anything that I can do? It really seems most hard to be treated in this way.'

Another appeal to the Duke of Beaufort's purse which his Grace passed on to Brett at this time came from young Allies, who wrote from his parents' home in Sudbury. In his letter, dated 6 July 1890, he began by asking for Lord Arthur Somerset's address, 'as I should like to explain myself to him of all the trouble and anxiety it must have caused you and I should like to impress upon you that it was not entirely my doing.' But the fact was, he went on, 'I am solely destitute and should be glad if anything could be done to help me.'

> You must understand when the effort was made to get me to go away I knew it was too late. I had given evidence which I knew I was compelled to give and his Lordship knows it was his mistake. Your Grace, I feel if you will do so, I feel sure I should not be doing any harm to anyone. I am sorry for his Lordship. Also you. But now I am Destitute. I ask you kindly to do something for me. And if this does not meet with approval, I shall not ask anything more because I shall think you Blame me for what has been done. But am sure his Lordship would help me a little.

'Of course,' the writer added in a postscript, 'you know who I am.' As if the Duke and every other member of the Somerset family could ever forget the name of Algernon Edward Allies.

What action was taken as the result of this begging letter Brett's papers do not reveal. It was most probably ignored and it is unlikely that Allies was supplied with Somerset's address. At all events he now disappears from view. It was otherwise with Arthur Newton, who was the recipient of considerable sympathy from clients and professional colleagues alike. His temporary setback did him no harm in the long term, as the speed with which he recovered his practice was to show. The fact that barely three years later he was the subject of one of the fashionable 'Spy' cartoons in *Vanity Fair*, accompanied by a flattering 'profile', was further evidence that his personal misadventure with the law had been forgotten and that he was once more on the crest of the wave of success in his profession.

CHAPTER V

The End of the Affair

I

BY THE TIME Newton went to prison, public interest in the Cleveland Street scandal had largely waned. It was at its height during the Parke trial in January 1890 and when Labouchere initiated a debate on it in the House of Commons on 28 February. The House was in committee of supply, and he moved the reduction of the vote by way of a procedural amendment, basing his motion, as he said, 'upon the fact that certain official persons, whose salaries are included in it, have conspired together to defeat the course of justice.' His case against the Government, and particularly the Prime Minister, on which he spoke for an hour and a quarter, he prepared beforehand with considerable care but not invariably with accuracy of detail. He was briefed among others by Brett, who shared his Party political sympathies.

'Pray remember that poor Arthur Somerset's family suffer agonies every time his name is mentioned,' Brett wrote to Labby before the debate.

> I am sure you will be as tender towards the feelings of his wretched mother and sister (who have suffered so much) as you can consistently with the unpleasant necessities of the case. Of course the harder you hit H.M.G. the better. . . .
>
> The evidence against Arthur Somerset (my Father tells me who was told by the Chancellor all about it) is no stronger than against

Euston in the Parke affair. All *tainted* evidence. No letters, not one. Nor any *police* evidence. So you had better be careful there. I take it that the evidence against him was no stronger than against the two men [Veck and Newlove] who were sent to prison on their own confession. I am sure that no warrant would ever have been issued if Arthur Somerset had not gone abroad. This *I know* is the case of H.M.G.

Labouchere replied: 'I agree with you. There were no letters.' At the same time he pointed out that, while he would do all he could 'to say nothing disagreeable to your friends', Somerset's name had already been before the public, 'and they will no doubt see that it is impossible not to allude to it in an indictment of Ministers, because their indictment hinges on their action in regard to the warrant.' Personally he believed Somerset to be guilty, having had the detailed proof 'from a diplomatist in Constantinople' who 'had never heard anything before about the matter.' A little later Labouchere sent Brett a copy of P.C. Hank's statement about his visit to Badminton at the time of the Dowager Duchess of Beaufort's funeral, which Somerset attended. 'Do not show it to Newton or anyone as it might cause inquiries as to how I got copies of such documents.'

Two days before the debate, Labouchere addressed a note to the Government Chief Whip, Mr. Aretas Akers-Douglas, 'in his official capacity', which the Chief Whip immediately gave Mr. W. H. Smith, the Leader of the House of Commons, to send on to the Prime Minister. 'I think it only right that I should tell you that when the Cleveland Street matter comes on,' wrote Labby,' 'I mean to refer to Lord Salisbury's interview with Sir Dighton Probyn on October 18, and show that the statement of Lord Salisbury on that occasion, that the warrant against Lord Arthur Somerset would be issued the next day, was conveyed to him, and was the direct cause of his flight. The warrant was only issued on November 9.'

Apart from the fact that the warrant was actually issued three days later, a minor slip which Salisbury did not notice, the Prime Minister minuted Smith's covering note with a strong denial of the statement attributed to him when asked by Probyn 'whether there was any truth in the imputations which had been made in certain newspapers against persons whom he named'. As has been seen, Salisbury was to repeat this denial publicly in the House of Lords. 'I said that as far as I knew there was not a vestige of evidence against any of those persons except one; and in his case the evidence of identity was not, I believed, in the judgment of the Law Advisers of the Crown sufficient. I said nothing whatever about the issue of a warrant. As long as the evidence was insufficient, such a statement would have been absurd.'

Immediately Labouchere rose to speak in the Commons chamber, a Tory backbench member, sensing that Labby might indulge in some scandalous revelations, tried to have the press and other galleries cleared so that the proceedings could not be reported in the newspapers; but his motion that 'strangers be ordered to withdraw' was negatived without a division. The gravamen of Labouchere's charge against Lord Salisbury and his Cabinet was that they had attempted to hush up the scandal but had only succeeded in aggravating it. As a result foreign newspapers had taken notice of the matter, 'and they have represented this country as a nation of hypocrites, and made very strong and, I believe, unjust reflections on persons in high stations.'

It is the common talk in the workshops in this country respecting the case that the law is not fairly administered as between the rich man and the poor man, that justice is not fairly meted out between man and man, regardless of rank and social position, and thus great harm has been done by the course which has been adopted.

We have heard a good deal lately about criminal conspiracy. What is this case but a criminal conspiracy by the very guardians of public morality and law, with the Prime Minister at their head, to defeat the ends of justice?

Neither the upper classes or the Treasury have any reason to thank Lord Salisbury for his action in the matter, for both have been considerable sufferers by it. Is it not a fact that during the time the matter was before the public the name of many a gentleman was

insidiously and unjustly whispered about as being concerned in the
scandals? I myself heard the names of several persons in high
position hinted at and whispered about in connection with the case,
and after what has occurred I feel it my duty to say that, so far as I
know—and as the result of close inquiry I know as much as any man
—not one of those gentlemen whose names have been mentioned
abroad and at the clubs was directly or indirectly in any sort of way
connected with the scandals. In short, no name was spared, however high the position of the man who held it.

Labouchere went on to refer to Prince Eddy and his father;
although he did not mention them by name, it was quite clear to
everyone who heard him, and later read him in the newspapers, to
whom he was alluding.

I have seen the name of a gentleman of very high position
mentioned in foreign newspapers in connection with the case, but
having, as I have just said, looked very narrowly into the whole
matter, I am absolutely certain that there is no justification for the
calumny. In connection with this I may add that a still more eminent gentleman, closely connected with the gentleman to whom I
have alluded, has used all his efforts to have the highest publicity
given. I think that it is due to that eminent gentleman that the
Government have at last been forced into the qualified action which
has been taken against Lord Arthur Somerset. I think this ought to
be known . . . I honour and respect the eminent gentleman to
whom I have alluded for his action in this matter. I consider it wise
and noble and worthy of the great position he holds.

Labouchere's narration of the facts was generally accurate.
Unfortunately the inferences which he drew from the known facts
were not—for instance, with regard to the Government's action
over Hammond. 'If it had not been intended to extradite Hammond,
if the Government had no plan by which they intended to get hold
of him,' Labby asked, 'what was their object in hunting this man
from France to Belgium and from Belgium to America and then
leaving him alone?' Labby proceeded to supply the answer himself.

'I think the object is pretty obvious,' he said. 'They wanted to send him away as far as possible from this country. Their object, in fact, was much the same as that of Mr. Newton, who gave him money and paid his passage, and also that of the boy with him, to America. Both of them, each for different reasons, wanted him not to turn up in England.'

With regard to the case of Veck and Newlove and their sentence at the Old Bailey, Labouchere put forward a similar argument.

> Whether this inadequate sentence was a condition of these men pleading guilty, or whether, as they did plead guilty, it happened that the depositions at the police court were not shown to the Recorder, and he did not know how monstrous the case was, I do not know. But I think it is pretty clear that the real object was to stop all further disclosures, hush the matter up, and get these men out of the way.
>
> I believe that Veck and Newlove would never have been prosecuted had it not been for the action of the Postmaster General and the Secretary of the Post Office. The matter occurred in the Post Office, and they—I know and respect them for it—insisted that action should be taken in the matter. The Solicitor to the Treasury, ... and I dare say the Home Secretary also, knew perfectly well by this time that certain persons had frequented this house in Cleveland Street, and they knew that certain names had been mentioned, and they determined, so far as they were concerned, that if they were obliged to prosecute these two men the case should go no further if they could prevent it.

In the course of his speech, Labouchere produced a copy of Constable Hanks's report of his visit to Badminton, where on instructions he attended the Dowager Duchess of Beaufort's funeral and noted Somerset's presence. 'I suppose it was thought desirable to give the Treasury one more opportunity of acting,' Labby remarked, causing a cry of 'Oh!' from the Government benches.

> The report Hanks made was sent to the Treasury and no doubt the Home Secretary has a copy of it. I believe that a suggestion was

made that action should be taken. The reply of the Treasury took the form of a direction to at once withdraw the constable. Finding no action was taken Lord Arthur Somerset remained in England, and went to his clubs as if nothing had occurred. During this time inquiries had been made of the police and the Treasury by the commanding officer of Lord Arthur Somerset's regiment and by a gentleman connected with the Household of the Prince of Wales. Lord Arthur Somerset himself being a member of that Household, the police refused to give any information in the matter, and about the middle of October the gentleman representing the Household of the Prince of Wales telegraphed to Lord Salisbury, asking for an interview with him.

As for the resultant meeting at King's Cross railway station between Lord Salisbury and Sir Dighton Probyn, Labouchere alleged—quite wrongly, as has been seen—that the Prime Minister told Probyn that a warrant was about to be issued for Somerset's arrest. 'I think this fact was communicated to the commanding officer of Lord Arthur Somerset's regiment, and Lord Arthur Somerset then fled the country.' But, Labby went on to ask, was any time lost in the issue of the warrant?

> Was it issued immediately? No. The conversation with Lord Salisbury took place on the 18th of October, and the warrant was not issued until the 12th of November, in order that it might be absolutely certain that Lord Arthur Somerset had received the information that a warrant was about to be issued to give him time to get out of the country . . . What further evidence was there on the 12th November than was known on October 18th? We know there was no further evidence. Why was not the warrant issued when Lord Arthur Somerset was in the country? Why was it put off to November 12th? Perhaps the Attorney General when he speaks will tell us that.

Although it was not published in any of the newspapers, Labouchere had managed to get hold of a copy of Constable Sladden's statement at Marlborough Street Police Court during the committal proceedings of Veck and Newlove. When Labby began to read from this document, the Attorney General interrupted him to ask what it was. Labouchere replied that it was Sladden's evidence, and added, 'I can understand why the honourable gentleman does not want this evidence read.'

This brought an objection from Webster and a rebuke by the chair, which, since the House was in Committee, was occupied by Mr. H. L. Courtney, Chairman of the Committee of Ways and Means. The Chairman described Labouchere's observation as 'a most offensive one, which ought not to be made across the floor of the House.'

'I will withdraw it,' Labby retorted, 'but perhaps I may be allowed to explain that my case is that the Government wish to hush the matter up.' He added that he had 'put the matter in a general way' and not in reference to the Attorney General in particular. He went on to quote from Sladden's account of the watch he had kept on 19 Cleveland Street.

> I commenced on July 9th. On that day I saw at 5.10 p.m. a corporal of the 2nd Life Guards arrive at the house. A gentleman arrived at 4.50 p.m., knocked at the door, and was answered from the door. He and the corporal shook hands, talked for about five minutes, and walked away without entering the house. On July 13th I saw the same men call again. The house was empty and they went away. On the same day a great many gentlemen called at the house. On July 14th a gentleman and a Royal Artilleryman called. On July 30th I saw other gentlemen come, and finding the house empty went away.

'Now I think I have proved my case,' said Labouchere. 'The house is in no obscure thoroughfare, but nearly opposite the Middlesex Hospital.'

> Surely it must have been known to the police, and if it was not known to them it ought to have been. In no other city in the world are such abominations openly carried on. Parliament has done its best to put down houses of ill fame, but compared with this place a house of ill fame is respectable. If it were desired to make an example of the offenders, why was not a policeman stationed at the

house to follow the persons who came there? The obvious answer is that it was not desired to follow them up and punish them. One person guesses the police were on his track. I do not wish to mention any names except those which have already been made public, but I will give the name of this person because a warrant is out for his arrest. It is Lord Arthur Somerset. A warrant is out for his arrest and he has fled . . .

The statement of Constable Sladden is perfectly astounding, but I do not think it can be contradicted. I think the Home Secretary can bear me out when I say that this offence has been on the increase of late, but every constable or inspector takes care not to arrest any cognate person, because they believe that by so doing they would make themselves marked men and be sent out to the suburbs. In the streets, in the music halls, you have these wretched creatures openly pursuing their avocation. They are known to the police, yet the police do nothing to stop this sort of thing . . . These poor and wretched creatures live to minister to the vices of those in a superior station. Is there any man who will not feel indignant that boys employed in one of our public offices should be tempted into indecencies more gross than were ever committed under Louis XV?

Labouchere concluded his speech by asking for a Select Committee to investigate his charge that the Prime Minister and others had entered into a criminal conspiracy to defeat the ends of justice. 'If it is granted, I am perfectly willing to withdraw my amendment,' he said, 'but I will not—and I do not think many in this House will—be satisfied with a mere *ex parte* denial on behalf of the incriminated persons. If the Committee is not granted, Lord Salisbury and others stand condemned by their own code of ethics.' He added that the Irish Nationalist leader, Mr. Parnell, was charged with writing certain letters condoning terrorism, and again and again Ministers and their backbench supporters in the House said he must be guilty because he had not courted an investigation. Mr. John Walter, the chief proprietor of *The Times* which published the letters, had certain proofs, but he did not submit them. 'For my own part,' Labouchere declared, 'I think I have shown more of a *prima facie* case for an inquiry than there was simply because Piggot sold forged letters to *The Times*. If the Government refuse this investigation, either they admit their guilt or they have two codes of ethics—one for an Irish leader and one for a Conservative leader. If the Government plead guilty, I shall deem it my duty to divide the House, because I think that this House ought to disconnect itself from any condoning of abominable offences of this kind, and ought to stand up for the principle of equal justice between man and man. If they do not admit their guilt, I shall divide, because a man cannot be judge, jury and defendant in his own case.'

2

It took the Attorney General over an hour and a half to reply to Labouchere in the debate. Much of what he said on this occasion was reflected in the official correspondence already quoted, so that it is unnecessary to repeat it here. On the whole he put up as credible a defence of the actions of the Government and its head as might be expected. 'The main sting of this charge,' he asserted, 'is that Lord Salisbury on a given night in October, with the purpose of allowing Lord Arthur Somerset to escape, made a communication which was intended to be conveyed to him, and that on receiving that communication Lord Arthur Somerset fled. Before I sit down I shall demonstrate that there is not a shadow of foundation for that charge.' By and large he succeeded.

First, he dealt with Labouchere's other charges, particularly concerning the trial of Veck and Newlove in which context he quoted the account subsequently written by the Senior Treasury counsel, Harry Poland. Webster went on to ask, did Labouchere intent to charge a judge like the Recorder of London with being a party to this criminal conspiracy?

Unless the honourable Member admits that the sentence was a sentence passed by the Recorder in the exercise of his discretion, he must contend that the Recorder also was a party to the conspiracy, and for some motive was willing to inflict a lighter sentence than should have been passed. The honourable Member affirms that the real object of the conspiracy which he alleges existed was to hush the matter up . . . All the depositions were before the learned Recorder as a matter of course. There is not a shadow of foundation for saying that anything but the ordinary course of justice was pursued in this case.

As regards Hammond, the Attorney General insisted that the authorities were 'extremely anxious' to have him extradited. But the only ground on which it could have been successfully demanded was aggravated or indecent assault, 'and unfortunately, in the case of Hammond, all the boys consented and were above the protected age.' As for Labouchere's charge that the Government wished to send Hammond away, Webster went on, 'there is not one scrap of evidence before me that the Government, directly or indirectly, took any step to prevent Hammond from being brought to justice. On the contrary, every act is in the other direction. But the honourable gentleman said that owing to the action of the police—and supposedly he meant the action of the police under directions—and the action of the Government, a poor miserable boy was abstracted from his parents and sent away to America. What did the honourable gentleman mean by suggesting that this was done by the action of the Government? Are such charges to be bandied about on the mere *ipse dixit* of any honourable gentleman who chooses to believe any claptrap he may hear?' The Attorney General thereupon challenged Labouchere to give the name of his informant, but Labby did not respond to the challenge.

'As to the circumstances under which Hammond did go to America,' Webster continued, 'my mouth is closed. I should be perfectly willing, and some day I shall be allowed, to state them.' Then, he added, with a glance at Russell on the Opposition Front Bench, 'The honourable and learned gentleman the Member for South Hackney knows them as well as I do.'

'I know nothing at all about them,' said Russell.

'The honourable and learned gentleman's memory misleads him,' Webster replied. 'He appeared for Newton on the application

THE END OF THE AFFAIR

to remove the case into the Queen's Bench; and on that occasion all the depositions and statements of Newton were brought up, and Newton's affidavit, in which he stated that he had been a party to getting Hammond to go away on account of the blackmail he was levying on people in England.'

'I am sorry that my name is being brought into the matter in this way,' Russell retorted, 'as I intimated to the honourable and learned gentleman early in the debate that I should take no part in it, for reasons which it is unnecessary to state in the House. I can assure the Attorney General that, although I may have seen some general statements, I had no connection with the case which required me in any way to examine them.'

Webster immediately accepted Russell's statement and withdrew his remark, adding that he was precluded from stating the facts of the case, because it was *sub judice* and he had to be the prosecuting counsel against Newton.

Finally, the Attorney General effectively refuted Labouchere's charge that the Prime Minister had connived at Somerset getting away, giving the substance of Salisbury's categorical denial which he had used to the Leader of the House of Commons and which he was to repeat publicly in the House of Lords a few days later. Webster went on to explain how he (Webster) had been considering 'with the greatest anxiety' for many months whether there was sufficient corroboration against Somerset or not, how he had consulted the Lord Chancellor who thought the evidence was 'wholly insufficient', and how several weeks elapsed before he eventually gave directions for the issue of the warrant for Somerset's arrest. Consequently there was no foundation whatever for the statement that Lord Salisbury had stated that the warrant was going to be issued immediately. At the same time Webster asked Labouchere to say who had warned Somerset of his impending arrest. Was it Sir Dighton Probyn?

However, Labby again refused to state the name of his informant, though he offered to write it down. A little later he did so and held out a small piece of paper to the Attorney General. 'I will leave him

[225]

to read it out to the House or not as he likes,' Labby said. 'Will the honourable and learned gentleman take it?'

'I insist on putting the question which I am entitled to put,' replied Webster, waving away the proffered paper. 'Does the honourable gentleman say he got the statement from Sir Dighton Probyn? Will he answer that question or not?'

'Look at the paper,' said Labouchere.

'I am entitled to continue my speech,' the Attorney General rejoined. 'Nobody is entitled to make such a charge as this on hearsay evidence.'

'It is not hearsay evidence,' Labby insisted.

Although the name on the paper was never publicly revealed, it is practically certain that it was that of the solicitor Arthur Newton.

'This I assert,' Webster went on, 'that Lord Salisbury does distinctly deny that he ever said a single word about a warrant being issued or directly or indirectly conveyed anything of the kind.' He had only one more fact to add, he said. 'The matter was most carefully considered, and I again saw the Lord Chancellor, and, not being convinced altogether, the Lord Chancellor told me I should act in the matter on my own responsibility . . . That was about the 1st or 2nd of November. I then gave directions that the warrant should be issued. I have been occupied with this matter for a long time, and I say that a more infamous charge than that made by the honourable member was never brought, without a shadow of foundation. I hope and believe that there are many on the other side of the House, who however bitter their Party feeling, will not by their vote support such an accusation as that which has been levelled by the honourable Member for Northampton.'

Webster then proceeded to make an important constitutional distinction, which he hoped Labouchere and other members would appreciate:

> It is a mistake to suppose that the Director of Public Prosecutions acts under the direction of the Home Secretary. The rule is that the action of the Public Prosecutor should in all matters, including the

instruction of counsel be subject to the Attorney General, and during the time I have had the honour of holding my present office I have had, practically speaking, in all such cases the evidence before me. If there were any attempt to prevent justice being done, it must have been known to me.

'This I will say,' he concluded. 'Examination was conducted step by step into the conduct of the persons in this matter; and though it may be easy to say that in the possible knowledge of guilt other steps might have been taken, yet in regard to the accusation made against Lord Salisbury and those connected with him that they have interfered with the course of justice, there is not the slightest foundation in any way for the allegations which the honourable Member has put forward.'

When Webster sat down, Labouchere rose and repeated his offer to submit the name of his informant which he had written down to the Attorney General, 'and if he, having seen the name, liked to read it to the House, he was at full liberty to do so.'

As Webster shook his head, there were cries from the Ministerial benches of 'Read it yourself!' But Labby refused to be drawn.

'I leave it to the honourable and learned gentleman,' he went on. 'The honourable and learned gentleman at first appeared to accept the proposal, but he thought better of it afterwards. I can perfectly understand why the honourable and learned gentleman did not accept the proposal. I am obliged to speak frankly and truly in this matter. I assert, if I am obliged to do it, that I do not believe Lord Salisbury.'

The Chairman of the Committee promptly intervened when he heard Labby's last remark. 'The honourable Member is aware that there is a certain courtesy due from Members of this House to Members of the other House. It would be intolerable for an honourable Member to use that language of a Member of this House, and he cannot be permitted to use it of a Member of the other House.'

'Sir, I repeat it,' said Labby.

'I must call on the honourable Member to withdraw the expression,' said the Chairman.

'I decline, Sir, to withdraw,' Labby persisted, amid cries of 'Name!'

'I shall have to exercise the authority vested in me if the honourable Member declines to obey my ruling,' the Chairman warned him. 'Does the honourable Member withdraw?'

'No, sir.'

On a point of order, T. P. O'Connor rose to ask whether there was any precedent for a Member of the House of Commons being asked to withdraw a statement he had made about a member of the Upper House. After the Chairman had ruled there was nothing in this, he again asked Labouchere whether he would obey the direction he had given him to withdraw what he had said about the Prime Minister.

'With all respect to you, Sir,' Labouchere replied, 'I must decline to withdraw.'

'Then I name you, Mr. Henry Labouchere,' said the Chairman.

This was the signal for Mr. W. H. Smith, the Leader of the House, to rise and move that 'Mr. Henry Labouchere be suspended from the service of the House'.

On the resolution being challenged by some members of the Opposition, a division was called, and the motion was carried by 177 votes to 96.

In accordance with practice, the Chairman left the chair to report the resolution of the House to Mr. Speaker Peel, who appeared in the chamber a few minutes later and resumed the chair. The question was now formally put and carried by a majority of 81 as before, after which the Speaker ordered Labouchere to withdraw. Labouchere did so, 'expressing at the same time my regret that my conscience would not allow me to say I believed Lord Salisbury.'

After Labby's departure, an attempt was made by a Scottish Liberal backbencher to have the debate adjourned. This led to another division, and the proposal was defeated. Mr. John Morley, who sat on the Opposition Front Bench, then tried to lower the temperature by suggesting that the discussion on Labouchere's motion should be continued when Labby was present and that the House should proceed with other business on the Order Paper. 'So far as the debate has gone,' said Morley, 'it seems to me that my honourable friend has done a good service in raising a subject around which a great cloud of rumour and mystery has gathered.' At the same time the effect of the Attorney General's speech would 'undoubtedly be to dissipate most of those rumours', although Morley cautiously added that in his view 'there were in it some gaps which may on some future occasion be criticised.'

But the Leader of the House insisted that it was impossible for him to allow Labouchere's motion to drop without a division. 'The Government cannot allow a charge of this kind to hang round the Prime Minister for an indefinite period until the honourable Member for Northampton is able to return to his place,' said Mr. Smith. 'If he is so ill-advised as to return to the charge at a future period, he may do so; but we must challenge a decision from the Committee now that we have heard the charges, and that which we claim to be a complete and absolute refutation from the Attorney General of one of the most odious charges that could by any possibility be brought against a Minister of the Crown.'

Consequently the debate was continued for the best part of two hours until it was automatically terminated at midnight under the Standing Orders of the House. Charles Bradlaugh, Labby's atheist colleague in the representation of Northampton, and T. P. O'Connor, the editor of *The Star*, which at this time was short of one member of its staff by reason of Parke being in prison, both took up the cudgels on behalf of the suspended MP. But nothing much new emerged from the debate, although a considerable amount of invective was employed by O'Connor and several other Irish Members. 'The Government can find detectives enough to dog the footsteps of the Irish Members,' O'Connor taunted the Treasury Bench; 'they cannot find a detective to dog the footsteps of a ruffian who for upwards of a year has kept a house in this city which has brought disgrace on the character of the city. They let Hammond go to France. They ought to have watched him within an hour of Newlove's confession, if they were serious in the business.' As for the conversation between Lord Salisbury and Sir Dighton Probyn, no amount of argument on the part of the Attorney General could explain the coincidence of Somerset's escape on the same day.

> The public will not stand inequality in the treatment of anyone. It will not stand a number of unfortunate wretches being sent year after year to long sentences of penal servitude for these offences when in the midst of our city a house is allowed to exist where titled people commit these offences, and when they are allowed to escape in the end.

The most constructive contribution to the debate was made by Mr. Charles Hall, the Attorney General to the Prince of Wales, who, it will be recalled, had almost certainly written the letter to the *New York Herald* about the case in the particular context of Prince Eddy, quoted above. His object in intervening was to clear Probyn's name from the imputation that he had alerted Somerset, by showing from his inside knowledge that it was impossible that the information resulting in Somerset's flight could have been communicated to him by Probyn or anyone else acting on Probyn's behalf, and further that Somerset's flight was 'the very last thing that any man connected with the household of Marlborough House wished.'

> The facts are simple, and I will recite them as far as I can without any expression of feeling. The interview between Sir Dighton Probyn and Lord Salisbury took place at King's Cross in the evening. When that interview was over Sir Dighton Probyn drove home to dress for dinner. It was then late, and having dressed he went to his club and commenced a late dinner. Before Sir Dighton Probyn had finished his dinner, and before he had spoken to anyone on the subject, Lord Arthur Somerset had left London, and it has since been ascertained that he gave orders to his servants to have his things ready for his leaving London before the interview between Lord Salisbury and Sir Dighton Probyn took place.
>
> Now, if that be the case how can it be suggested that Lord Arthur Somerset's flight was in any way connected with the information given by Sir Dighton Probyn, or through Sir Dighton Probyn? I have only to add that Sir Dighton Probyn and Lord Arthur Somerset's colleagues in the Household believed him to be

innocent, and it was their most anxious desire that he should take steps to clear his character from what they believed to be a base and scurrilous accusation made against him; and on that very day Sir Dighton Probyn had urged him, pressed him, to vindicate his character, and Lord Arthur Somerset said he would take steps to do so.

Before the debate ended, the Leader of the House announced the Government's refusal to appoint a Select Committee 'to inquire into the truth or falsehood of the rumours that have prevailed in connection with these charges'; it would be wrong that people who, in the opinion of the Law Officers had been falsely accused, should be dragged before the Committee or some similar body, and there 'pilloried and gibbeted and perhaps injured and ruined for life' by such an inquiry. 'I will say at once that the Government will not be a party to such a proceeding,' Mr. Smith declared. 'I can also say that we rely upon the completeness and fullness of the answer given by the Attorney General, and that we claim the judgement of the House upon the matter.'

So the matter eventually went to a division after a debate lasting some seven hours. In the result Labouchere's amendment was defeated by 206 votes to 66, a majority of 140 for the Government.

3

Labouchere took his suspension in good part, although he thought that it was not in accordance with parliamentary practice. 'I was delighted with the chance, all the more as Courtney was all wrong,' he told Brett next day. 'It is a well known rule that when an individual is the subject matter of a discussion, any speaker may say what he likes about him, because this is part of his case. Nothing could have suited me better than to be suspended wrongfully for not believing that august being Lord Salisbury. I dare say that in private life he is the soul of honour, but as a public man Cranmer was not in it with him.'

The Prime Minister took the first opportunity of making a

personal statement in the House of Lords, in the terms quoted above. This was generally accepted by the press except, as might be expected, *Truth* and *Reynold's Newspaper*. The latter denounced Salisbury's 'explanation' as 'nothing better than a shuffling and quibbling attempt to wriggle himself out of the mess into which he had gotten.' Labouchere, who was anxious that his suspension should not be prolonged beyond the customary one week, contented himself with stating that 'Lord Salisbury did not mend his case by his admissions in the House of Lords on Monday,' a statement which he proceeded to develop in relatively mild language, stressing the constitutional aspect of his action. 'Why I declined to withdraw the words which led to my suspension,' he wrote in the issue of 6 March, 'was to convince Lord Salisbury and other Noble Lords that, when they take the people's money, they are responsible to the representatives of the people for all and everything they do as public men. It is a strange comment upon three years of Tory rule that the chief of our Tory rulers should have to be taught this; for without this responsibility to the House of Commons, the voting by that House of salaries to Ministers in the House of Lords be a farce.'

Otherwise he urged the Government to take more resolute steps than they had done hitherto against homosexual offenders:

> Various opinions are, no doubt, entertained in regard to the debate last Friday in the House of Commons. But I think that the Tory and Liberal-Unionist press are hardly doing good service to public morals by insisting that the Government came out of it triumphantly. Their triumph was much that of the *Times* before the Royal Commission. They were shown to be guilty of most of the facts that were alleged against them; but they demurred to the inferences drawn from these facts. It cannot be expected that these journalistic toadies and lickspittles should condemn them. This would be much like the counsel for the defendant taking the part of the plaintiff. But they might, I should have thought, have suggested that the guardians of public morality should in future do their utmost to stamp out what has become a national disgrace by energetic actions against offenders. Anyhow, I trust that this will be the result

of the debate, and that it will not be necessary to call attention again to a most unsavoury subject.

The commission to which Labouchere referred was the celebrated Special Commission which the Government had appointed to inquire into the terrorist charges brought by *The Times* against Parnell and other Irish Nationalist MPs, based largely on letters which appeared to have been written by Parnell but which were afterwards shown to have been forged by an Irish journalist named Richard Pigott, who broke down in the face of Sir Charles Russell's devastating cross-examination before the Special Commission. Pigott thereupon fled to Spain where he killed himself in a Madrid hotel, but before leaving England he sought an interview with Labouchere to whom he confessed that he had forged the letters. Since the debate on the Special Commission's Report began in the House of Commons on 3 March, the same day as Salisbury made his statement in the Upper House, Labouchere was debarred by his suspension from taking part in the proceedings, which in the circumstances of Pigott's confession was a disappointment to him. However, he had plenty of other matters to occupy his attention, particularly the hoaxes and practical jokes of which he was the victim at this time. The perpetrator of many of these subsequently turned out to be a respectable member of a London West End club.

The clubman was responsible, among other pranks, for sending two hearses with mourning coaches to Labby's house, together with a representative of a cremation company to arrange for his cremation. Vast quantities of goods were ordered in his name from various West End stores, including a wedding-cake, a bed and other furniture, a billiard table, beer, spirits and wines, and an umbilical belt for hernia. Cabins were also engaged for him for trips to India and the United States. A salmon was delivered in his name to Mr. Gladstone, a Stilton cheese to Sir William Harcourt and sundry other gifts to other politicians, including a travelling bag for Mr. Asquith. However, the identity of the sender of a curious communication to Labby on the day after his suspension has not been determined. This purported to be a letter from the secretary of the Tory Primrose

League, enclosing a letter from the Prime Minister to Lord Arthur Somerset.

Primrose League Central Offices
Victoria Street

Sir,

I enclose you an autograph letter of Lord Salisbury. I obtained it from a man of the name of Hammond, whom I promised to reward if he could get me any letters likely to injure the character of Tory leaders. He tells me that a client of his in Cleveland Street called upon him and produced it from a black bag. He did not ask the man what his name was, but the man took him to a neighbouring public-house where there were others, who confirmed his statement, but declined to give their names, and obliged me to take a solemn oath not to mention the name of my friend with the black bag. I have already offered the letter to Lord Hartington and to the Editor of the *Pall Mall Gazette* but they have both declined to have anything to do with it. If you use it, I must request you to send me a cheque for £1,000 and you must pledge yourself never to give up the name of Hammond. He is a very worthy man, and he fears that if it were known that he had given me the letter some Tory would shoot him.

Your obedient servant,
E. C. HOUSTON

The enclosure read as follows:

Hatfield House,
October 17

My dear Lord Arthur,

There is a good deal of evidence against you, although the Lord Chancellor and the Attorney General have decided that the evidence of identity is not sufficient, but I hear a rumour that more evidence can be obtained. I can count upon the Chancellor standing to his guns, but I am not quite so sure of Webster. He, you know, will have to answer to that scoundrel Labouchere in the House of Commons, when he brings on the subject, and he is getting shaky. Perhaps he will be forced to issue a warrant.

Yours very truly,
SALISBURY

'Evidently someone is trying to Pigott me,' Labby wrote in the same issue of *Truth* which contained his article on Salisbury, and in which he published the letters. 'I do not hesitate to say that the letters are not from those from whom they profess to be written. It is really shameful that two such good men and true as Lord Salisbury and Mr. Houston should be selected for this reprehensible hoax.'

During the next month, the editor of *Truth* made only two brief references to the Government's action over Somerset, and thereafter he dropped the subject altogether. The first appeared on 20 March:

> I observe that I am now charged with 'gross impertinence' in Tory newspapers for having raised the question of the action of the Government in the case of Lord Arthur Somerset, and I make no doubt that there are many persons who really think that it was an impertinence of the grossest kind. That there should be one law for a nobleman and another for a man of low estate is so rooted in the mind of every flunkey and lickspittle, that he is unable to understand how any one can take a different view. I can only say that if I again catch Lord Chancellors, Attorney-Generals, and Prime Ministers putting their heads together, with the result that, whilst poor men are sent to prison, a warrant against a nobleman, charged with the same offence, is held over for months, and then only issued when it is known that he has escaped from the country, I shall expose this perversion of justice.

Labouchere's final swipe at the Establishment was delivered a fortnight later when he wrote that 'the name of Lord Arthur Somerset having been removed from the commission of the peace for Monmouthshire, the Duke of Beaufort, who is Lord Lieutenant of the County, has consoled himself by making eleven new magistrates, of whom only three are Liberals.'

On 21 March, Mr. W. H. Smith called at the Treasury Solicitor's office in order to find out how Labouchere had been able to secure so many details for his speech in the House of Commons. The Assistant Public Prosecutor, Hamilton Cuffe, was consequently asked to prepare a report. Much had been obtained from the various police court proceedings and also probably from Newton, Cuffe told the Leader of the House. One remark of Labby's particularly exercised Smith's mind, namely that the Public Prosecutor knew that the police had got certain clues as to who frequented the house in Cleveland Street and that certain names had been mentioned. 'As regards Lord Arthur Somerset,' Cuffe commented, 'this might be known to Mr. Labouchere from the newspapers or through Mr. Newton;' but, as regards others, the names mentioned 'ought only to have been known to the police and ourselves.' Cuffe suggested that Saul, who had given evidence in the Parke trial, 'may have made some communication', based on his statement to the police, which reached Labouchere. However, Cuffe assured Smith that, although copies of the statement had been sent to the Attorney General and the Home Secretary, 'it has always been kept under lock and key in this Department.'[1]

Then there was the allegation that Constable Hanks, who had been sent down to Badminton for the Dowager Duchess of Beaufort's funeral, was withdrawn by the Public Prosecutor after the policeman had made his report. For Smith's information, Cuffe recalled how he had sent the Lord Chancellor a telegram on 6 October asking for his opinion as to whether the contemplated prosecution of Somerset should proceed. Anticipating, as he then did, instructions to proceed on the 7th, Cuffe said he warned Inspector Abberline at Scotland Yard to be within reach. Two days later he received the Lord Chancellor's opinion, advising no proceedings on the existing evidence.

> On the 10th I wrote to Mr. Monro, I think saying I had no instructions to arrest. My action, or inaction was of course known to the police and though I do not remember anything being said about the withdrawal of the constable my inaction may have produced that result.

But Cuffe gave no indication of how Labouchere could have obtained a copy of Hanks's report to Abberline that he had attended the

[1] The originals of Saul's statements are in the Public Record Office (DPP1/95/4). Other names mentioned besides the Earl of Euston were Major Moet, 'a brother of the firm of wine merchants', Colonel Hosier, Mr. George Cavendish Bentinck, and a banker named Bevan.

funeral at Badminton on 8 October and how Somerset had been present.

Finally on the question of responsibility for Hammond being allowed to escape, Cuffe exonerated both the Metropolitan Police and his own office. 'If there was any *laches*,' he assured Smith, 'it was certainly with the Post Office Police, not Scotland Yard, in not giving notice or preventing Newlove from communicating with Hammond.' Nor was the Director of Public Prosecutions in any way to blame, said Cuffe, since on the date Hammond got away the Public Prosecutor 'had never heard of the occurrence at the Post Office.'

Incidentally it was widely believed at the time that the 'certain clues' in the possession of the police, to which Labby referred in his speech, consisted of a ledger containing Hammond's accounts with his aristocratic customers and that the police, 'acting on the orders of a high personage whose name was in the book of sin,' destroyed it. This was a fabrication. It is true that there was a book belonging to Hammond which was seized by the police, probably at the time they arrested Veck, but according to Avory's clerk, who should have been in a position to know, 'there was no name in it of any person in society or public life. The book was burnt, but it could never have been of any use to the prosecution.'[1]

From Somerset's point of view, it was a great pity that he did not return and face the music, as his father and other members of his family urged him to do. No doubt his sudden and precipitate flight on 18 October 1889 added to the presumption of his guilt, though whether the Government would not have eventually issued the warrant for his arrest had he remained in England (as Brett believed) is open to question. As late as the beginning of November the Lord Chancellor still doubted whether there was enough evidence to justify the issue of the warrant, but he left the final decision to Webster, who decided to go ahead with it, as we have seen. The greatest point in Somerset's favour was that the evidence against him was 'tainted', that is to say it was the testimony of accomplices who if

[1] F. W. Ashley. *My Sixty Years in the Law* (1936), p. 114. There is no mention of the book in the DPP papers in the Public Record Office.

it was true were equally guilty, and such testimony is always rightly open to suspicion, particularly in the absence of corroboration. The police had none of the incriminating letters which Allies told the Public Prosecutor that Somerset had written to him, since they had been destroyed. It is true there were the postal orders, but Somerset could always have pleaded that he had taken a fatherly interest in Allies and had been helping him since his dismissal from the Marlborough Club for theft.

If he had gone to George Lewis and retained a leading counsel like Russell or Lockwood to defend him, he might well have been acquitted, just as Euston was cleared of the charge Parke had made against him. In this case there was more credible evidence against Euston than that given by the male prostitute Saul, although it was not called. This was the statement of Newlove that Euston had visited the house more than once, and Newlove had no ulterior motive for incriminating Euston any more than he had Somerset. But with his family and friends, Somerset stuck to his excuse for having to leave England. This was, as Sir Dighton Probyn put it, that he had been forced to do so to screen another and that his lips were closed. The only conclusion therefore that could be drawn was that he was sacrificing himself to save Prince Eddy. Who else was there for whom he could make such a sacrifice?

Lord Arthur Somerset realised that in the circumstances he could never return to England, and that as a fugitive from justice he must face a long, dreary exile. In the event it was to last for thirty-six years. His sister, Lady Waterford, spent the latter part of March 1890 with him in the Paris suburb where he had settled under another name. She 'found the poor dear very much aged, but very quiet and natural and cheerful, and if only no one molests him to signify—i.e. if they don't insist on his moving on—he is better here than anywhere, and is as nearly happy as one could hope. This is such a snug rabbit hole, and he has done it up capitally and made all his surroundings as cheerful as possible.' He had been joined by his English servant, Farrow, who had looked after him for the past two years, but 'Arthur is really looking after Farrow who knows no French which is a terrible bore. There is no doubt it would be far better if he had a French servant . . .' On 20 March, Lady Waterford wrote to Brett from Paris:

> Unfortunately we were driving yesterday in a street cab, when Charlie Montagu walked by (some way off too in a broad street). I'm afraid he recognised Arthur—at least we thought he jumped. However, he is probably on his way to his father who is ill in Naples, so let us hope he won't talk, and at any rate he does not know where he lives.[1]

Although his name remained in Debrett and other reference books, Somerset's address did not appear, and his whereabouts and new name were to remain a closely guarded secret known only to his family and intimate friends like Brett. On her way back to Ireland Lady Waterford stopped briefly at Badminton to report to her parents and to write again to Brett:

> I left my poor dear Friday night, and we made up our minds to behave well. Poor thing! What a life—but he gets used to it, he says, and except for the misery to Father, Mother, etc., could get on if he could presently find something to do. Perhaps later he may manage some buying of horses for dealers but I have told him he *must* be patient. So he is, I must say, poor heart. I talked to Farrow who said he thought he should like to stay on very much and Arthur says he could not send him away which I quite see . . .
>
> My people are going out very soon *in bits*—not all at once—so as to spin themselves out, and I hope to go again in July. Arthur looks 1,000 but won't turn grey which is a pity and would disguise him better than anything. I will look for some stuff that would turn his hair gradually. It must not be done at once or the few people (shopkeepers) who know him in his new name would become suspicious.
>
> Of course, the most pitiable thing *of all* is my Mother's state—no wonder. She is as good and plucky as she can be; but her misery is so far beyond description that I don't see how her brain can stand it. However, God knows, and it is no use *my* bothering who don't

[1] Lord Charles Montagu (1860–1939) was a younger son of the 7th Duke of Manchester, who died in Naples at this time. His sister, Louisa, Countess of Gosford, was a Lady-in-Waiting to the Princess of Wales.

know anything. It is the knowledge of this misery that kills Arthur—for himself he says he is getting used to this wretched life. His rooms are so nice, not a bit overdone, but so simple and clean and pretty. I'm sure you will approve.

For Reginald Brett the painful business was now virtually over. On 20 November 1890, he made this brief entry in his journal: 'From June 1889 onwards, certain events in connection with a great sorrow to a personal friend and his unfortunate family occupied nearly all my time. They ended disastrously for all concerned in the closing months of last year. The worry of them was maintained through the first half of the present year.'

4

The publication of the original version of Oscar Wilde's tale of youthful corruption, *The Picture of Dorian Gray*, in *Lippincott's Monthly Magazine* in July 1890 attracted several hostile reviews, of which one showed that Cleveland Street had not been forgotten. 'Mr. Wilde has brains, and art, and style,' wrote the Tory journalist, Charles Whibley, in an unsigned notice for *The Scots Observer*, then edited by the poet, W. E. Henley; 'but if he can write for none but outlawed noblemen and perverted telegraph boys, the sooner he takes to tailoring (or some other decent trade) the better for his own reputation and the public morals.' There is no evidence that Wilde ever went to the house in Cleveland Street, but Henley may have heard some gossip to the effect that he had done so, since the editor is on record as having asked Whibley what was the nature of 'this dreadful scandal about Mr. Oscar Wilde'.

With the exception of the correspondence, official and otherwise, of those concerned, which has already been quoted in this book, the Cleveland Street scandal, though a burning topic in the London clubs and newspapers while it lasted, was not a subject to lend itself to general discussion or comment outside Government and legal circles, and in the conventional atmosphere of the period it was generally ignored by Victorian letter writers, at least in their published correspondence.

An exception who followed the case with obsessive interest from his home in Switzerland was the homosexual writer, John Addington Symonds—'Mr. Soddington Symonds', as the poet Swinburne irreverently called him. At this time he was engaged in writing *A Problem of Modern Ethics*, a monograph which he had privately printed in a strictly limited edition of fifty copies and in which he attacked the 'Labouchere amendment' to the Criminal Law Amendment Act of 1885 as an encouragement to the kind of blackmail in which Hammond and others indulged. Symonds used to visit Venice where he befriended a young gondolier, but this attachment did not prevent him from being invited to official functions. In a letter to the critic, Edmund Gosse, later librarian of the House of Lords, who was also tortured by homosexual longings, Symonds described how a fellow guest at a state banquet, who was an officer from a P. & O. ship then in port, brought up the subject of Cleveland Street 'and volunteered the opinion that it was absurd to disqualify by law passions which seemed so harmless and instructive, although he added that his own (I suspect very free) self-indulgences were in the opposite direction.' This led Symonds to confess to Gosse that 'the way of thinking among the proletariat, honest citizens, etc., in Italy and Switzerland, where I alone have fraternised, is all in favour of free trade.'

On his return from his tour of India in May 1890, Prince Eddy was created Duke of Clarence and Avondale and Earl of Athlone, as a mark of his grandmother the Queen's confidence. Labouchere, who had never believed that the Prince had anything to do with the disreputable goings on in Cleveland Street, attacked the new creation in a characteristic editorial in *Truth*.

> The titles selected for Prince Albert Victor are certainly not well chosen. The only Duke of Clarence who is known in history is the numskull who was deservedly drowned in a butt of malmsey, and during the present century the title was associated with the aberrations and extravagances for which William IV was unenviably notorious until he ascended the throne. The last Earl of Athlone was Ginkle, the General of William III who fought at the Boyne, and

who defeated the Irish at Athlone and at Aughrim, and whose memory was execrated in Ireland for more than a century on account of the shameful violated treaty. The Scotch title is utterly meaningless, for it is taken from an unknown village in Lanarkshire. George III was considerably more felicitous in his decisions when choosing titles for his sons.

No wonder Queen Victoria disliked 'that horrible lying Labouchere', as she referred to him, a sentiment shared by the Prince of Wales, who called him 'that viper'. It was the Queen's objection to Labby's association with *Truth*, rather than his opposition to the Royal Grants by Parliament, that was to prove fatal to his prospects of office, since when the Liberals came back to power in 1892 Gladstone dared not include him in the Cabinet. However, he was consoled with a Privy Councillorship when he retired from political life in 1905 to settle in Florence. Here the presence of Lord Arthur Somerset's brother Henry no doubt served to remind him from time to time of Cleveland Street. 'One of the very few quite honest MPs who always told the truth and was always most amusing', was how his parliamentary colleague, Wilfred Scawen Blunt, described him.

What susequently befell the other principal characters in this narrative is also worth brief mention. In June 1890, James Monro, the Metropolitan Police Commissioner, sent in his resignation, which was accepted. The principal reason for his action was his belief that the Police Pensions Bill, which the Home Secretary was about to introduce into Parliament, did not meet the just claims of the force. He was also dissatisfied with the Government's handling of the Cleveland Street case. Another reason was the Home Secretary's intention to appoint his (the Home Secretary's) Private Secretary to the post of Assistant Commissioner, vacant by the sudden death of Colonel Pearson, who had 'blabbed' about Somerset, instead of the Chief Constable whom Monro had recommended. 'My views as to the police administration unfortunately differ in many important respects from those held by the Secretary of State,' Monro wrote in his letter of resignation to Matthews, 'and I have received clear indication that the duties of the successor of Colonel Pearson are to be entrusted to a gentleman, who however estimable personally has no police, military or legal training.' Incidentally, the latter was a brilliant young civil servant named Evelyn Ruggles-Brise, then aged thirty-two. However, the Home Secretary had second thoughts and did appoint Monro's nominee to the vacancy. It was fortunate for the public service that he did so, since it enabled Ruggles-Brise to become Chairman of the Prison Commission a few years later and to found the famous Borstal system of juvenile-delinquent reform. As for Monro, he returned to India and devoted the rest of his active life to founding and carrying on a medical mission in Bengal.

Inspector Abberline retired in 1892, his salary at the time amounting to the incredible sum of £206 13s. 4d. a year.

Nothing more is known of Veck, Newlove, Allies and the telegraph boys. On 10 March 1890, Hammond was reported in the *New York Herald* as saying that 'if the parties implicated' in the Cleveland Street scandal 'knew what was to their interest, they would communicate immediately by cable to a person known to them by an initial, and whose present residence is 2232½ Front Street, Seattle.' This was in fact where Hammond was living with a retired professional 'Madam' named Adele Gayet, as already noted. Hammond was also said to have mentioned the name of a man who visited his house in Cleveland Street and whose father occupied 'a prominent position' in London. 'It is observed from these remarks that Hammond wants money,' the *Herald* correspondent in Seattle cabled his New York office. 'He has torn off the mask and now threatens to disclose the names of several other men high in station who were, as he alleged, customers at his house of crime. Seattle is undoubtedly fast becoming a place of interest to certain men in London, and the end is not yet.' In the event, that was the end of the matter, since in spite of anything Hammond may have said, the authorities in London took no further steps to prosecute anyone else whose name had been mentioned.

As for the Duke of Clarence and Avondale, he did not enjoy his new titles for long and he never came to the throne. Towards the end of 1891 he became engaged to be married to Princess Mary of Teck, who was afterwards to marry his younger brother George. The wedding was fixed for 27 February 1892. But it was not to be. On 7 January, the day before his twenty-eighth birthday, the royal Duke went out shooting at Sandringham. On getting back to the house he collapsed with influenza. Pneumonia quickly developed and a week later he was dead.

'A most harrowing day down here,' wrote Oliver Montagu, who had hastened to Sandringham to offer his condolences to the grief-stricken family. 'The Prince broke down terribly at our first meeting; as did also the poor Princess, but they all got calmer after and took me to see the poor boy 3 different times before I left again. He looked quite peaceful and calm. The funeral is military at Windsor on Wednesday [20 January]. The Princess thought she could not bear it and I don't think she will go. I also saw Teck and poor Princess May who has behaved beautifully throughout.'

Montagu himself barely lived another twelve months. He had re-tired on half pay in the previous year, at the age of forty-seven. Shortly after the Duke of Clarence's death, he had a bad attack of bronchial influenza. On medical advice he decided to spend the following winter in Egypt, then much favoured by English tourists thanks to the enterprise of Thomas Cook & Son. He was taken ill again in Cairo a few weeks after his arrival, this time with pneumonia, and he died in the Hotel Continental there on 24 January 1893. 'He proved himself an excellent officer and the Queen's service has to mourn a very great and valuable comrade,' wrote Prince George to the dead man's brother, the Earl of Sandwich. Another letter of sympathy came from that Prince's imperial cousin in Berlin. 'I knew him well and always liked him for his open manly ways,' the Kaiser wrote of his 'so untimely end' to his other brother, Rear-Admiral Victor Montagu. 'There is now since his death a gentleman less in England! And a thorough one too! God bless him!'

Princess Alexandra of Wales, whose great friend Oliver Montagu had been, was naturally much affected by his death. 'It is indeed terrible to think that we shall never see his dear face on earth again,' she wrote on learning the news, 'but thank God he is at rest and peace with our Father in Heaven.' To her whom he had loved with a peculiarly unselfish devotion, he was 'the best and truest of men, one to be relied on in every relation of life, faithful, discreet and trust-worthy.' He had certainly been so with his friend and fellow officer, Arthur Somerset. And on the first anniversary of Oliver's death the Princess wrote again to his brother, Lord Sandwich: 'I wanted you so much to know how constantly my thoughts were with you on that dreadful day.' At the same time she sent flowers which she asked should be laid on his grave, a tribute which she continued to pay without fail on each anniversary until his brother's death twenty-two years later, the brother whom Oliver would have succeeded as Earl of Sandwich had he lived.

Nor did Lord Euston succeed to his titled inheritance. However, his admission of his interest in *poses plastiques* in the Parke trial had no adverse effect upon his subsequent career. Already a prominent Freemason, he became Grand Master of the Mark Masons. He was also appointed an ADC by King Edward VII in the coronation year. But he never became Duke of Grafton, since he died of dropsy in 1912 when his father was still alive. On the other hand, in spite of serving a twelve months prison term, Ernest Parke lived to become a respected member of the National Liberal Club and a Justice of the Peace for his native Warwickshire, to which he retired after a success-ful career as a provincial newspaper editor and director of the Northern Newspaper Company in Darlington.

It was otherwise with Arthur Newton. For twenty years after his short spell in prison, he enjoyed a very lucrative practice, culminating in his defence of the poisoner Crippen, which attracted world-wide interest and brought him an immense amount of advertisement. But the Crippen case proved to be the beginning of his undoing. For what the Law Society held to be unethical proceedings in the conduct of Crippen's defence, he was suspended from practice for twelve months in 1911. Two years later he was charged, along with two con-federates, one of whom absconded, with obtaining by fraud and false pretences in connection with land deals in Canada a large sum of money from a young Austrian who had come into a big fortune. The case was tried at the Old Bailey where Newton insisted on conducting his own defence, although there must have been many able counsel who would gladly have given their services to a solicitor who had in his time delivered many highly-marked briefs to them. In the event Newton was found Guilty and sentenced to three years penal servitude. Naturally this brought his professional career to an end, since he was struck off the rolls at the instance of the Law Society.

The solicitor's former client, Lord Arthur Somerset, continued to live incognito in France, eventually moving from his rooms in the Paris suburbs to a villa in Hyères. This was the oldest and most southerly of the French Riviera resorts, situated on the slope of a steep hill some three miles from the sea between Toulon and St. Raphael and sheltered from the cold north and north-east winds by the Maures mountains. Besides a British Vice-Consul, the town had an English church, a casino, a good public library and public gardens, a fine avenue of palms, and a large square where the municipal band would play twice weekly in the season. It was here, in the Villa Sophie, that Somerset lived out his life, tended by a French cook and servants and an English companion named James Andrew Neale. By this time his elder brother Henry had moved from Monaco to Florence, but they were still able to meet from time to time. However, unlike Henry, Arthur Somerset never returned to England, even for the briefest visit, since the warrant for his arrest remained on the record until his death. Their sister Blanche died in 1897, followed two years later by 'The Old Blue 'Un' and in 1906 by the Duchess of Beaufort. Arthur Somerset himself died at the Villa Sophie on 26 May 1926. To his nephew, the Marquess of Worcester, who had succeeded to the Dukedom and Badminton two years previously, he left the residue of his estate, sworn for English probate at under £17,500, in addition to his property in France, which was disposed of separately as required by French law. He was buried in the 'English section' of the town cemetery in Hyères under a headstone recording his true name and paternity, the dates of his birth and death, and the text 'The Memory of the Just is Blessed.' So far as the present writer has been able to ascertain, no obituary notice was published in any English newspaper.

Why Lord Arthur Somerset's remains were not brought back to England and interred in the family burial vault at Badminton is unclear. Since the warrant for his arrest had never been rescinded, there may have been a fear of possible complications with the English customs authorities, if the coffin had been opened for purposes of identification on arrival at the port of entry. Incidentally, a 'notice of abandonment' has recently been affixed to the grave by the local authorities in Hyères, but this would appear to be illegal since the municipal records indicate that the grave was purchased in perpetuity by the Somerset family and belongs to the Duke of Beaufort or his heirs and assigns.

Reginald Brett, who had striven so hard to help his friend in his trouble, survived him by four years, having long before succeeded his father as the second Viscount Esher. Few men of his time could have wielded more power behind the scenes through his influence with the royal family and the leading contemporary political figures than Lord Esher until his retirement at the end of the First World War. But there was nothing more that he could do for Arthur Somerset. Perhaps Esher might have done something had he accepted the vice royalty of India which he was offered by King Edward VII and which he turned down on the ground that with his opportunity for influencing vital decisions at the centre, the post of proconsul 'would be (it sounds vain, but it isn't) parochial.'

In his old age, in the year after Somerset's death, Esher produced *Cloud-Capp'd Towers*, a volume of his impressions of some of the men and women whom he had known in his Victorian and Edwardian heyday and of the period generally from his time as a schoolboy at Eton with Somerset. It could hardly be expected that there could be anything about Cleveland Street and his friend in such a discreet work. Some things are best left unsaid. Yet it was a world with its royalties and intrigues and scandals, of which the Cleveland Street affair was perhaps the most scandalous, a world which vanished with their lives.

Who's Who

ABBERLINE, Chief Inspector Frederick (1840–1916). Detective at Scotland Yard in charge of Cleveland Street case. Had previously investigated the 'Jack the Ripper' murders in 1888. Joined the Metropolitan Police, 1863. Appointed one of the first Divisional Inspectors when the CID was formed in 1878, covering the Whitechapel and Bethnal Green area where he acquired an unrivalled knowledge of London's East End. Transferred to Scotland Yard, 1887; promoted Chief Inspector, 1889: retired, 1892.

ALBERT VICTOR, H.R.H. Prince (1864–1892). Elder son of Prince and Princess of Wales. Familiarly known as Prince Eddy until he was created Duke of Clarence in 1890. *Educ:* Trinity College, Cambridge. Captain in army and A.D.C. to Queen Victoria. Engaged to Princess Mary of Teck but died of pneumonia before marriage.

ALLIES, Algernon Edward (*b.* 1870). Ex-waiter at Marlborough Club. Son of William Allies, coachman, of Sudbury, Suffolk. Befriended by Lord Arthur Somerset who gave him money after he had been dismissed by the club for theft, and against whom he subsequently swore an information. Under police protection for several months. Wrote to the Duke of Beaufort in July 1890 that he was 'destitute'.

AVORY, Horace (1851–1935). Junior Treasury Counsel. Son of Henry Avory, Clerk of the Central Criminal Court. *Educ*: King's College, London; Corpus Christi College, Cambridge. Barrister, Inner Temple, 1875. Judge of the High Court, 1910–35.

BARRINGTON, Hon. Eric (1847–1918). Private secretary to the Marquess of Salisbury at Foreign Office. Younger son of 6th Viscount Barrington. *Educ*: Eton. Later Assistant Under-Secretary of State. K.C.B., 1902.

BEAUFORT, Henry Charles FitzRoy Somerset, 8th Duke of (1824–1899). Lord Lieutenant of Monmouth and large land-owner. *Educ*: Eton. Former army officer, Conservative MP, and Master of the Horse. Married Lady Georgiana Curzon, daughter of 1st Earl Howe, and was father of Lord Arthur Somerset. Well known as sportsman and inventor of game of badminton, so-called after his estate in Gloucestershire. Nicknamed 'The Old Blue 'Un' and notorious for his love affairs.

BRETT, Hon. Reginald Baliol (1852–1930). Son of 1st Viscount Esher, Master of the Rolls, and friend of Lord Arthur Somerset. *Educ*: Eton; Trinity College, Cambridge. Private Secretary to the Liberal leader Lord Hartington, 1878–85. Liberal MP 1880–85. After losing seat, he retired for some years to his house near Windsor, where he was admitted to Queen Victoria's private circle. As Secretary to the Office of Works, he organised the Queen's Diamond Jubilee and King Edward VII's coronation. Later as Chairman of War Office Reconstruction Committee he recommended creation of Army Council and General Staff. Knew everyone in politics and society and wielded great influence behind the scenes. Succeeded father as 2nd Viscount, 1899. Refused vice-royalty of India. Author of *Cloud Capp'd Towers* (1927) and co-editor of Queen Victoria's correspondence, with A. C. Benson.

CAVE, Sir Lewis (1832–1897). Judge of the High Court. *Educ*: Rugby; Lincoln College, Oxford. Barrister, Inner Temple, 1859. Edited Law Reports and legal text-books.

CHAMBERS, Sir Thomas (1814–1891). Recorder of London. *Educ*: Clare Hall, Cambridge. Barrister, Middle Temple, 1840. Sat in House of Commons as Liberal for 25 years. Advocated legal reforms.

COURTNEY, Leonard Henry (1832–1918). Chairman of Committees and Deputy Speaker of House of Commons. Created Lord Courtney of Penwith, 1906.

CRANBROOK, Gathorne Gathorne-Hardy, Viscount (1814–1906). Lord President of the Council. *Educ*: Eton; Oriel College, Oxford. Created Earl of Cranbrook, 1892. Ardent sportsman and broad churchman.

CUFFE, Hon. Hamilton (1848–1934). Assistant Director of Public Prosecutions, 2nd son of 3rd Earl of Desart. *Educ*: Radley; Trinity College, Cambridge. Served in Royal Navy, 1860–63. Barrister, Inner Temple, 1872. Treasury Solicitor and Director of Public Prosecutions, 1894–1909. Prosecuted Oscar Wilde, 1895. Succeeded elder brother as 5th and last Earl of Desart, 1898.

DE GALLO, Adolphe. Interpreter at Great Marlborough Street Police Court. Also acted as inquiry agent for solicitor Arthur Newton. Grand Jury refused to bring in a true bill against him for conspiracy, February 1890.

EUSTON, Henry James Fitzroy, Earl of (1848–1912). Eldest son of 7th Duke of Grafton. *Educ*: Harrow. Commissioned in Rifle Brigade. Married variety actress Kate Cooke, whom he divorced. Succeeded in prosecuting Ernest Parke to conviction for criminal libel, January 1890. A prominent Freemason. Died during his father's lifetime, so never succeeded to Grafton dukedom.

GILL, Charles (1851–1923). Junior Treasury Counsel. *Educ*: Royal School, Dungannon. Barrister, Middle Temple, 1874. Recorder of Chichester, 1890–1921. Knighted, 1921.

HALL, Charles (1843–1900). QC and Conservative MP. Attorney General to Prince of Wales. *Educ*: Harrow; Trinity College, Cambridge. Barrister, Lincoln's Inn, 1866. Knighted, 1890. Succeeded Sir Thomas Chambers as Recorder of London, 1892.

HALSBURY, Hardinge Stanley Giffard, Lord (1823–1921). Lord Chancellor. *Educ*: Merton College, Oxford. Barrister, Inner Temple, 1850. Occupied Woolsack with two short breaks for 18 years. Created Earl, 1898. Diehard Conservative.

HAMMOND, Charles (*b.* 1854). Professional male prostitute, blackmailer and brothel-keeper. Married a French prostitute known as 'Madame Caroline', by whom he had two sons. Occupied house at 19 Cleveland Street from latter part of 1885 until his flight on 6 July 1889. In October 1889 went to America where he settled in Seattle.

HANKS, Constable Luke. Attached to Post Office.

HANNAY, James (1826–1903). Magistrate at Great Marlborough Street Police Court. *Educ*: St. John's College, Cambridge. Barrister, Inner Temple, 1852. Retired, 1898.

HAWKINS, Sir Henry (1817–1907). Judge of the High Court. *Educ*: Bedford School. Barrister, Middle Temple, 1843. Best known for his trial of criminal cases, being unjustly nicknamed 'Hanging Hawkins', though he favoured leniency, particularly for first offenders. Created Lord Brampton, 1899. Fond of horse racing and was a convert to the Roman Catholic Faith.

KNOLLYS, Sir Francis (1837–1924). Private secretary to Prince of Wales. Created Viscount Knollys, 1911.

LABOUCHERE, Henry Du Pré (1831–1912). Editor of *Truth* and Liberal MP with Charles Bradlaugh for Northampton. *Educ*: Eton; Trinity College, Cambridge. Spent 10 years in diplomatic service before becoming a journalist. One of the most powerful Radicals in the House of Commons. Took leading part in exposing Cleveland Street scandal.

LENNOX, Lord Algernon (1847–1921). Colonel, Grenadier Guards, and ADC to Commander-in-Chief, Duke of Cambridge. Younger son of 6th Duke of Richmond and Lennox.

LOCKWOOD, Frank (1847–1897). QC and Liberal MP. *Educ*: Caius College, Cambridge. Barrister, Lincoln's Inn, 1872. Solicitor General, 1894–95. Well known caricaturist and contributor to *Punch*. Knighted, 1894.

LUSHINGTON, Godfrey (1832–1907). Permanent Under-Secretary, Home Office. *Educ*: Rugby; Balliol College, Oxford. Barrister, Inner Temple, 1848. Knighted, 1892.

MATHEWS, Charles Willie (1850–1920). Senior Treasury Counsel. *Educ*: Eton. Barrister, Middle Temple, 1872. Knighted, 1907. Director of Public Prosecutions, 1908. Created baronet, 1917.

MATTHEWS, Henry (1826–1913). Home Secretary. First Roman Catholic to become a cabinet minister since passing of Emancipation Act. *Educ*: Paris and London Universities. Barrister, Lincoln's Inn, 1850. QC, 1868. Created Lord Llandaff, 1895.

MONRO, James (1838–1920). Commissioner of Metropolitan Police. *Educ*: Edinburgh High School; Edinburgh and Berlin Universities. Entered Bengal Civil Service, 1857, later serving as magistrate, judge and Inspector-General of Police. Assistant Commissioner, Scotland Yard, 1884–88. Resigned, 1890, and returned to Bengal where he founded and ran the Ranighat Medical Mission.

MONTAGU, Hon. Oliver (1844–1893). Colonel commanding the Royal Horse Guards. Younger son of the 8th Earl of Sandwich. Devoted admirer and friend of the Princess of Wales. Died of pneumonia in Cairo.

NEWLOVE, Henry Horace (*b.* 1871). Post Office employee. Lived with his mother in Camden Town. Convicted of homosexual offences and procuring at Central Criminal Court and sentenced to four months in the House of Correction with hard labour, September 1889.

NEWTON, Arthur John Edward (1860–1930). Son of Edward Newton, manager of the Legal and General Assurance Society. *Educ*: Hawtrey's School and Cheltenham College. Admitted solicitor, 1884. Practised largely in the police courts. Defended Veck and Newlove and acted for Lord Arthur Somerset; also assisted Hammond in going to America. Sentenced by Mr. Justice Cave to 6 weeks imprisonment for conspiracy to obstruct

[252]

the course of justice, May 1890, but not suspended by Law Society. Acted for Alfred Taylor, Oscar Wilde's co-defendant, in the Wilde trials in 1895. Suspended for 12 months in 1911 in connection with his defence of the poisoner Crippen. In July 1913 was sentenced to three years penal servitude for fraud and obtaining money by false pretences, and was subsequently struck off the rolls.

O'CONNOR, Thomas Power (1848–1929). Irish Nationalist MP and editor of *The Star*, the London evening paper which he founded in 1887. Son of a garrison billiard-marker in Athlone. *Educ*: Queen's College, Galway. First President of Board of Film Censors, 1917. For many years 'Father' of the House of Commons.

PARKE, Ernest (1860–1944). Editor of the *North London Press*; also worked on *The Star*. *Educ*: Stratford-on-Avon Grammar School. Later director of the Northern Newspaper Co., Darlington and JP for Warwickshire. Fervent Radical and friend of T. P. O'Connor.

PEARSON, Lt.-Colonel Richard (1831–1890). Assistant Commissioner of Metropolitan Police. *Educ*: Eton; Sandhurst. Commissioned in Grenadier Guards and served in Crimean War, in which he was highly decorated. Appointed to Scotland Yard, 1881. Moved in society circles.

PERKINS, William Meech. Telegraph boy at General Post Office. Lived with his mother in Pentonville. Procured by Newlove for Hammond. Suspended from duty and dismissed, December 1889.

POLAND, Harry Bodkin (1829–1928). Senior Treasury Counsel and adviser to Home Office in criminal matters. *Educ*: St. Paul's School. Barrister, Inner Temple, 1851. Recorder of Dover, 1874–1901. Knighted, 1895.

PROBYN, Sir Dighton (1833–1924). Comptroller and Treasurer to Prince of Wales. Previously had distinguished army career, winning Victoria Cross in 1857 and retiring with rank of General.

RUSSELL, Sir Charles (1832–1900). QC and Liberal MP. *Educ*: Trinity College, Dublin. Barrister, Lincoln's Inn, 1859. First Roman Catholic Attorney General since the Reformation, 1886, 1892–94. Leading counsel for Parnell in the Parnell Commission, in which he exposed the Pigott forgeries. Created Lord Russell of Killowen, 1894. Lord Chief Justice of England, 1894–1900.

SALISBURY, Robert Arthur Talbot Gascoyne-Cecil, 3rd Marquess of (1830–1903). Prime Minister and Foreign Secretary. *Educ*: Eton; Christ Church, Oxford. Lived at Hatfield House in Hertfordshire.

SAUL, John (*b.* circa 1854). Professional male prostitute known as 'Dublin Jack.' Principal defence witness in the Parke trial. Previously involved in the Dublin Castle scandals, 1884. Made two statements to police about the Cleveland Street case, August 1889.

SLADDEN, Constable Richard. Detailed to keep watch on suspect house in Cleveland Street.

SMITH, William Henry (1825–1891). First Lord of the Treasury and Leader of the House of Commons. *Educ*: Tavistock Grammar School. Partner in father's news-agency business, which he developed enormously by securing railway-bookstall monopoly. As First Lord of the Admiralty in Disraeli's Government, he was good humorously lampooned by Gilbert and Sullivan in *H.M.S. Pinafore*. Died of overwork. His widow was created Viscountess Hambledon, 1891.

SOMERSET, Lord Arthur (1851–1926). Major in Royal Horse Guards and superintendent of the Prince of Wales's stables, known familiarly as 'Podge'. 3rd son of 8th Duke of Beaufort. *Educ*: Eton. Served with distinction in Egyptian and Nile campaigns, 1882–84, being wounded and decorated. Unsuccessfully contested Chippenham Division of Wiltshire as Conservative in 1885 election. Left England permanently, 18 October 1889, resigning his commission and appointment in the Prince of Wales's household prior to the issue of a warrant for his arrest. Eventually settled at Hyères on the French Riviera, where he died and was buried.

SOMERSET, Rt. Hon. Lord Henry (1849–1932). 2nd son of 8th Duke of Beaufort; known familiarly as 'Penna'. *Educ*: Eton. Former Conservative MP and Controller of Queen Victoria's Household. After his wife, Isabel, daughter and heiress of the 3rd and last Earl Somers, secured a judicial separation with the custody of their only child, he settled in Monaco and later in Florence, where he achieved some reputation as a popular song-writer. Most of the poems in his *Songs of Adieu* (1889) are said to have been inspired by his love for a young man named Henry Smith who was the cause of the break up of his marriage and subsequently emigrated to New Zealand.

STEAD, William Thomas (1849–1912). Editor of the *Pall Mall Gazette*. His 'Maiden Tribute of Modern Babylon' articles exposing juvenile prostitution led to the passing of the Criminal Law Amendment Act, 1885, and also to his own trial and imprisonment. Drowned in the sinking of the *Titanic*.

STEPHENSON, Sir Augustus (1827–1904). Treasury Solicitor and Director of Public Prosecutions. *Educ*: Caius College, Cambridge. Barrister, Lincoln's Inn, 1852. Retired, 1894.

SWINSCOW, Charles Thomas (*b*. 1874). Telegraph boy at General Post Office. Lived with his mother at Highbury. Swore information against Lord Arthur Somerset. Suspended and dismissed from duty, December 1889.

TAYLORSON, Frederick. Managing clerk to solicitor Arthur Newton. Indicted with him for conspiracy, but insisted on pleading not guilty and was acquitted, May 1890.

THICKBROOM, Charles Ernest (*b*. 1872). Telegraph boy at General Post Office. Swore information against Lord Arthur Somerset. Suspended from duty and dismissed, December 1889.

TYRWHITT, Hon. Harry (1854–1891). Equerry-in-waiting to Prince of Wales. Eldest son of Sir Henry Tyrwhitt, Bart, and Baroness Berners.

VAUGHAN, James (1814–1906). Magistrate at Bow Street Police Court. *Educ*: Worcester College, Oxford. Barrister, Middle Temple, 1839. Knighted, 1897. Retired, 1899.

VECK, George Daniel (*b.* 1849). Ex-Post Office employee. Posed as clergyman and lived with Hammond in Cleveland Street. Convicted of homosexual offences at Central Criminal Court and sentenced to nine months imprisonment with hard labour, September 1889.

WATERFORD, Blanche Marchioness of (1857–1897). Only sister of Lord Arthur Somerset, whom she stood by most loyally. She married John Henry, 5th Marquess of Waterford (1844–95), as his second wife in 1874. 'It is impossible to convey to anyone how delightful and ridiculous both my parents were,' wrote their daughter Lady Clodagh Anson in *In Victorian Days*, 'so quick-witted that nobody ever had to explain anything, and yet so humorous and kind, no pretence or affectation and absolutely free from all hypocrisy.'

WEBSTER, Sir Richard Everard (1842–1915). Attorney General. *Educ*: Charterhouse; Trinity College, Cambridge. Barrister, Lincoln's Inn, 1868. Created Lord Alverstone, 1900. Lord Chief Justice of England, 1900–13.

WEGUELIN, Hugh. Stockbroker. Friend of Brett and Somerset, with office in Bartholomew Lane and rooms in Sackville Street. Brother of painter John Weguelin, R.W.S.

WRIGHT, George Alma (*b.* 1872). Telegraph boy at General Post Office. Procured by Newlove for Hammond. Suspended from duty and dismissed, December 1889.

Note on Sources

A COLLECTION OF official papers on the Cleveland Street case, formerly in the custody of the Director of Public Prosecutions, has recently been transferred to the Public Record Office, where it is now open without restriction. The collection is contained in seven boxes (DPP 1/95/1–7) and comprises correspondence, legal opinions, police reports and statements, transcripts of court proceedings, sworn informations, indictments and newspaper extracts. The two extant bundles of Home Office files on the case (HO 144/477/X24427 and X24427a) are officially closed to the public until 1991 and 1992 respectively. But in exceptional circumstances they may be made available for research by special permission of the Home Secretary, and they have been so used in this book.

The important correspondence of the second Viscount Esher (then the Hon. Reginald Brett) has been bound up in a volume labelled 'The Case of Lord Arthur Somerset' and is now preserved with the rest of the Esher Papers in Churchill College, Cambridge. The Salisbury Papers, which also contain a number of important letters, formerly in the library of Christ Church, Oxford, are now at Hatfield. Some letters from and about Lord Arthur Somerset's commanding officer, the Hon. Oliver Montagu, are in the possession of his great-nephew, Mr. Victor Montagu, at Mapperton, Dorset.

The Halsbury Papers, which have likewise been consulted, are in the British Museum.

The most important printed source is *The North London Press*, which published Hammond's letters (in the issues of 21 December 1889 and 11 January 1890) as well as accounts of the prosecution of Parke and of Newton. Labouchere's editorials and articles in *Truth* are particularly relevant. Other journals which gave accounts of the scandal and legal proceedings with comments include *Reynold's Newspaper*, *The Star*, *The Pall Mall Gazette*, *The Daily News*, *The Times*, *The Illustrated Police News*, and *The New York Herald*.

The report of the debate in the House of Commons initiated by Labouchere on 28 February 1890 and replied to on behalf of the Government by the Attorney General (Sir Richard Webster) is in *Hansard's Parliamentary Debates*, 3rd Series, vol. 341, cols. 1534–1611, and that of Lord Salisbury's 'Personal Explanation' in the House of Lords is in the same volume, cols. 1618–19. These two parliamentary reports are essential source material.

The following printed books contain useful background information on the period and its leading personalities: Lady Clodagh Anson. *In Victorian Days* (1957); Georgina Battiscombe. *Queen Alexandra* (1969); E. F. Benson. *As We Were* (1930); Horatia Durant. *The Somerset Sequence* (1951); Lord Esher. *Cloud Capp'd Towers* (1927); Kathleen Fitzpatrick. *Lady Henry Somerset* (1924); Michael Harrison. *Clarence* (1972); H. Montgomery Hyde. *Their Good Names* (1970); Philippe Jullian. *Edward and the Edwardians* (1967); Philip Magnus. *King Edward the Seventh* (1964); J. F. Moylan. *Scotland Yard and the Metropolitan Police* (1929); T. P. O'Connor. *Memoirs of an Old Parliamentarian* (1929); Cecil Roberts *Alfred Fripp* (1932); Timothy d'Arch Smith. *Love in Earnest* (1970); and J. E. Vincent, *H.R.H. The Duke of Clarence* (1893).

Index